Best Hikes Raleigh, Durham, and Chapel Hill

Help Us Keep This Guide Up to Date

Every effort has been made by the author and editors to make this guide as accurate and useful as possible. However, many things can change after a guide is published—trails are rerouted, regulations change, techniques evolve, facilities come under new management, etc.

We appreciate hearing from you concerning your experiences with this guide and how you feel it could be improved and kept up to date. While we may not be able to respond to all comments and suggestions, we'll take them to heart and we'll also make certain to share them with the author. Please send your comments and suggestions to the following address:

Globe Pequot Press
Reader Response/Editorial Department
246 Goose Lane, Suite 200
Guilford, CT 06437

Thanks for your input, and happy trails!

Best Hikes Raleigh, Durham, and Chapel Hill

The Greatest Views, Wildlife, and Forest Trails

Second Edition

Johnny Molloy

FALCONGUIDES

GUILFORD, CONNECTICUT

An imprint of The Rowman & Littlefield Publishing Group, Inc.
4501 Forbes Blvd., Ste. 200
Lanham, MD 20706
www.rowman.com
Falcon and FalconGuides are registered trademarks and Make Adventure Your Story is a trademark
of The Rowman & Littlefield Publishing Group, Inc.

Distributed by NATIONAL BOOK NETWORK

Copyright © 2016 The Rowman & Littlefield Publishing Group, Inc.
This FalconGuide Edition 2020

Photos by Johnny Molloy
Maps by Melissa Baker

British Library Cataloguing in Publication Information available

Library of Congress Control Number: 2020940019

ISBN 978-1-4930-4854-0 (paper : alk. paper)
ISBN 978-1-4930-4855-7 (electronic)

∞™ The paper used in this publication meets the minimum requirements of American National
Standard for Information Sciences—Permanence of Paper for Printed Library Materials, ANSI/NISO
Z39.48-1992.

The authors and The Rowman & Littlefield Publishing Group, Inc. assume no
liability for accidents happening to, or injuries sustained by, readers who engage in
the activities described in this book.

This book is for all the hikers who ply the trails of the Triangle and the greater capital region.

Little waterfall (hike 4)

Contents

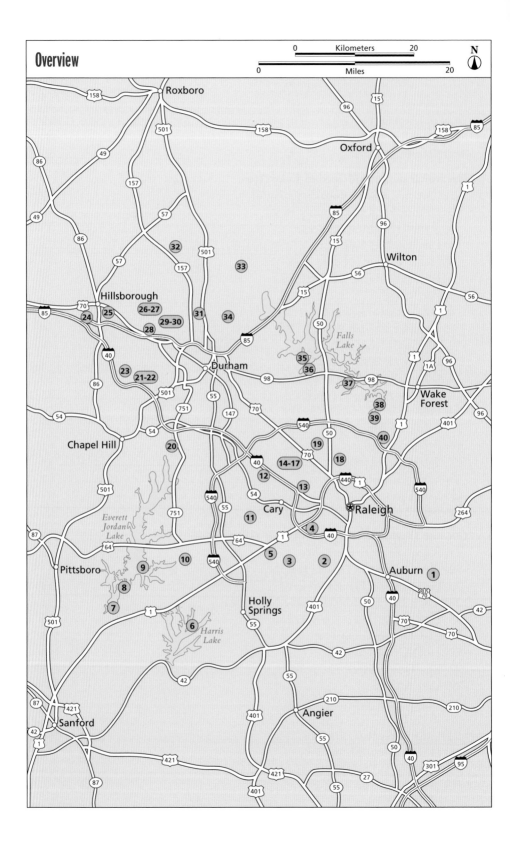

Overview

Acknowledgments

Thanks to my wife, Keri Anne, for her help. Thanks also to those who build and maintain Triangle trails, and to the folks at FalconGuides. Also thanks to Sierra Designs for their fine tents, sleeping bags, and other camping gear used while exploring the trails of the Triangle.

Introduction

Welcome to the second edition of this hiking guide. The capital region of North Carolina, well known as the Research Triangle, or simply the Triangle, is blessed with a range of hikes that explore North Carolina's biodiversity. It all started with area residents acknowledging and preserving central North Carolina's scenic splendor. The citizenry could see that the special places would remain special if they were held by the public for the public to use and enjoy. North Carolina state parks were formed first, such as Umstead State Park. Other city and county parks and preserves were expanded or created, from Historic Yates Mill County Park to Wilkerson Nature Park.

With their backdrop the rolling Piedmont of central North Carolina, Triangle hikers can immerse themselves in the capital region's forests, hills, lakeshores, and river valleys laced with hiking trails. Occoneechee Mountain, west of Durham, has far-reaching views, while the Historic Occoneechee Speedway presents one of the most unusual and scenic hikes anywhere, as trail trekkers trace a track from the inaugural 1949 NASCAR race season. Farther east the New Hope Creek watershed has several trail-laden nature preserves and parks within its bounds, from Duke Forest properties to state game lands. Duke Forest presents a disparate yet collectively large parcel of land offering still more green space and trails—and some superlative scenery blending the hills and hollows of the Piedmont. North Carolina State is represented with a hike at Schenck Memorial Forest, one of their properties memorializing one of the first scientific foresters in the United States.

Big Jordan Lake is peppered with trail-laden recreation areas such as Ebenezer Church and Poe Ridge, where you can enjoy gorgeous shoreline vistas as well as glimpse the area's past. Other area outdoor sanctuaries, such as Horton Grove Nature Preserve, offer other hiking destinations.

Metro Raleigh, the biggest city of the Triangle and the state capital of North Carolina, has an ever-growing greenway system linking city parks. Within the park system are paved greenways and natural surface trails, both of which primarily follow the tributaries of the Neuse River, flowing just north and east of the city. Still other hikes encircle watershed impoundments, such as Lake Johnson and Lake Crabtree. Part of the Neuse is dammed as Falls Lake, a huge impoundment laced with more pathways along its shores, as well as developed parks with paths of their own. Hemlock Bluffs Nature Preserve in Cary harbors an outpost of evergreens and other plants rare for central North Carolina. Bond Park presents a mix of stream and lakeside hiking on its interconnected trail network.

Chapel Hill has a mix of wooded trail parks, greenways, and nature preserves. I applaud Triangle residents with the foresight to establish these natural gems, such as Johnston Mill Nature Preserve, with its rocky rapids, old mill sites, and richly wooded hills.

And then there are the North Carolina state parks within the Triangle, such as Eno River State Park with its history predating the Revolutionary War, milldam relics, settler homesites, and miles of trails coursing through wetlands, woodlands, high hills, and steep-sided creeks. The establishment of Umstead State Park extends back to the Great Depression of the 1930s, when the Civilian Conservation Corps came in and built campgrounds, picnic shelters, and other facilities to enhance the already verdant beauty. Of course, they built hiking trails to explore hills and valleys, vistas, and rapids. Now both Eno River and Umstead are virtually enveloped in civilization, and have thus become preserves that are even more important. Clemmons Educational State Forest presents an informative venue to hike. Hikers today benefit from a cornucopia of parkland throughout the capital region. It all adds up to an impressive array of hiking destinations!

The hikes in this book are found in Raleigh, Durham, and Chapel Hill, along with the greater capital region. After having the privilege of researching potential routes for this book—hiking the hikes, taking photographs, finding the ones that made the grade (and the ones that didn't), exploring the parks beyond the trails, mapping the hikes, then actually writing and completing this compendium— I couldn't help but reflect on the wealth of places found within the scope of this guide. I recalled time spent on the Laurel Bluffs Trail. It presents an ideal mix of land and water, hills and bottoms, where the human history of the Triangle's past mixes

The view from Occoneechee Mountain (hike 24)

with the natural history and the flora and fauna that make hiking in the Triangle a singular experience.

From Gebel Rock on the Laurel Bluffs Trail, I reflected on other destinations, recounting all the scenic hikes of the Triangle. I thought of the Eagle Spur Trail, a forgotten rail line cutting deep into bottomlands near Jordan Lake. Speaking of rail trails, the long American Tobacco Trail comes to mind, with its many miles of trails connecting the Triangle from one end to the other. The hike at Cox Mountain provides vertical variation, wildflowers, and a cool swinging bridge over the Eno River. The Peninsula Trail on Harris Lake provides another aquatic trailside venue, settler history, and everywhere-you-look beauty.

I recalled the ingenious way trail builders constructed a path around the entirety of Lake Crabtree, using boardwalks, sewer line right-of-ways, pedestrian bridges, even the top of the dam holding the lake back. The trails circling Lake Lynn use extensive boardwalks that offer first-rate still water walking. The path around the waters of Eno Quarry is all-natural.

I came again to the scene at hand, the Eno River and Gebel Rock, and considered the preserved stream valley where generations past lived in mill-centered communities. Those that came after them helped establish Eno River State Park, where generations present and future hike through nature. I hope the trails offered in this book will help you explore, understand, and appreciate the natural and human history of the Triangle. Enjoy.

Weather

The Triangle experiences all four seasons in their entirety. Summer is usually warm, with occasional downright hot spells. Morning hikers can avoid the heat and the common afternoon thunderstorms. Electronic devices equipped with Internet access allow hikers to monitor storms as they arise. Hikers increase in numbers when the first northerly fronts of fall sweep cool, clear air across the Piedmont. Crisp mornings, great for vigorous treks, give way to warm afternoons, more conducive to family strolls. Fall is drier than summer. Winter brings frigid, subfreezing days and chilling rains, even occasional snow, and fewer hours of daylight. However, a brisk hiking pace and wise time management will keep you warm and walking. Each cold month has a few days of mild weather. Make the most of them. Spring is more variable. A warm day can be followed by a cold one. Extensive spring rains bring regrowth, but also keep hikers indoors. However, any avid hiker will find more good hiking days than they will have time to hike in spring and every other season. A good way to plan your hiking is to check monthly averages of high and low temperatures and average rainfall for each month in Raleigh. Below is a table showing each month's averages. This will give you a good idea of what to expect each month.

Temperature Chart

Month	Average High (°F)	Average Low (°F)	Precipitation
January	49°	29°	3.5"
February	53°	31°	3.2"
March	62°	39°	4.1"
April	72°	46°	2.9"
May	78°	55°	3.3"
June	85°	64°	3.5"
July	88°	68°	4.7"
August	87°	68°	4.3"
September	81°	61°	4.3"
October	72°	48°	3.2"
November	63°	39°	3.1"
December	52°	34°	3.1"

Flora and Fauna

The landscape of the Triangle varies from hilly terrain west of Durham to the river valleys of the Eno River, Neuse River, and New Hope Creek. Parts of the streams are dammed as lakes, and their shores contain hiking trails aplenty. A wide variety of wildlife calls these landscapes home. Deer is the land animal you most likely will see while hiking Triangle trails. They can be found throughout the capital region. Deer in some of the parks are remarkably tame and may linger on or close to the trail as you approach. A quiet hiker may also witness turkeys, raccoons, or even a coyote. Do not be surprised if you observe beavers, muskrats, or a playful otter along streams and lakes. When encountering any critter, keep your distance and they will generally keep theirs. Be thoughtful when pulling out your phone to photograph wildlife, not harassing them just to get a shot.

Overhead, many raptors ply the skies for food, including hawks, falcons, and owls. Depending upon where you are, other birds you may spot range from kingfishers to woodpeckers. Look for waterfowl in lakes. Songbirds are abundant no matter the habitat.

The flora offers just as much variety. Along the trails you'll find verdant hardwood forests rich with maple, oak, and hickory. Pines and cedars are the primary evergreens. In moister areas sycamores and beech predominate, thriving along nearly every stream in the Triangle. Wildflowers can be found in spring, summer, and fall along watercourses and in drier, site-specific situations.

Mountain laurel blooms in scads during May along the Eno River (hike 26).

Wetlands provide unique habitats and occur naturally and with a little help from park personnel.

Wilderness Restrictions/Regulations

Hiking in the greater Research Triangle is done primarily in city, county, and state parks and also nature preserves and US Army Corps of Engineers land. Raleigh, Durham, and Chapel Hill each have fine park systems. They are well-run, well-maintained facilities with a little bit of everything for everyone, from hiking to team sports to golfing. Entrance is free, and visitor guidelines keep the parks in the best shape possible.

North Carolina state parks offer natural getaways with an emphasis on recreation. They also protect special areas such as the nature preserves within them. Area state parks—Falls Lake State Recreation Area, for example—are often centered on a reservoir built by the US Army Corps of Engineers. These man-made lakes were built primarily for flood control and water storage. The recreational aspect of the lakes is an important but secondary function. Trails are laid upon the shoreline of the reservoirs. Entrance to state parks and their trails are free part of the year and carry a charge at other times, but you will have to pay to camp, golf, or overnight in a cabin. As a whole, the state park trail systems are in good shape.

Then there are the nature preserves. North Carolina has a special program designating state natural areas, whereby land is set aside for protection. These lands usually have unique ecological characteristics that deem them worthy of saving. The preserves are the most restricted in terms of usage. Luckily for us, hiking is considered passive recreation. Camping is generally not allowed on these lands. Other preserves are privately held and also emphasize passive recreation, which includes hiking.

Getting Around

Area Codes
The greater Triangle area codes are 919 and 984.

Roads
For the purposes of this guide, the best hikes near Raleigh, Durham, and Chapel Hill are confined to a 1-hour drive from the greater metro region. Northerly, this stretches to Falls Lake, northwest to Hillsborough, southeast to Clayton, southwest to the Cape Fear River, and west to the west shore of Jordan Lake. The entire hiking area is considered the Research Triangle, or simply the Triangle, in the Piedmont heart of central North Carolina.

A number of major interstates converge in the greater capital region. Directions to trailheads are given from these arteries. They include I-40, I-85, I-540, and I-440—the main loop around Raleigh.

By Air

Raleigh-Durham International Airport (RDU) is 6 miles northwest of downtown Raleigh, off I-540 and I-40.

To book reservations online, check out your favorite airline's website or search your favorite travel site for the best price.

By Bus

Capital Area Transit (known as "CAT") operates bus service throughout Raleigh and its suburbs. Visit www.raleighnc.gov or call (919) 485-RIDE. In addition to CAT, Durham, Chapel Hill, Cary, and Wake Counties also have public transit lines. Greyhound serves many towns in the region; visit www.greyhound.com for more information.

Visitor Information

For general information on the Research Triangle, visit North Carolina's official website of the area, www.visitnc.com/raleigh-durham-the-triangle, or call (800) VIS-ITNC (800-847-4862). This site links you to the various Triangle community tourism sites.

How to Use This Guide

Take a close enough look, and you'll find that this guide contains just about everything you'll ever need to choose, plan for, enjoy, and survive a hike near Raleigh, Durham, and Chapel Hill, and the rest of the Triangle. Stuffed with useful central North Carolina–area information, *Best Hikes Near Raleigh, Durham, and Chapel Hill* features forty mapped and cued hikes. The hikes are grouped into three units that neatly fit within the three primary urban areas that comprise the Triangle. "Greater Raleigh and Jordan Lake Area" covers paths in the capital city area and around Jordan Lake. "Greater Durham, Chapel Hill, and Hillsborough Area" details hikes around the home of the University of North Carolina, the home of Duke University, and history-laden Hillsborough. "Wake Forest and Falls Lake Area" harbors hikes in the vicinity of the big impoundment of the Neuse River and the Wake Forest zone. These sections give you an idea of where in the Triangle the hikes are situated.

Here's an outline of the book's major components: Each hike starts with a short **summary** of the hike's highlights. These quick overviews give you a taste of the hiking adventures to follow. You'll learn about the trail terrain and what surprises each route has to offer. Following the overview you'll find the **hike specs:** quick, nitty-gritty details of the hike. Most are self-explanatory, but here are some details on others:

Distance: The total distance of the recommended route—one-way for loop hikes, the round-trip on a there-and-back or balloon loop hike, point-to-point for a shuttle. Options are additional.

Hiking time: The average time it will take to cover the route. It is based on the total distance, elevation gain, and condition and difficulty of the trail. Your fitness level will also affect your time.

Difficulty: Each hike has been assigned a level of difficulty. The rating system was developed from several sources and personal experience. These levels are meant to be a guideline only and may prove easier or harder for different people depending on ability and physical fitness.

> **Easy**—Five miles or less total trip distance in one day, with minimal elevation gain and paved or smooth-surfaced dirt trail.
>
> **Moderate**—Up to 10 miles total trip distance in one day, with moderate elevation gain and potentially rough terrain.
>
> **Difficult**—More than 10 miles total trip distance in one day, with strenuous elevation gain and rough and/or rocky terrain.

Trail surface: General information about what to expect underfoot.

Best seasons: General information on the best time of year to hike.

Other trail users: Horseback riders, mountain bikers, inline skaters, etc.

Canine compatibility: Know the trail regulations before you take your dog hiking with you. Dogs are not allowed on several trails in this book.

Land status: Metro park, county park, state nature preserve, etc.

Fees and permits: Whether you need to carry any money with you for park entrance fees and permits.

Maps: This is a list of other maps to supplement the maps in this book. USGS maps are the best source for accurate topographical information, but the local park map may show more recent trails. Use both.

Trail contacts: This is the location, phone number, and website URL for the local land manager(s) in charge of all the trails within the selected hike. Before you head out, get trail access information, or contact the land manager after your visit if you see problems with trail erosion, damage, or misuse.

The **Finding the trailhead** section gives you dependable driving directions to where you'll want to park. **The Hike** is the meat of the chapter. Detailed and honest, it's a carefully researched impression of the trail. It also often includes lots of area history, both natural and human. Under **Miles and Directions,** mileage cues identify all turns and trail name changes, as well as points of interest. **Options** are also given for many hikes to make your journey shorter or longer depending on the amount of time you have. Don't feel restricted to the routes and trails that are mapped here. Be adventurous and use this guide as a platform to discover new routes for yourself. **Green Tips** are included to help you help the environment we all share. A **sidebar** is included with some hikes. This is simply interesting information about the area or trail that doesn't necessarily pertain to the specific hike but gives you some human or natural tidbit that may pique your interest to explore beyond the simple mechanics of the trek. Enjoy your time in the outdoors and remember to pack out what you pack in.

How to Use the Maps

Overview map: This map shows the location of each hike in the area by hike number.

Route map: This is your primary guide to each hike. It shows all the accessible roads and trails, points of interest, water, landmarks, and geographical features. It also distinguishes trails from roads, and paved roads from unpaved roads. The selected route is highlighted, and directional arrows point the way.

Map Legend

Transportation

══(25)══	Interstate Highway
══(24)══	US Highway
══(67)══	State Highway
══[621]══	County/Forest Road
══ ══ ══	Local Road

Trails

------	Featured Trail
- - - -	Trail

Water Features

⬭	Body of Water
⸰⸰	Marsh
∿	River or Creek
⸰⸰⸰	Intermittent Stream
⩘	Waterfall

Land Management

▭	Forest/Park/ Preserve/Game Lands

Symbols

▥	Boardwalk
⇟	Boat Ramp/Launch
⏝	Bridge
■	Building/Point of Interest
⛺	Campground
▲	Campsite
✪	Capital
○	City/Town
—	Dam
•—•	Gate
▲	Mountain/Peak
◈	Overlook/Viewpoint
🅿	Parking
⛉	Picnic Shelter
🛈	Ranger Station
⛨	Restroom
⏛	Tower
①	Trailhead
⊢──⊣	Tunnel
❓	Visitor/Information Center

Trail Finder

To get you started on the hikes that best suit your interests and abilities, this simple trail finder indicates the best features for each hike in the book. Hikes may fall under more than one category. Choose the categories that are most appropriate for your area of interest.

Hike #	Hike Name	Best Hikes for Waterfalls	Best Hikes for Great Views	Best Hikes for Children
1	Clemmons Educational State Forest			●
2	Historic Yates Mill County Park	●		
3	Swift Creek Bluffs Preserve		●	
4	Lake Johnson Loop	●		
5	Hemlock Bluffs Nature Preserve			●
6	Peninsula Trail		●	
7	Poe Ridge		●	●
8	New Hope Lakeside Loop			
9	Ebenezer Church Walk			●
10	American Tobacco Trail		●	●
11	Bond Park Hike			●
12	Lake Crabtree County Park		●	
13	Schenck Memorial Forest			●
14	Loblolly Trail			
15	Company Mill Loop			
16	Sycamore Trail			
17	Sals Branch Loop			●
18	Shelley Lake Loop		●	●
19	Lake Lynn Loop		●	

Best Hikes for Dogs	Best Hikes for Stream Lovers	Best Hikes for Lake Lovers	Best Hikes for Nature Lovers	Best Hikes for History Lovers
•	•	•		
	•	•		•
	•		•	
•		•		
	•		•	
•		•		•
•		•	•	
•		•	•	
		•		•
•			•	
•	•	•		
		•		
	•		•	
•			•	•
	•		•	•
	•		•	•
	•		•	•
		•		
	•	•		

Hike #	Hike Name	Best Hikes for Waterfalls	Best Hikes for Great Views	Best Hikes for Children
20	Eagle Spur Trail		•	
21	Rhododendron Bluff Hike			
22	Piney Mountain Double Loop			
23	Johnston Mill Nature Preserve			•
24	Occoneechee Mountain State Natural Area		•	
25	Historic Occoneechee Speedway Hike			•
26	Cox Mountain Hike			•
27	Holden Mill Circuit			
28	Eno Quarry Hike		•	•
29	Cole Mill Loop			
30	Laurel Bluffs Trail		•	
31	Eagle Trail		•	•
32	Little River Regional Park Hike			
33	Horton Grove Nature Preserve			
34	Pennys Bend Nature Preserve			•
35	Falls Lake Trail at Rollingview	•	•	
36	Falls Lake Trail from Boyce Mill			
37	Blue Jay Point County Park		•	•
38	Falls Lake Trail at Falls Lake Dam		•	•
39	Wilkerson Nature Park			•
40	Durant Nature Preserve		•	•

Best Hikes for Dogs	Best Hikes for Stream Lovers	Best Hikes for Lake Lovers	Best Hikes for Nature Lovers	Best Hikes for History Lovers
•		•	•	
	•		•	•
•	•		•	•
	•		•	•
			•	•
•	•			•
•	•		•	•
•	•		•	•
		•		•
•	•			•
	•		•	•
•		•		•
	•	•		•
	•		•	
•	•		•	•
		•	•	•
•		•	•	•
		•		
		•	•	
			•	
•		•	•	

Autumn comes to Sals Branch (hike 17).

Greater Raleigh and Jordan Lake Area

The Forest Demonstration Trail at Clemmons Educational State Forest is bordered by spring greenery (hike 1).

1 Clemmons Educational State Forest

The destination not only has great trails, but also fine facilities for hands-on learning about forestry and the Piedmont environment. Plan to spend extra time enjoying the facilities, in addition to hiking around the forest pond and along one of the streams coursing through the forest. The last part of the hike takes the Talking Rock Trail, which explains the stony underpinnings of the land.

Start: Parking lot near the forest pond
Distance: 4.6-mile triple loop
Hiking time: 2.5–3.0 hours
Difficulty: Moderate
Trail surface: Natural
Best season: Spring through fall
Other trail users: None
Canine compatibility: Leashed dogs allowed
Land status: State forest

Fees and permits: No fees or permits required
Schedule: Open Mar 1–Nov 30, closed Mon, open Tues–Fri 9 a.m.–5 p.m., Sat–Sun 11 a.m.–5 p.m. EST, 11 a.m.–8 p.m. Daylight Savings Time
Maps: Clemmons Educational State Forest
Trail contacts: Clemmons Educational State Forest, 2411 Old US 70 W., Clayton, NC 27617; (919) 553-5651; www.ncesf.org

Finding the trailhead: From exit 306 on I-40, southeast of downtown Raleigh, take US 70 Business East toward Clayton for 1 mile to a traffic light. Turn left on Auburn Knightdale and follow it for 0.3 mile to Garner Road/Old US 70. Turn right on Garner Road and follow it for 3.7 miles to the forest, on your left. Follow the main forest road to the trailhead. Trailhead GPS: N35 41.247', W78 29.174'

The Hike

The greater Raleigh area is fortunate to have North Carolina's first state educational forest in its midst. Although Clemmons is primarily geared toward informing students about the Tar Heel State's forests, the property, trails, and learning opportunities are open to the public. This includes hiking trails with specific educational themes, such as the Talking Tree Trail, whereby visitors learn about the types of trees growing in the area, and the Talking Rock Trail, which explores the geological aspects of the land. My favorite, the Forest Demonstration Trail, presents information about forestry practices and management.

Clemmons Educational State Forest began as a 1930s Civilian Conservation Corps work project. First the federal government purchased around 800 acres of eroded farmland and built a tree nursery. Young men lived in camps on the forest and not only propagated trees for planting elsewhere but also built an infrastructure to manage the nursery. Later the nursery was turned over to the North Carolina Division of Forest Resources, which continued to manage Clemmons as a nursery.

Looking over the state forest pond

Things changed in 1976 when the state tree nursery was moved to Goldsboro. The Division of Forest Resources decided to establish the state's first educational forest at Clemmons. The land was close to Raleigh and thus would be convenient for area school kids to learn about natural resources management. Clemmons Educational State Forest was born. Resource management includes not only timber, which you would expect on a state forest, but also water that is affected by forestry practices. The cleanest water flows out of forested lands, so when logging is done here, a wooded buffer is retained along the streams to keep the water unpolluted. Soil is another component of forest management. When this land was farmed, it was done in an irresponsible manner, causing extensive erosion. Today forest personnel take steps to prevent runoff because keeping soil in place helps grow better trees.

Wildlife enhancement is another important component of forest management; therefore practices shown to improve habitat for deer, turkeys, and even songbirds are part of the forest mission. Finally, forest managers are also continuing flora restoration on parts of the terrain. After being historically used as farmland and a tree nursery, the once vast longleaf pine savannas are being reestablished, using a combination of planting and prescribed fires.

These are the things you can learn about when visiting Clemmons Educational State Forest. Your exploratory hike takes you first by the forest pond, where songbirds can be heard. The serene pond adds a scenic component to the area. You then join the Forest Demonstration Trail, passing by planted tree plantations for harvest, small open fields known as food plots where special grasses and vegetation are raised for wildlife, large pieces of equipment used to control wildfire, and other aspects of forest management. Informational signs add to your understanding of what forestry management is all about.

Next you join the Watershed Extension Loop, a circuit trail that traverses the "back 40" of the forest. This trail travels along Beddingfield Creek and its tributaries and is a lesser-visited part of the forest. An unbridged creek crossing makes the loop an unappealing high-water option, but the flowery bottoms, wooded wetlands, and forested hills make the Watershed Extension Loop a bonus trail and an additional opportunity to see wildlife. The hike then rejoins the Forest Demonstration Trail, where you enjoy more interpretive information while making your way back to the forest pond to appreciate a little more aquatic beauty.

Finally, walk the Talking Rock Trail, with its numerous interpretive stops that head up a small spring branch feeding the lake. The final part of the trek takes you through the mini-maze of walkways, educational buildings, and forestry exhibits near the trailhead. This is a fine area to end your hike, as a picnic shelter, restrooms, and interpretive information will keep you lingering. The Talking Tree Trail, not included on this hike, is another option should you want to extend your walk and/or learn more about the specific trees that grow in this slice of Carolina.

Before you leave, climb the old North Carolina Division of Forest Resources fire tower. The tower has been cut off and is much shorter, but it is still fun to walk up and imagine watching for forest fires up here, as they did in the old days.

Miles and Directions

0.0 As you face the picnic area and facilities entrance to the state forest, leave right, away from the facilities entrance, to pass around a pole gate on a closed doubletrack. Descend to come alongside the forest pond, only a few acres in size, ringed with birdhouses and a mix of environments for wildlife. Cross the pond dam, stay left, then turn right, away from the water.

0.2 Reach a four-way intersection. Turn right here, joining the Forest Demonstration Trail. Walk northerly on a doubletrack path, passing some firefighting vehicles and behind the outdoor amphitheater. Bisect an unmarked fire management road and come near a wildlife food plot.

0.6 Drop off a hill to come alongside Beddingfield Creek. Turn left, upstream. Come near the remains of an old bridge that once spanned the stream.

0.8 Come to a trail intersection. Head right here, joining the Watershed Extension Loop. Continue up Beddingfield Creek. Step over clear, spring-fed, sandy branches.

Clemmons Educational State Forest

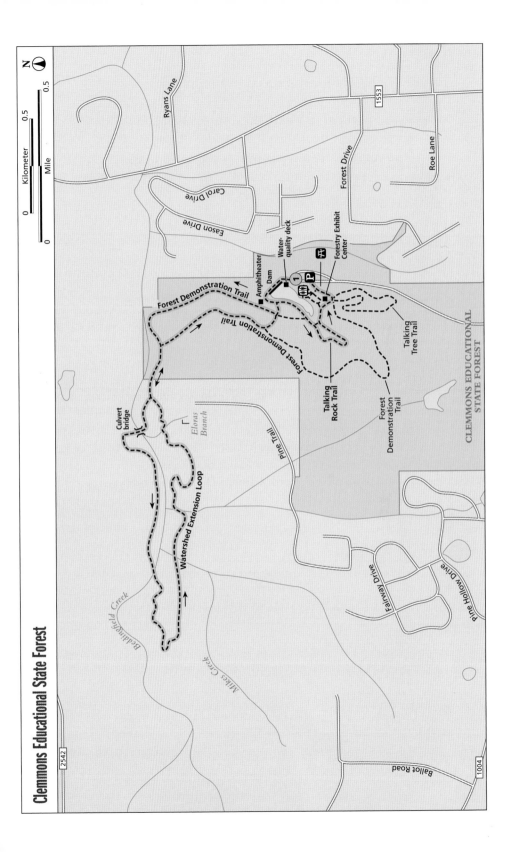

1.0 Rise to the edge of a fast-disappearing clearing, populated in youngish trees. Begin the loop portion of the Watershed Extension Loop by heading right. Cruise along the edge of the former field next to trees.

1.2 Span Beddingfield Creek via a culvert bridge. Curve west in rich bird habitat on the edge of the forest.

1.7 Open onto a gas line clearing. Cross Beddingfield Creek on a bridge. Soon reenter pine-dominant woods.

2.1 Curve back east in pines.

2.2 Cross back through the gas line clearing. Meander through a piney ridge separating Beddingfield Creek from Mikes Creek.

2.6 Make an unbridged crossing of Mikes Creek—easily doable at normal water flows.

2.8 Curve away from the bottomland then drop to cross Eloras Branch.

3.3 Complete the loop portion of the Watershed Extension Loop. Backtrack.

3.5 Turn right here, back on the Forest Demonstration Trail. Climb south on a hill. Absorb more interpretive information. Top out in rocky woods.

3.9 Reach another intersection. Head left on the Forest Demonstration Trail shortcut toward the forest pond. Descend.

4.0 Come to the forest pond and head right along the water.

4.1 Join the Talking Rock Trail. Make a loop, enjoying interpretive geological information. Circle a spring branch.

4.4 Complete the Talking Rock Trail. Head toward the trailhead and the Forestry Exhibit Center.

4.5 Reach an intersection. The Talking Tree Trail heads right and offers 0.8 mile of additional interpretive path. You head left, weaving through the mini maze of walking paths connecting the facilities, trails, and pond. The state forest has numerous displays and information in this locale.

4.6 Return to the trailhead after passing through the picnic area, completing the hike. Make sure to climb the fire tower, just for fun, if you have enough energy.

Spring comes alive at Clemmons State Forest.

2 Historic Yates Mill County Park

This hike not only explores historic and photogenic Yates Mill and its adjacent pond, but also nearby wetlands, tributaries, and hills on well-marked and maintained foot trails. The nature center here is worth a visit too.

Start: Nature center parking lot
Distance: 3.5-mile loop with spurs
Hiking time: 2.0–2.5 hours
Difficulty: Easy
Trail surface: Natural
Best season: Year-round
Other trail users: None
Canine compatibility: Pets not allowed
Land status: Wake County park

Fees and permits: No fees or permits required
Schedule: 8 a.m. to sunset
Maps: Yates Mill County Park; USGS Lake Wheeler
Trail contacts: Historic Yates Mill County Park, 4620 Lake Wheeler Rd., Raleigh, NC 27603; (919) 856-6675; wakegov.com/parks/yatesmill

Finding the trailhead: From exit 297 on I-40, south of downtown Raleigh, take Lake Wheeler Road south for 3 miles to the park on your right. Official address: 4620 Lake Wheeler Road. Trailhead GPS: N35 43.229', W78 41.258'

The Hike

Yates Mill County Park truly deserves the "Historic" moniker at the beginning of its name, for it is the only operating mill left in Wake County of the seventy that were once scattered throughout the district. A mill, dam, and pond were first located here at Steep Hill Creek back in the mid-1700s, when North Carolina was still a British colony. As with other mills, nearby residents would gather to grind their corn and wheat into meal and flour, visit with the neighbors, and maybe do a little business as well. In other words the mill served as a combination trading post, community center, and communication location.

A dam held back the creek to ensure a regular flow of water—thus power—to the mill, creating the pond behind it. The impoundment was popular for fishing, swimming, and family picnicking. Located at a crossroads, Yates Mill was a regular gathering place and an integral part of the fabric of Wake County for two centuries.

The original owner and mill builder, Samuel Pearson, passed it on to his son Simon Pearson in the opening days of the 1800s. However, the younger Pearson was a poor money manager and lost the mill to debt. He was forced to sell the mill at a sheriff's auction. A man named William Boylan, a banker and newspaper owner, then purchased Yates Mill. It sounds like an inside job since Mr. Boylan was the director of the bank that held Simon Pearson's loan. Whether he obtained the mill by hook or crook, Mr. Boylan expanded the mill, adding a sawmill to the meal-grinding operation.

This log cabin stands next to the dam at Yates Mill.

After Mr. Boylan's day, a partnership of prominent Raleigh businessmen purchased the mill, operating it during the days before the Civil War and into the conflict between North and South. Interestingly, one partner, Thomas Briggs, started a business operation that continues to this day as Briggs Hardware in Raleigh, the oldest hardware store in the Triangle. The key to Mr. Briggs's business success was his converting Confederate currency into silver before the South lost the war and the rebel money became worthless.

Phares Yates bought the mill in March 1863, as well as 94 acres around it. It was during his forty-year operation of the mill that the name as we know it today finally stuck. Phares's son, Robert E. Lee Yates, inherited the mill in 1902 and owned it for thirty-five more years before his passing.

Times were changing, and by the 1930s local residents were purchasing their own bread or not getting meal ground on a regular basis. Sawmills were using gas-powered engines, and electric power was spreading throughout the land, eliminating the need for small-scale mill-driven power. Yates Mill finally closed in the 1950s for lack of business, and the grounds became a company retreat. In 1963 North Carolina State University bought the mill and a thousand adjacent acres as an experimental farm. The mill building sat empty and slowly deteriorated right before the eyes of passing locals. It was then that area residents rallied to form the Yates Mill Association. Eventually the mill, now on the National Register of Historic Places, was restored and a park established by Wake County. The preserve was opened in 2006 and is once again a gathering place for area residents to enjoy the millpond, the trails, the Finley Center, and the history of this special spot in the Triangle.

Yates Mill Dam

Make your first stop the Finley Center, where the history of Yates Mill comes to life, and where you can also learn about the nature of the 157-acre park. There is over 2,200 square feet of exhibition space filled with fascinating information and displays explaining the park's past existence. To this day the pond remains a popular fishing locale, especially the Pond Boardwalk, which stretches over the impoundment.

You start your hike by bridging Yates Mill Pond on the Pond Boardwalk then crossing ecologically important wetlands while heading up the valley of Steep Hill Creek. After your return trip, walk the shoreline of Yates Mill Pond then visit the mill itself. Inside tours are available on weekends; otherwise you can simply admire the mill building, the dam, and the historical nature of the location, as well as a nearby log cabin. The final part of the hike loops through adjacent hills on the High Ridge Trail and back to the start. After your visit you will become yet one more fan of the beauty and history of Yates Mill.

Miles and Directions

0.0   From the north side of the Finley Center parking lot, pick up the trail leading to and across the Pond Boardwalk. This wide boardwalk is a popular fishing area, so you may see anglers vying for bream and bass.

0.1   Reach a trail intersection after crossing Yates Mill Pond. Turn right here on the Creekside Trail, as the Mill Pond Trail goes left.

Historic Yates Mill County Park

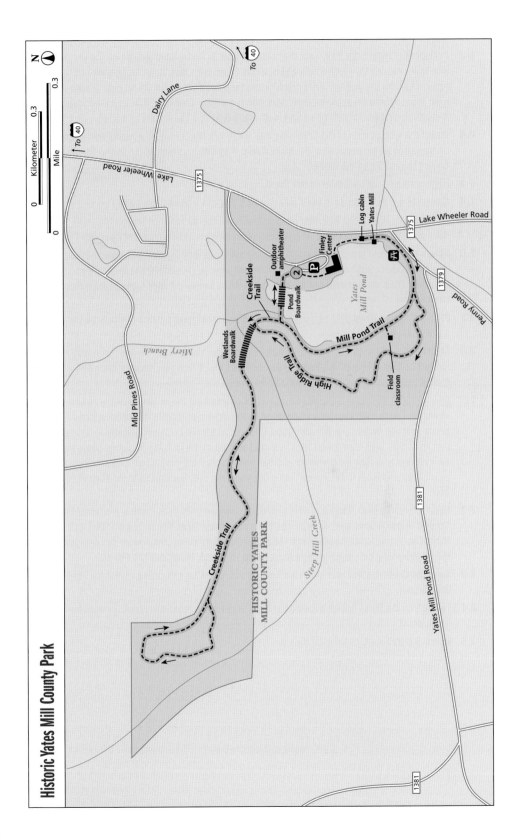

N

Kilometer
0   0.3   0.3

Mile
0

To 40

To 40

Dairy Lane

Lake Wheeler Road

1375

Mid Pines Road

Miery Branch

Outdoor amphitheater

Finley Center

2

P

Creekside Trail

Pond Boardwalk

Wetlands Boardwalk

High Ridge Trail

Log cabin

Yates Mill

Lake Wheeler Road

1375

Yates Mill Pond

Mill Pond Trail

Penny Road

1379

Field classroom

Creekside Trail

HISTORIC YATES MILL COUNTY PARK

Steep Hill Creek

1381

Yates Mill Pond Road

1381

0.2 Intersect the High Ridge Trail. Save that path for later. For now, keep straight on the Creek-side Trail, crossing the Wetlands Boardwalk over Steep Hill Creek. Look for beavers and other wildlife in the wetland. After reaching the far side of Steep Hill Creek, pass a spur road going right to an adjacent farm. Stay with the narrow Creekside Trail as it meanders through sloping woods with open farmland to the right and the stream to the left.

0.8 Reach the loop portion of the Creekside Trail. Head left. Numerous boardwalks and plank bridges span wetter sections of the rocky forest. Intermittent channels cut across the trail, flowing toward Steep Hill Creek.

1.1 Begin turning back toward Yates Mill Pond in pines.

1.4 Complete the loop portion of the Creekside Trail. Backtrack toward Yates Mill Pond.

1.9 Return to the High Ridge Trail after passing back over the wetlands of Steep Hill Creek. Keep straight on the Creekside Trail, reentering woodlands, heading toward Yates Mill Pond.

2.0 Return to the Mill Pond Trail after passing the High Ridge Trail. The Pond Boardwalk is to your left. Keep straight on the natural surface path and begin walking the shoreline of Yates Mill Pond. An accompanying brochure identifies twenty different types of trees along the trail here. Gaze across the shoreline at the mill and the Finley Center.

2.2 Pass a spur trail going right to the field classroom. School groups frequently use the park for environmental education.

2.3 Meet the south end of the High Ridge Trail. You will return here later. For now, continue straight on the Mill Pond Trail, heading toward Yates Mill. Come very close to Yates Mill Pond Road as you pass through a small picnic area.

2.5 Reach Yates Mill. This is a favorable angle for photographing the historic building, water-wheel, and dam. Take the stone steps down to the stream and cross the wooden foot-bridge that lies under Lake Wheeler Road (the footbridge will be closed if water is flowing over it). Climb away from Steep Hill Creek and you are at the mill. This is a good place to walk around and view the buildings and the pond itself. From here a trail leads through a picnic area and back to the Finley Center. However, our hike backtracks to the High Ridge Trail.

2.7 Head left on the High Ridge Trail. The ambitiously named path does climb a moderate hill cloaked in hardwoods and winds across intermittent drainages flowing toward Yates Mill Pond. Cross a park maintenance road accessing the field classroom. Toward the end you will be straddling the ridgeline separating Steep Hill Creek from Yates Mill Pond.

3.3 Meet the Creekside Trail and Mill Pond Trail yet again. Turn right, heading toward the Pond Boardwalk.

3.4 Turn left on the Pond Boardwalk, walking amid anglers one more time. Look for waterfowl in the pond.

3.5 Reach the trailhead, completing the hike.

3 Swift Creek Bluffs Preserve

Check out huge old-growth beech trees overlooking scenic Swift Creek on this relatively short but biologically diverse hike in a small preserve. First you reconnoiter bottomlands and Swift Creek then come alongside Beech Bluff, where the old trees—and wildflowers—grow. Next, climb the bluff to view Swift Creek from above, then loop back to drop off the bluff and explore Overcup Oak Swamp.

Start: Holly Springs Road parking area
Distance: 1.8-mile triple loop
Hiking time: 1.0–1.5 hours
Difficulty: Easy, but has steep sections
Trail surface: Natural
Best season: Spring for wildflowers
Other trail users: None
Canine compatibility: Leashed dogs allowed

Land status: Nature preserve
Fees and permits: No fees or permits required
Schedule: Sunrise to sunset
Maps: Swift Creek Bluffs Trail Map; USGS Apex
Trail contacts: Triangle Land Conservancy, 514 S. Duke St., Durham, NC 27701; (919) 908-8809; www.triangleland.org

Finding the trailhead: From exit 295 on I-40, southwest of downtown Raleigh, take Gorman Street south just a short distance to reach Tryon Road. Turn right on Tryon Road and follow it west for 2.2 miles to turn left on Walnut Street, which becomes Holly Springs Road. Reach the preserve parking lot on the right after 2.1 miles, just after the bridge over Swift Creek. Address: 7800 Holly Springs Rd., Raleigh, NC 27606. Trailhead GPS: N35 43.061', W78 45.188'

The Hike

Swift Creek Bluffs Preserve packs a lot of punch in its 23 acres. Held by the Triangle Land Conservancy, the preserve is bordered by Lochmere Golf Course, Holly Springs Road, a water pumping station, and a neighborhood. Yet you will be surprised by the beauty contained within it—the bottomlands along Swift Creek, the stream itself as it courses beneath bluffs, the steep bluffs, the swamp, and the stars of the show, the massive old-growth beech trees upwards of 200 years old.

The precipitous bluffs and swampy terrain were part of what protected the land in the first place—the tract was not easy to develop. The smallish parcel was off the radar as a park development for local governments, but was right up the alley for the mission of the Triangle Land Conservancy, which is to improve our lives through conservation by safeguarding clean water, protecting natural habitats, and connecting people with nature.

Since the trail mileage is relatively short, take your time to appreciate the efforts of the Triangle Land Conservancy, for there is much to see, especially the wildflowers in spring—from spring beauties to trout lilies to jack-in-the-pulpits. A series of mini loops take you through the multiple environments. First, leave the trailhead and work

THE TRIANGLE LAND CONSERVANCY

Swift Creek Bluffs Preserve is just one nature preserve held by the Triangle Land Conservancy. The organization also holds primitive conservation lands that have no developed trails or obvious recreation opportunities on them, but are simply protecting the flora and fauna within them. The group has collaborated with state, county, and local parks in acquiring and managing lands in six counties of the greater Raleigh area. It all started back in the early 1980s when a group of citizens foresaw the future explosive growth that was to take place in the Triangle. They believed that some places should be preserved for nature. A land trust was formed, and by 1987 the first tract, White Pines Nature Preserve, was purchased. Since then they have identified and preserved nine other nature preserves, all with high ecological or natural value. Johnston Mill Nature Preserve, another Triangle Land Conservancy parcel, is detailed in this guide too.

Public enjoyment of these preserves is an important tenet for the Triangle Land Conservancy, for they realize that citizens are more likely to be engaged in conservation if they can actually see, feel, touch, and smell the habitats around them. The group helps restore lands by removing invasive species and reestablishing native habitats. Finally, they realize they cannot do it alone, and thus encourage and help other organizations in protecting these wild places of the Triangle. For more information about the Triangle Land Conservancy, please visit www.triangleland.org.

your way through forested bottomland to come alongside aptly named Swift Creek. Swift Creek drains 66 square miles of the Triangle area, flowing southeasterly from Apex and Cary. Here the tributary of the Neuse River flows easterly in alternating shoals and pools, bordered by sand and mud bars, meeting the Neuse near Smithfield, after being dammed as the well-known Triangle impoundments of Lake Wheeler and Lake Benson.

This part of the hike traverses the upper watershed, though Swift Creek is decent-sized already. The trail leaves Holly Springs Road and curves to come alongside Swift Creek. Here you walk alongside the stream in wooded flats, passing a shortcut back to the trailhead before reaching the hilly bluff part of the preserve. It is here in the flats just below the bluff where the biggest beech trees rise from the woodland floor. A

Jack-in-the-pulpit

narrowing flat finally closes and you backtrack to then climb the bluff above you via the Stairway to Heaven. Trout lilies by the thousands bloom here in spring. The forest changes to oaks once atop the bluff, but before you get used to the new habitat, the trail drops off to bottoms again within sight of Lochmere Golf Course. This is where you join a greenway toward Birkhaven Drive, climbing a hollow. A natural surface footpath leads back into the preserve, and from here it is mostly a backtrack to the trailhead, save for the section passing through Overcup Oak Swamp. A boardwalk over the wetland is your final highlight before returning to the trailhead.

Miles and Directions

0.0   From the parking area on the west side of Holly Springs Road, just south of the bridge over Swift Creek, join the main trail leaving the parking area to cross a bridge over a small ditch. Ahead, reach a trail intersection and head right, toward Swift Creek. The trail at this juncture can be a little mushy after rains, as it traverses wooded bottoms.

0.2   Reach a trail intersection. Here a shortcut leads left back toward the trailhead. Stay straight, crossing an old ditch and continuing up Swift Creek.

0.3   Cross a sewer right-of-way. Continue up Swift Creek under loblolly pines, dogwoods, and sycamores.

0.4   The trail becomes squeezed in by the stream on your right and bluffs to your left. Reach a trail intersection here and head right, still continuing up Swift Creek. Look for big beech trees. Just ahead, the trail splits and the Stairway to Heaven leads left up the bluff. For now, stay straight in a slender flat along Swift Creek. More old-growth beech trees tower above you. The north-facing bluffs harbor wildflowers aplenty. Bottoms stretch across the stream.

0.6   The flat closes in. Loop back to the Stairway to Heaven. Do not continue up Swift Creek, perpetuating a user-created erosive trail.

0.8   Make the steep climb up the Stairway to Heaven, literally wood and earth stairs ascending sharply. Admire more beech trees. Curve into a hollow then level out. Peer down to the creek, now 100 feet below. Houses can be seen through the woods to your left.

1.0   Reach a trail junction atop the bluff. Keep straight here, making another loop. Slowly descend among oaks.

1.2   Reach a short paved greenway back in bottoms, leaving right and left, near Lochmere Golf Course. Head left, away from the golf course on a paved path, climbing.

1.3   Join a natural surface path leading acutely left, back into the preserve, before the paved greenway comes to Birkhaven Drive and ends.

1.4   Complete this hilltop bluff loop, returning to the intersection at 1.0 mile. Backtrack toward the trailhead, descending the Stairway to Heaven.

Swift Creek Bluffs Preserve

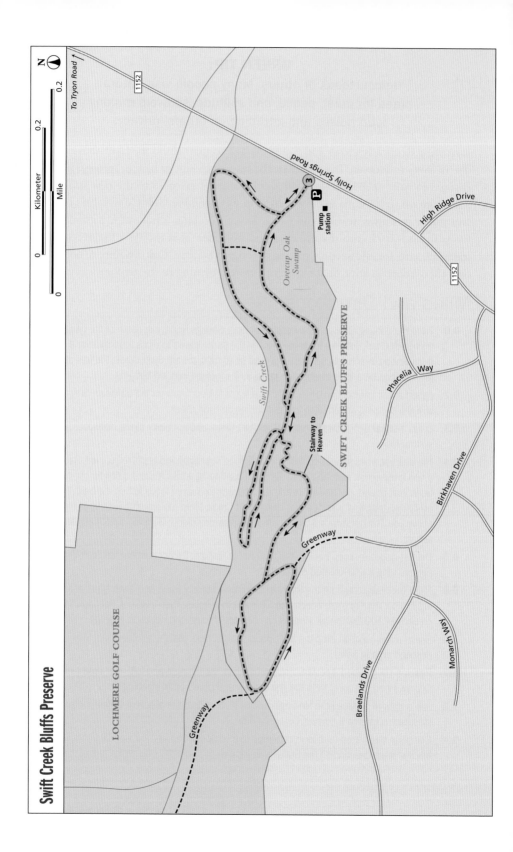

1.6 Return to Swift Creek, back in bottoms at the base of the Stairway to Heaven. Turn right here, easterly, walking downstream along Swift Creek. Ahead, reach another intersection and stay right, joining a new trail. Keep east, then turn away from the bluff to cross Over-cup Oak Swamp on a boardwalk bridge. Depending on recent precipitation and the time of year, the swamp could be all water or dry.

1.8 Reach the Holly Springs Road trailhead, finishing the hike.

4 Lake Johnson Loop

This is a sizable circuit hike around a big lake at a big Raleigh city park. Popular with hikers, joggers, and other outdoor enthusiasts, a paved path follows the shoreline undulations of the east half of the lake, while a natural surface path leads you around the quieter west half of the impoundment. Be prepared for plenty of views and aquatic scenery at this urban oasis.

Start: Boathouse/concessions parking area
Distance: 5.0-mile loop
Hiking time: 2.5–3.0 hours
Difficulty: Moderate
Trail surface: Asphalt, natural
Best season: Year-round
Other trail users: Joggers, bicyclers on east half

Canine compatibility: Leashed dogs allowed
Land status: Raleigh city park
Fees and permits: No fees or permits required
Schedule: Dawn to dusk
Maps: L J Park Map
Trail contacts: Lake Johnson Park, 4601 Avent Ferry Rd., Raleigh, NC 27606; (919) 233-2121; www.raleighnc.gov/parks/

Finding the trailhead: From exit 295 on I-40, southwest of downtown Raleigh, take Gorman Street north for 1.1 miles to turn left on Avent Ferry Road. Follow Avent Ferry Road for 1.3 miles to the main entrance to Lake Johnson Park on your left, just before Avent Ferry Road crosses Lake Johnson. Trailhead GPS: N35 45.766', W78 42.836'

The Hike

Lake Johnson Park is a popular place, but the 300 acres can handle it. Hikers, joggers, and water enthusiasts flock to this city of Raleigh preserve on nice days. Although the 5-plus miles of trails easily accommodate the amount of users, the problem comes with parking. On those idyllic days that you really want to get out and enjoy a Carolina outdoor experience at Lake Johnson, others will have had the same idea, and there will simply be too few convenient parking spots for the number of visitors. However, there are five parking areas scattered throughout the park, with three of them near the Lake Johnson Trail, the loop that takes you around the impoundment. If you can't get in one of these, you may have to park up by the pool and stadium, located in the northwest part of the park. An access trail leads from the stadium parking area to the main loop.

On your average day, parking is not troublesome at all, and I recommend the boathouse/concessions parking area at 4601 Avent Ferry Road, which is where this hike starts. As you make your 5-mile loop around Lake Johnson, you will conclude that it is a big lake. It stretches over 150 surface acres with many coves and bays. Adjacent wooded hills rise from the water and enhance the scenery. Wetlands spread

A boardwalk crosses Walnut Creek.

along the upper stretch of the lake. Though surrounded by civilization, Lake Johnson provides a true oasis of nature for Triangle outdoor enthusiasts.

The impoundment came to be in 1952, when Walnut Creek was dammed for flood control, upstream of Lake Raleigh, itself dammed in 1914 for the capital city's drinking water. Today, Lake Johnson is thought of as a scenic park body of water, rather than for flood control. This is reflected in the park's rental of pedal boats, johnboats, canoes, kayaks, and even sailboats. The park also offers free fishing tackle, but you must fish from the boathouse dock area. Park visitors can bring their own nonmotorized craft but must pay a modest launch fee. Wading and swimming in the lake is not allowed; however, the park has a pool open during the warm season.

Non-aquatic pastimes here at Lake Johnson Park include hiking, bicycling, jogging, and picnicking. The trail system has paved and natural surface paths, and also links to the Walnut Creek Greenway, which itself links into the greater Capital Area Greenway System that courses throughout the Raleigh area.

You do not have to do the entire loop around Lake Johnson, as a long boardwalk pedestrian bridge crosses the lake near the Avent Ferry Road crossing. The 5-mile loop begins at the boathouse area. Here the paved portion of the Lake Johnson Trail begins its journey around the east half of Lake Johnson. The boundaries of the park are very close to the lake during the first part of the hike, so you are cruising a wooded strip of land with the water off your right and dwellings within sight to your left. The wide asphalt trail meanders under pines, where it passes the impoundment dam.

The hike then enters a larger part of the park that offers a woodsier atmosphere. A few hills spice up the hike. Downtown Raleigh seems a world away from this part of Lake Johnson Park. Ahead, a scenic route provides an alternate loop. The path then

A wild azalea brightens the springtime woods at Lake Johnson Loop.

turns westerly, as it is hemmed in by I-40. Road noise filters through the trees, but the scenery remains forested. Here the trail passes near an attractive creek that makes a waterfall when flowing strongly, adding to the beauty.

The loop next curves north and takes a spur trail that makes a small circuit of its own to reach the tip of a peninsula overlooking the water. Beyond here the hike cuts across Avent Ferry Road and becomes natural surface and much less used. If you want to shortcut the loop, the long boardwalk bridge running parallel to Avent Ferry Road returns to the parking area.

The trek then becomes more remote as it joins a hiker-only natural surface trail, skirting the increasingly hilly shores of Lake Johnson. Enjoy a few vistas of the lake then turn into the upper part of the impoundment, where willow trees and other vegetation create a marshy wetland. Here a boardwalk crosses the upper reaches of this marsh and Walnut Creek. Beyond here a trail leads up to the large parking area near the park stadium, which is a good parking area when the crowds descend on Lake Johnson. The balance of the hike cruises along the north shore of the impoundment under tall pines. Finally, a second crossing of Avent Ferry Road returns you to the trailhead.

Miles and Directions

0.0   From the parking area just north of the boathouse on the north side of Lake Johnson, take the paved Lake Johnson Trail easterly, passing a trailside kiosk, bridging a little creek, and curving around a small cove. Pass picnic shelter #2.

0.5   The Lake Johnson Trail curves around a deep cove. Continue along the north side of Lake Johnson.

0.8   Reach a trail intersection. Here the Walnut Creek Greenway goes left to alternate parking off Lake Dam Road. Stay right and join the dam holding back the waters of Lake Johnson. Far-reaching aquatic views extend westerly.

1.0   Cross the dam spillway then intersect a spur greenway heading north to link to the Walnut Creek Greenway. The trail reenters woods and is back a little bit from the lake.

1.1   Curve around an intimate cove then roll through mild hills.

1.6   Pass a spur trail leading left to the Magnolia Cottage, a park meeting facility available for rental. Just ahead, the Lake Johnson Trail splits. Stay right with the Scenic Loop as it curves around a hill above the lake, amid copious dogwood trees.

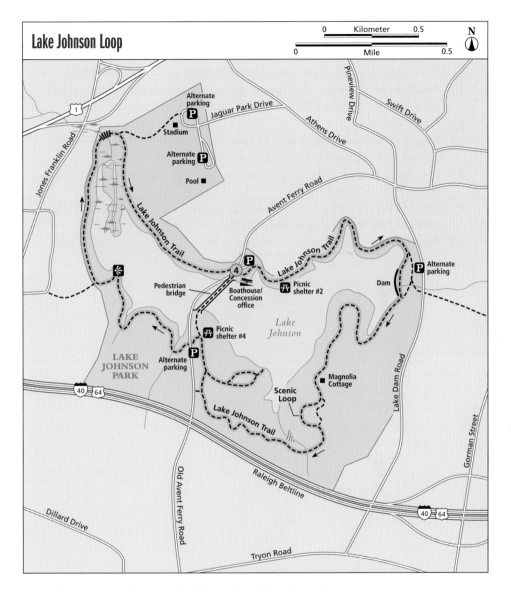

Lake Johnson Loop

0	Kilometer 0.5
0	Mile 0.5

N

1.8 Rejoin the Lake Johnson Trail. Keep right, still southbound but soon to curve westerly.

1.9 Dip to bridge a stream by a culvert. Down from the trail, this stream displays a few cascades and waterfalls at higher flows.

2.1 Cross a second stream by a culvert then climb a hill away from the watercourse.

2.4 A short spur leads left to Avent Ferry Road. Keep straight on the Lake Johnson Trail.

2.5 Come to a trail intersection. Turn right here and make a mini loop and spur reaching out to an overlook of Lake Johnson and a small picnic area. This makes a good stopping point halfway along the hike.

2.9 Return to the Lake Johnson Trail, northbound.

3.0   Come to another trail intersection. Here a paved spur keeps straight and passes picnic shelter #4 to your right, then becomes a boardwalk bridge spanning a narrow segment of Lake Johnson. This is a shortcut if you do not feel like making the entire circuit. However, to do the whole loop, split left here and descend to a parking area and Avent Ferry Road.

3.1   Cross Avent Ferry Road and reach alternate parking. Join a natural surface hiker-only path rolling westerly along the south shore of Lake Johnson after bridging a small branch.

3.4   Cross another creek.

3.7   Come to a view atop a knob. Continue the loop. Cross another branch then stay right as a spur trail leads left toward Jones Franklin Road. Walk a wide path.

4.2   Cross Walnut Creek on a long, wooden boardwalk–type bridge. The willow-bordered stream courses in braids below the bridge.

4.3   Reach the end of the bridge. A paved path heads straight to the stadium parking lot, which rarely fills. Our hike turns right, on a natural surface trail cruising beneath tall pines.

5.0   Reach Avent Ferry Road. Cross the road and arrive at the trailhead, completing the hike.

5 Hemlock Bluffs Nature Preserve

Explore this first-rate preserve harboring unique Piedmont habitat, now nestled in the heart of Cary. A kid-friendly nature center presents programs that enhance the well-marked and maintained trails sightseeing the state preserve, from the bluffs clad in Eastern hemlock to wildflower-filled flats to oak-topped hills.

Start: Stevens Nature Center
Distance: 2.4-mile double loop
Hiking time: 1.5–2.0 hours
Difficulty: Easy, but has steep sections
Trail surface: Mulch, wood steps
Best season: Year-round
Other trail users: None
Canine compatibility: Dogs allowed on 6-foot or less leash

Land status: State-owned, city-operated preserve
Fees and permits: No fees or permits required
Schedule: 9 a.m. to sunset
Maps: Hemlock Bluffs Nature Preserve; USGS Apex
Trail contacts: Hemlock Bluffs Nature Preserve, 2616 Kildaire Farm Rd., Cary, NC 27518; (919) 387-5980; www.townofcary.org

Finding the trailhead: Take exit 293 from I-440 toward Cary. Then join US 1 South toward Sanford and take exit 98-A to join Tryon Road eastbound. Go to the third stoplight and turn right onto Kildaire Farm Road. Go through two stoplights (past Lochmere Golf Course and a shopping center on your left). Cross over a bridge and round a curve. Turn right into the preserve on your right. Official address: 2616 Kildaire Farm Road. Trailhead GPS: N35 43.413', W78 47.005'

The Hike

Hemlock Bluffs Nature Preserve has arguably the best laid out, marked, and maintained trail system in the greater Triangle area. You will be amazed at the wide mulch paths complemented by elaborate stairs on several steep sections. Other portions of pathway have uber-sturdy boardwalks over wetlands. Sumptuous overlook decks enhance the footpaths. It seems the state of North Carolina, complemented by the town of Cary and the Friends of Hemlock Bluffs, as well as volunteers, are sparing no expense and effort in keeping Hemlock Bluffs—an official state natural area—a first-rate hiking experience. Then when you add wildflower gardens and the large Stevens Nature Center, with an on-site staff that leads hikes and executes nature programs, you end up with one of the best environmental education experiences in the Tar Heel State.

During the last ice age, plants that grew in the North Carolina mountains migrated to lower terrain in the Piedmont. The peaks became barren and treeless, covered in hardy sedges and low-growing plants suited for an arctic-type climate, while the Piedmont endured a climate much like the highest peaks of today's Appalachians. When the climate warmed back up, most of these plants, including the eastern

23

Swift Creek is the centerpiece of this park.

hemlock, migrated back toward the mountains or else died out. However, on the nearly sheer north-facing bluffs above Swift Creek in Wake County, a relic stand of eastern hemlocks survived to our day. Their unusual presence on the Piedmont has been recognized by the state of North Carolina with the establishment of a state natural area that is operated by the town of Cary. The initial tract was first protected in 1976. Later a 36-acre parcel and a 29-acre parcel were added, expanding the preserve to the 140 acres of today.

The park's centerpiece flora, the eastern hemlock, is under attack in the North Carolina mountains and beyond up the Appalachians. These hemlocks are imperiled by the invasive bug known as the hemlock woolly adelgid. This critter from Asia, specifically southern Japan, is devastating the hemlocks. They feed on the evergreens. Their signatures are tiny, white, round "golf balls"—egg sacs of the adelgid—on the undersides of hemlock needles. Trees normally die within four to ten years of infestation. There is hope, however, as another insect, a beetle that kills the adelgid, is being propagated and let loose to eliminate the adelgid. Soapy insecticides can also slow the adelgid but require lots of manpower to apply. The verdict is still out on the long-term viability of unprotected hemlocks, a staple tree in moist creekside hollows of the North Carolina mountains. This outlier stand of hemlock is somewhat protected from the spread of the adelgid, but park personnel remain vigilant. Otherwise, hemlocks will go the way of the decimated chestnut tree in the early 1900s, victim of the chestnut blight.

The isolated nature of this stand of approximately 200 hemlocks combined with their precarious existence beyond the Piedmont ought to give you added appreciation of this nature preserve. After examining the Stevens Nature Center, the hike takes you directly to some of these fascinating evergreens. A superlative trail leads out a ridge-line then down steps to a pair of observation decks where you can peer down—and directly at—a stand of hemlocks as they lord over Swift Creek well below. The hike then drops off the north-facing bluff into flats stretching along Swift Creek. Briefly join the breached dam of a long-abandoned mill. It is hard to believe that where you stand overlooks what once was underwater. Beyond, what seems undisturbed forest that wasn't underwater was formerly farmland. The recuperative powers of nature are amazing here at Hemlock Bluffs Nature Preserve. Take a long boardwalk along Swift Creek then turn back to the bluff, where you cruise a wildflower-rich margin before climbing back toward the nature center.

The hike then joins the Chestnut Oak Loop Trail as it explores a lesser-heralded portion of the preserve before returning to Swift Creek and its bluffs. Interestingly, despite being nearly encircled by urbanization, park personnel use prescribed fire in maintaining the upland oak forest along the Chestnut Oak Loop Trail, as well as burning to reduce fuel loads, preventing forest fires from getting out of control. These burns also help native wildlife dependent on the oak habitat, decrease invasive plants, and keep the natural plant order, for chestnut oak forests need fire to maintain their characteristics.

The final part of this hike takes you to overlooks of regal beech trees as well as another impressive stand of hemlocks, clinging to a nearly sheer slope. A little more walking leads uphill back to the nature center, where there is always something new cooking with the staff and facilities. By the way, park naturalists are happy to custom-ize a nature program for your scout group, church organization, or for birthday parties and other special occasions.

Miles and Directions

0.0 From the rear of the Stevens Nature Center, take the mulched path leading west, away from the wildflower gardens and hemlock trees. Quickly reach a trail intersection, where you can go right or left. Head right toward the Swift Creek Loop Trail. Begin heading down-hill to shortly reach wooden steps and decks overlooking a stand of eastern hemlocks.

0.2 Come to a trail intersection after continuing down wooden steps to reach flats along Swift Creek. Head left, beginning the Swift Creek Loop Trail. Quickly come alongside Swift Creek then join a long and elaborate boardwalk bordered in tulip trees. Ritter Park is across Swift Creek, but there is intentionally no access to Ritter Park in order to keep the nature preserve a bastion of passive, nature-oriented activity versus other parks that have ball fields and such. Pass the old milldam.

0.3 Turn to come alongside the bluff in a wildflower-rich flat returned to forest from farmland.

0.4 Complete the Swift Creek Loop Trail. Backtrack up the bluff, passing the first stand of hemlocks again.

Hemlock Bluffs Nature Preserve

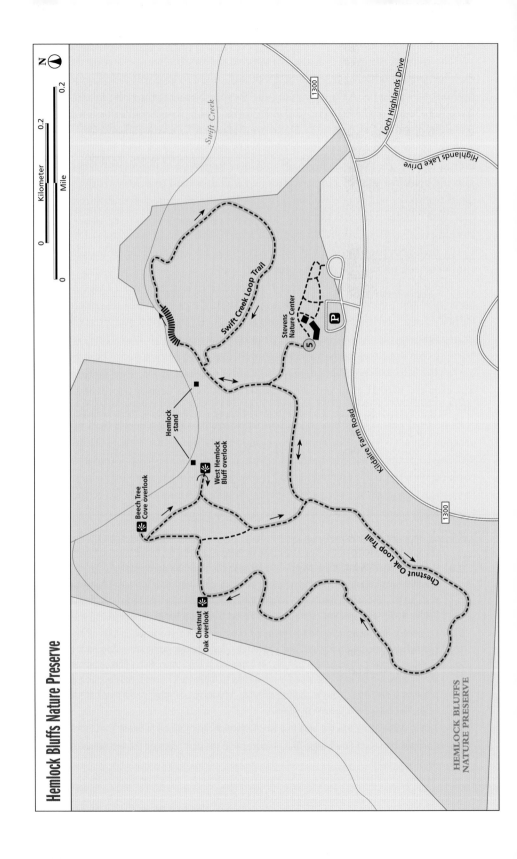

This boardwalk makes passing through the Swift Creek bottoms easy.

0.6 Come near the spur to the nature center. Continue on new trail, heading toward the Chestnut Oak Loop Trail.

0.9 Reach an intersection and the Chestnut Oak Loop Trail. Head left, southbound through fire-managed oak woods on a superlatively maintained trail. Look for white quartz outcrops emerging from the woodland floor.

1.1 Curve back north, dropping to a hollow. Continue wandering ferny draws separated by oak ridges.

1.5 Come to the Chestnut Oak Overlook, where you can peer down into a ravine of a Swift Creek tributary.

1.6 Reach a trail junction. Stay left toward the Beech Tree Cove Overlooks.

1.7 Come to the stairs leading to the lower Beech Tree Cove Overlook. Here you can view the Swift Creek bottoms and a large lightning-damaged beech tree, as well as a big tulip tree. Backtrack to pass the upper Beech Tree Cove Overlook. Continue ascending.

1.8 Take the spur trail leading left to reach the second major stand of hemlocks. Here an observation deck overlooks hemlock trees precariously perched on a sheer slope above Swift Creek. Backtrack and resume the Chestnut Oak Loop Trail.

1.9 Pass a shortcut bypassing the overlooks. Stay left here, gently climbing.

2.0 Complete the Chestnut Oak Loop Trail. Backtrack toward the trailhead.

2.4 Reach the nature center, completing the hike.

6 Peninsula Trail

This trek skirts the shores of Harris Lake, a scenic impoundment in southern Wake County. The hiker-only path never runs far from shore, except to cross the peninsula on which it lies. You'll see ponds, old homesites, and a restored longleaf pine forest amid nearly constant quality scenery.

Start: Near cartop launch and Longleaf Picnic Shelter
Distance: 4.3-mile loop
Hiking time: About 2.5 hours
Difficulty: Moderate
Trail surface: Natural
Best season: Year-round
Other trail users: None
Canine compatibility: Pets on 6-foot leash only

Land status: Wake County park
Fees and permits: No fees or permits required
Schedule: 8 a.m. to sunset
Maps: Harris Lake County Park; USGS Cokesbury
Trail contacts: Harris Lake County Park, 2112 County Park Dr., New Hill, NC 27562; (919) 387-4342; www.wakegov.com/parks/harrislake

Finding the trailhead: From exit 89, New Hill/Jordan Lake, on US 1 southwest of Raleigh, take New Hill Holleman Road south for 2.9 miles to turn right into the park, then follow the main park road to the Longleaf Picnic Shelter. The Peninsula Trail starts near the shelter parking area and runs in conjunction with the path to the cartop boat launch access trail. Trailhead GPS: N35 37.205', W78 55.641'

The Hike

Overshadowed by Jordan Lake and Falls Lake, Harris Lake can hold its own in splendor, as proven by a hike on the Peninsula Trail. True to its name, the Peninsula Trail circles an arrow-shaped point of land jutting into Harris Lake. In fact, the entirety of Harris Lake County Park is situated on this peninsula dividing the Oak Creek arm of the lake from the Little Branch arm. Duke Energy dammed Beaver Creek just before it flows into its mother stream, the Cape Fear River, to provide water for the Harris Nuclear Power Plant, creating Harris Lake. The cooling tower, which you will see during this hike, needs water. The lake provides a continuous, reliable source of water and an opportunity for outdoor recreation, from boating to fishing to waterfowl hunting to waterskiing. Landlubbers like us enjoy hiking along the preserved shore. As you hike, the massive concrete cooling tower will be a beacon much of the way.

Harris Lake stretches over 4,100 surface acres and averages 18 feet in depth, with a maximum depth of 58 feet. There are 40 miles of shoreline, much less than Jordan Lake and Falls Lake.

You gain multiple views of this cooling tower along the hike.

This is the primary park on Harris Lake, though it does not have a boat ramp, just a cartop launch for canoes and kayaks. Other ramps are located on Harris Lake outside the park. In addition to the Peninsula Trail, the park also boasts a set of mountain biking trails ranging from beginner to advanced. It also features a disc golf course. Furthermore, park visitors can enjoy picnicking, a playground, and environmental education programs. On the natural side, part of the peninsula is being managed for longleaf pine, restoring a now rare habitat that once ranged over much of the Carolina Piedmont.

The Peninsula Trail is one of the better hikes in the Triangle. You are never far from water. It leaves a large picnicking area, complete with multiple shelters and shaded picnic sites. Hikers have to navigate through several trail intersections at the hike's beginning before breaking off and wandering the peninsula shoreline. These various intersections, however, allow hikers to shorten the loop if they so choose. The last of these so-called short loops circles around a small waterfowl impoundment, and you actually walk across the dam of this pond, providing an interesting contrast between the small pond to your right and big Harris Lake to your left.

Just as you get your legs going, the numerous intersections are behind you and you enter the Longleaf Pine Management Area, the locale where longleaf pines are being restored to their former glory. Parts of the trail are actually used as fire breaks in managing the longleaf pines, creating different types of forest on each side of the trail in places. The path continues circling around the peninsula, gaining views of the lake and cooling tower, then heads inland, where it visits the Womble Homesite, adding a historical element to the trek, before returning to the trailhead.

Miles and Directions

0.0 Leave the parking area at the trailhead kiosk, following the trail toward the cartop boat launch. After a few feet the Peninsula Trail splits right, bridges a ditch, then quickly reaches another trail intersection. Here the Red Fox Run Trail makes a loop around a small pond. Stay left with the Peninsula Trail and quickly meet another trail intersection. Here the Peninsula Trail leaves right and will be your return route. For now, stay straight with the Peninsula Trail, beginning a clockwise loop.

0.2 Reach another trail junction after passing under a power line. Stay left, as a shortcut leaves right. Come alongside Harris Lake, looking south over the impoundment. Curve into a dammed, marshy embayment.

0.4 Cross a boardwalk over the upper part of the embayment you are circling around. Hike through pine-oak-sweetgum woods through gently rolling terrain.

0.5 Enter a tall pine grove then come back alongside Harris Lake. Just ahead, an unnamed trail leaves right and makes a short loop. Keep straight on the Peninsula Trail.

0.8 Bridge a ditch. Keep westerly along the south shore of the lake.

LONGLEAF PINES

Longleaf pines are being restored at Harris Lake County Park. You pass them on the hike. They really do have long leaves, er—needles. In fact, they have the longest needles and largest cones of any pine east of the Mississippi River. Longleaf pines grow primarily in the eastern half of North Carolina, but their native habitat has been diminished in the Tar Heel State.

This pine is recognized by its straight, tall trunk, few lower branches, thick stout twigs—and long needles. Longleaf pines are valued as naval stores—straight trunks are used for masts and sap is turned into turpentine. However, standing longleaf forests offer regal beauty—where towering trunks contrast with the long green needles and tawny wiregrass stretches between widely dispersed trees. When first emerging from the ground, longleafs are at the "grass" stage, just needles rising from the forest floor. Then a spindly "trunk" rises, topped with a single bulb-like expanse of needles emerging from the top of the plant. These pines are using all their energy to grow their trunk high enough to be able to withstand a low-intensity, lightning-caused ground fire, like those that often sweep through longleaf pine forests. Once they are tall enough, the longleaf begins to branch out and gain height.

The longleaf/wiregrass ecosystem once covered more than 50 million acres in the Southeast and now grows in less than 3 million acres. These nearly level pine woods are easy to develop or alter and thus have been cut over, changed, or allowed to evolve into other forest types due to fire suppression. But with proper management the longleaf pines here at Harris Lake County Park are rising again.

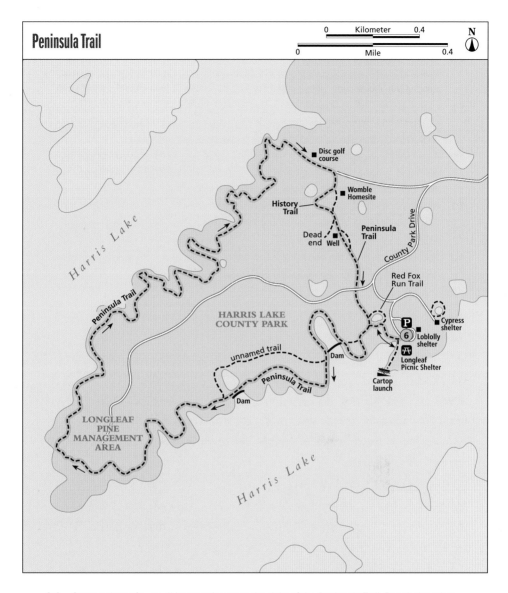

0.9 Cross a dam of a small impoundment to the right of the Peninsula Trail. Reach the other end of the unnamed loop trail and keep straight on the Peninsula Trail.

1.2 Pick up a doubletrack road and reach the Longleaf Pine Management Area. Soon split left, back on singletrack into woods. Harris Lake is still visible through the trees. This is a good place to see deer. Watch for old roadbeds from pre-lake days.

1.7 The trail turns easterly, fixing to traverse the north side of the peninsula. Grab your first views of the Harris Nuclear Power Plant cooling tower. Bridge occasional intermittent streams on wooden bridges. The longleaf pines are left behind.

2.8 Cross the dam of a small farm pond.

3.1 Cut through the power line clearing a second time. Reenter woods then curve out to a peninsula. Soak in more views of the cooling tower.

3.6 Seize a final view of Harris Lake and the cooling tower. Now turn easterly away from the lake to soon turn right again and join a doubletrack road closed to all but park vehicles. Pass near the park's disc golf course.

3.8 Split right from the doubletrack you have been following, then reach the Womble Homesite to your left. The original house was built in 1807. After exploring the homesite, split right on the History Trail. Pass a pond once used for livestock and recreation.

4.0 Rejoin the Peninsula Trail then split left. Reenter woods and come to a covered well. Rainwater from a building ran off here and was captured in the well then reused. Beyond this well, the main trail goes left, but stay right with the History Trail.

4.1 The History Trail and the Peninsula Trail rejoin again.

4.2 Pass under a power line then cross the access road to the Longleaf Pine Management Area.

4.3 Pass the other end of the Red Fox Run Trail just before completing the loop portion of the hike. Turn left here and soon reach the trailhead, completing the hike.

7 Poe Ridge

This hike explores the shoreline and hills of Jordan Lake, near where this impoundment is dammed. Start behind the US Army Corps of Engineers office, where you can enjoy fine lake views, then drop steeply to trace the shoreline, where more aquatic vistas can be had. Turn away from the lake to climb Poe Ridge, traversing great oak forests back to the trailhead. Two shortcut paths allow you to alter the route.

Start: US Army Corps of Engineers visitor center
Distance: 3.5-mile loop
Hiking time: About 2.0 hours
Difficulty: Moderate
Trail surface: Natural
Best season: Year-round
Other trail users: None
Canine compatibility: Leashed dogs allowed
Land status: US Army Corps of Engineers property

Fees and permits: No fee charged at dam visitor assistance center; fee charged at boat ramp parking area
Schedule: Parking area open 8 a.m.– 4:30 p.m., trail also accessible from 24-hour boat ramp parking area
Maps: Jordan Dam Visitor Assistance Center Trails
Trail contacts: US Army Corps of Engineers—Jordan Lake, 2080 Jordan Dam Rd., Moncure, NC 27559; (919) 542-4501; www.saw.usace .army.mil/Locations/DistrictLakesandDams/ BEverettJordan

Finding the trailhead: From exit 79 on US 1, southwest of downtown Raleigh, take Moncure-Pittsboro Road north for 0.2 mile to turn right on Jordan Dam Road. Follow Jordan Dam Road for 2.1 miles to reach the Jordan Dam Visitor Center. Trailhead GPS: N35 39.286', W79 4.228'

The Hike

Back in 1945 the devastating Homestead Hurricane cut a swath through the Southeast. It first landed in South Florida, where its winds tore through greater Miami. The hurricane then moved up the East Coast, leaving Florida briefly for the Atlantic Ocean. It then returned inland and struck North Carolina. This time its winds were not the most harmful aspect. Rather it was copious rain causing extensive flooding along the Haw River and much of the Cape Fear River basin.

After that the US Army Corps of Engineers stepped in with a plan to dam the Haw River southwest of Raleigh, for flood control among other reasons. The Corps acquired land in and around what became the lake. It took twenty-two years for construction to begin on Jordan Dam. Finally, the waters of Jordan Lake began filling in 1981. This federal property has since become an outdoor playground for boaters, hikers, and other outdoor enthusiasts, as well as a wildlife refuge.

This particular hike takes place on that property. Poe Ridge runs northeast–southwest very near Jordan Dam. A fine loop trail was created atop the ridge and along

WHAT IS HERPETOLOGY?

This trail has a "herp habitat." Herpetology is a part of zoology focusing on the study of reptiles and amphibians. "Herps" is a term used by biologists that encompasses all amphibians and reptiles. The most commonly known characteristic of reptiles and amphibians is being cold blooded. This means their body temperature depends on the environment in which they live, as opposed to having a constant temperature like humans do. The herp habitat located along the trail may help you learn a few more facts about North Carolina's amphibians and reptiles, perhaps becoming a junior herpetologist.

Jordan Lake, starting at the Army Corps of Engineers Visitor Center. However, the parking lot has limited hours, so if you cannot get your hike in during the hours the visitor center gates are open, there is an alternative access. The Poe Ridge Boat Ramp is open 24 hours a day, but there is a parking fee.

No matter where you park, expect to enjoy some superior lake views on a singletrack hiking path that has a fair amount of undulation. The hike starts behind the visitor center. Make sure and soak in the view from the observation deck overlooking Jordan Dam. This elevated vista gives you an idea of the massiveness of the lake and the forested shores that surround it. After leaving the visitor center, the Poe Ridge Trail enters dense hardwood forest and soon begins its loop. The path shortly leads to Jordan Lake. Here the trail follows an arm of the lake, curving in and out of hollows where rocky branches flow only after rains. Along the way, pass a pair of shortcuts where marked and maintained trails allow hikers to shorten their loop if they please.

The forest is rich with a wide variety of evergreen and deciduous trees, from scraggly cedar and holly to magnificent shagbark hickories and white oaks. Interestingly, after crossing a fire road, the forest morphs to managed pine habitat, complemented with tulip and sweetgum trees. Here the Army Corps of Engineers uses fire in managing this more open woodland.

The trail passes the second shortcut before reaching the boat ramp parking area. This is where you can park any time of day, without fear of being gated in. Beyond the boat ramp the trail splits and passes a "herp habitat." Herpetology is the study of reptiles and amphibians; thus this area is devoted to those critters. Beyond the herp habitat the trail ascends Poe Ridge then makes its return journey to the visitor center. This part of the hike is easier as you roll under rich forests. Don't forget to grab that view of the lake again from the deck northeast of the visitor center building.

◀ *Keep your feet dry on this footbridge, enveloped in fall color.*

Miles and Directions

0.0 From the rear of the US Army Corps of Engineers Visitor Center, pick up the Poe Ridge Trail. Descend a wide track, passing an outdoor amphitheater. Break left and join a blazed singletrack path. Interpretive information about the value of trees is located along the path.

0.1 Reach the loop portion of the hike. Stay straight here as the return part of the trek leaves left. Cruise underneath flanks of oaks, hickories, and beeches. Ferns spread along the ground.

0.2 Come to a now closed area. You are very near the lake. This was the former visitor center area boat ramp. The Poe Ridge Trail crosses the asphalt road and reenters woods on a steep slope. Ahead, cross the first of many intermittent stream drainages. Many of these drainages have little wooden bridges across them, as this one does.

0.4 Leave the no hunting safety zone that encircles the visitor center and dam area. Partial lake views are easily had. If you cannot stand waiting for a clear view, simply break off the trail for the shoreline. Here you can look up the main body of the lake, with the Haw River arm running due north and the New Hope Creek arm of the lake running northeasterly.

0.7 Briefly follow an old woods road. Continue turning into small coves and out to drier ridges.

0.8 Reach a kiosk with a trail map in the middle of the woods. Continue past the unexpected information locale, crossing another wooden bridge over an intermittent streambed. The lake is nearby.

0.9 Turn away from the lake and span a long wooden bridge. Just ahead, join a closed fire road. Here the Two Mile Shortcut leaves left, tracing the old fire road. Continue straight on the main loop, now in managed, pine-dominant forest.

1.2 Reach another trail intersection. Here the Three Mile Shortcut leaves left to angle up Poe Ridge. Keep straight, bridging a seasonal wetland on a boardwalk. Here the trail turns away from the lake, routing above an old trail segment that flooded. Roll through piney woods, bridging more streambeds.

1.5 Follow a gravel trail segment lined with rocks to keep you in the right direction.

1.7 Emerge near the Poe Ridge Boat Ramp. Here is a large alternate parking area, along with a restroom. The loop turns left, heads directly in front of the restroom, then leaves the lake area. Pass under a power line, eastbound.

1.8 The trail splits. The left fork goes through the herp habitat, which highlights reptiles and amphibians of the Lake Jordan area. The main loop stays right and climbs the northwest side of Poe Ridge.

2.0 Come very near Jordan Dam Road then meet the other end of the herp habitat access. Continue northeast along Poe Ridge, running roughly parallel to Jordan Dam Road, in classic hickory-oak woods.

2.5 The Three Mile Shortcut enters on your left. Stay forward with the main loop. The trail turns away from Jordan Dam Road in a hilly area. Hike through rock-lined trail amid tall pines and oaks.

2.9 Meet the wide fire road that is the Two Mile Shortcut. Stay straight on the main loop, a hiking trail.

3.2 Reenter the no hunting safety zone.

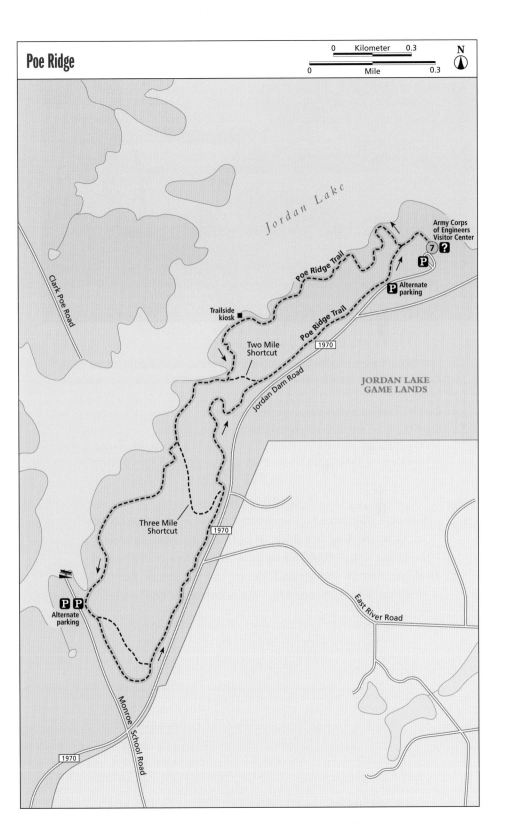

Poe Ridge

0 Kilometer 0.3

0 Mile 0.3

N

Jordan Lake

Clark Poe Road

Army Corps
of Engineers
Visitor Center

7 ?

P

Alternate
parking

P

Poe Ridge Trail

Poe Ridge Trail

Trailside
kiosk

Two Mile
Shortcut

Jordan Dam Road

1970

JORDAN LAKE
GAME LANDS

Three Mile
Shortcut

1970

East River Road

P P

Alternate
parking

Monroe School Road

1970

Looking out on a cove of Jordan Lake

3.3 Come near an alternate parking area on Jordan Dam Road. Cross a gated asphalt road that once led down to the former boat ramp. Circle left around a maintenance building on a steep slope.

3.4 Complete the loop portion of the hike. Backtrack uphill.

3.5 Reach the visitor center, completing the hike.

GREEN TIP:

Minimize the use and impact of fires. Use designated fire spots or existing fire rings (if permitted). When building fires, use small sticks (less than 1.5 inches in diameter) that you find on the ground. Keep your fire small, burn it to ash, put it out completely, and scatter the cool ashes.

8 New Hope Lakeside Loop

This is a fun hike. Explore the shoreline of Jordan Lake on a peninsula encircled by water on three sides. The trek takes you to the tip of the peninsula and a fine view before following the shoreline in deep forest. The loop then reaches a shortcut, offering a lesser circuit. However, the longest loop continues along more scenic shoreline, entering hilly terrain before ending. Consider adding tent camping or boating to your adventure at this multifaceted recreation area.

Start: New Hope Overlook Boat Ramp parking area

Distance: 5.1-mile loop

Hiking time: About 2.5 hours

Difficulty: Moderate

Trail surface: Natural

Best season: Year-round

Other trail users: None

Canine compatibility: Leashed dogs allowed

Land status: State recreation area

Fees and permits: Seasonal entrance fee

Schedule: Jan, Feb, Nov, Dec: 8 a.m.–6 p.m.; Mar, Apr, Sept, Oct: 8 a.m.–8 p.m.; May, June, July, Aug: 8 a.m.–9 p.m.

Maps: New Hope Overlook Trails

Trail contacts: Jordan Lake State Recreation Area, 280 State Park Rd., Apex, NC 27523; (919) 362-0586; www.ncparks.gov

Finding the trailhead: From exit 59 on I-540, west of Raleigh, take US 64 west for 5.9 miles to Beaver Creek Road. Turn left on Beaver Creek Road and follow it 3.2 miles to turn right on Pea Ridge Road. Follow Pea Ridge Road for 2 miles to W. H. Jones Road. Turn right on W. H. Jones Road then reach the New Hope Overlook entrance station after 0.5 mile. Turn right at the entrance station and follow it 0.2 mile toward the boat ramp. After entering the boat ramp parking area, look left for the trailhead. Trailhead GPS: N35 40.949', W79 2.887'

The Hike

This trek makes a fine circuit along an extensive peninsula of Jordan Lake known as the New Hope Overlook area. The hike is the centerpiece of land- and water-based recreation that presents not only hiking but also walk-in tent camping and boating. There are two camping areas here. Both offer campsites strung out along a trail, so you have to carry your stuff from the parking area to the campsite. Each campsite has a picnic table, fire ring, and lantern post. I have camped here myself and pronounce it a fine, rustic experience.

Jordan Lake State Recreation Area is composed of several different locales along the shores of big Jordan Lake, located west of Raleigh and south of Chapel Hill. The New Hope Overlook area is one of the prettiest, in my opinion. Being on a peninsula in the New Hope Creek arm of the lake adds an additional aquatic aspect to the land. At the same time, its limited amenities keep New Hope the domain of hikers and primitive campers. However, during the warm season there will be boaters on every

Trail markers show the way through colorful woods.

portion of Jordan Lake. Speaking of warm season, this trail is in deep enough forest that you can stay relatively cool during a morning hike even in summer's swelter.

A restroom and water fountain are at the trailhead. The hike immediately enters thick woods of pine, sweetgum, and maple. The forest is relatively young and densely growing. The Red Trail is marked throughout both the northern and southern loop, and the Blue Trail is blazed just on the northernmost loop.

It isn't long before you turn north and begin heading for the tip of the peninsula. Rock piles and low rock fences in this area reveal the hard work of long-ago farmers who cleared and used this land for pasture or field. The owner was what we now call a subsistence farmer. He grew crops and raised livestock for his family's use, to survive, to grow enough food to make it through the winter. Then do it all over again. A typical subsistence farmer might have a couple of pigs, some chickens, a few cows, and hopefully a horse for transportation and farm work. A vegetable garden always got the best spot and was close to the house. Fruit trees shaded the yard. Row crops such as corn were grown to consume over the winter. Tobacco was often raised to bring a little income in for things that could not be grown, such as coffee, sugar, and maybe a yearly new pair of shoes. Nothing went to waste. The native trees have since risen again, and the former farm is part of Jordan Lake State Recreation Area.

The trail leads through rich forest, with a mix of hardwoods. Evergreens such as pine, holly, and cedar add a year-round splash of green. The hike heads north before emerging at a cove, where a warm-up view awaits. Continuing the quest for the New Hope Overlook, you take a spur trail to the northern tip of the peninsula. Here the balance of the lake stretches north in a horizon of water and trees. The beach of the Ebenezer Church area is easily visible in the near northeast. In the far distance the US 64 bridge spans Jordan Lake. Coves, inlets, and other peninsulas stretch into the yon. This view is worth the hike itself. In winter all will be quiet, but a sunny summer Saturday may be a noisy chaos of boats out there.

Your hike down to the south end of the peninsula first passes near camping Area A then crosses its access road before coming alongside the New Hope Creek channel of Jordan Lake, where New Hope Creek once flowed free. The channel remains narrow, giving Jordan Lake a riverine aspect here. The hike gives plenty of lake viewing opportunities as it comes to the water's edge numerous times. In other places the trail turns inland up shallow vales. You also have a chance to cut the hike in half with a shortcut.

The longer loop eventually leaves the shoreline for good, climbing a hill known as Merry Oaks, where camping Area B is located. The path turns away before reaching the crest of the hill and meanders over more hills. The final quarter of the hike has the most undulations before taking you back to the trailhead.

Miles and Directions

0.0 Leave west from the trailhead on a singletrack path into thick pine woods. The trail is blazed in both red and blue.

0.1 Reach the loop portion of the hike. Turn right here, heading northbound. The trail continues to be blazed in red and blue.

0.2 Cross a wooden bridge over an intermittent streambed. The peninsula has no perennial streams, but you will pass over other bridges like this, spanning watercourses that flow only during wetter periods.

0.4 Briefly view the Area A campground access road to your left.

0.6 Reach a cove and unobstructed view of Jordan Lake. Here you can look easterly at a small arm of the impoundment.

0.8 Come to a trail intersection. Turn right here and walk out to the peninsula tip. Here you can gaze north onto the New Hope Creek arm of Jordan Lake. Sit a spell on the observation bench then backtrack, resuming the loop.

1.0 Bisect the gravel Area A access road.

1.1 Drop off a hill and slip over to the New Hope Creek channel of the lake. Views open of the serpentine body of water. Turn uphill and away from the water before dropping again.

1.5 A short spur trail leads right, down to the lake. Turn away from the water here, heading up a hollow.

1.8 Rock piles reveal the agricultural past of this now forested land.

2.2 Come to a trail intersection. Here you can shortcut the loop by going left, or stay right with the Red Trail and make the longer loop. Stay right, heading south and coming along the shoreline again, following red blazes only. This part of the trail shows lesser use.

2.5 Bridge the largest stream of the peninsula. Watch for beech trees in the ravines here.

3.4 A user-created spur trail leads right down to the water. This is your last chance to access the lake, as the Red Trail turns easterly and begins working up the west side of Merry Oaks Hill.

3.6 Dip to a drainage and keep climbing.

New Hope Lakeside Loop

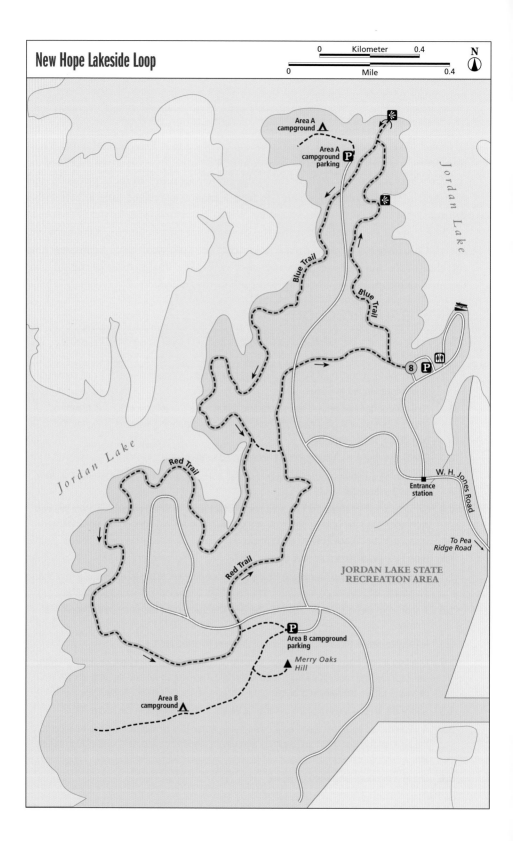

Kilometer 0 0.4

Mile 0 0.4

N

Area A campground

Area A campground parking

Blue Trail

Blue Trail

Jordan Lake

8 P

Jordan Lake

Red Trail

Red Trail

W. H. Jones Road

Entrance station

To Pea Ridge Road

JORDAN LAKE STATE RECREATION AREA

Area B campground parking

Merry Oaks Hill

Area B campground

3.9 Reach a trail intersection on the slope of Merry Oaks Hill. Here a spur trail leads right to the parking lot of Area B campground. Just ahead, cross a gravel road and keep straight, still on the Red Trail. Cruise through tall oak woods.

4.5 Come to another trail junction after surmounting a hill. You are at the shortcut. Stay right here, rejoining the Blue Trail, again following red and blue blazes.

4.8 Cross the Area A access road a second time. Climb over a final hill then descend through young woods, passing a small clearing on trail right.

5.0 Complete the loop portion of the hike. Keep straight.

5.1 Reach the trailhead, finishing the hike.

9 Ebenezer Church Walk

This pair of short loops wanders through the heart of Ebenezer Church Recreation Area, on the shores of Jordan Lake. Leave the often lively swim beach area and join the Ebenezer Church Trail. Visit the site of an 1820s church and later homestead then wander past a bucolic farm pond before returning to the trailhead. Your second walk first passes through a picnic area then makes a loop on the Old Oak Trail, where interpretive information and yet another pond awaits.

Start: Ebenezer Church Recreation Area swim beach parking
Distance: 0.9-mile loop and 1.6-mile loop
Hiking time: About 1.5 hours
Difficulty: Easy
Trail surface: Natural
Best season: Fall through spring
Other trail users: Picnickers
Canine compatibility: Leashed dogs allowed

Land status: State recreation area
Fees and permits: Seasonal entrance fee
Schedule: May, June, July, Aug: 8 a.m. to 9 p.m.; Sept, Oct, Mar, Apr: 8 a.m. to 8 p.m.; Nov, Dec, Jan, Feb: 8 a.m. to 6 p.m.
Maps: Ebenezer Church Recreation Area
Trail contacts: Jordan Lake State Recreation Area, 280 State Park Rd., Apex, NC 27523; (919) 362-0586; www.ncparks.gov

Finding the trailhead: From exit 59 on I-540, west of Raleigh, take US 64 west for 5.9 miles to Beaver Creek Road. Turn left on Beaver Creek Road and follow it 2.1 miles to turn right into Ebenezer Church Recreation Area. (Do not turn into Ebenezer Boat Ramp, 0.5 mile south on Beaver Creek Road.) Pass the gatehouse and then turn left into the swim beach parking area. The Ebenezer Church Trail starts in the southeast corner of the parking lot. Trailhead GPS: N35 42.442', W79 1.448'

The Hike

What we see today as Jordan Lake, enveloped in vast forests and interspersed with recreation areas, was not always so. This part of North Carolina has been pioneered since the 1700s. Simple farms were once scattered throughout the New Hope Creek valley. One hand-hewn log home, measuring 21 by 18 feet, started out as a house in the late 1700s, but was dismantled and moved to a hilltop clearing in pine woods, just off Beaver Creek Road. That year, 1827, Ebenezer Church was established, meeting in the former log home. Settlers and slaves, black and white, came in wagons, on horses, and on foot to worship together in Ebenezer Church. The house of worship soon outgrew the small building and moved. By 1840 the log structure had become a farmhouse again. The farm thrived, and other buildings were built around the old log house, including corncribs, tobacco barns, and a kitchen. By the early 1900s the log structure was no longer inhabited, and a new farmhouse was built nearby. Passersby lamented the abandonment of the familiar log structure as it fell into decay. Eventually the Ebenezer Church area was condemned and purchased as part of the

Trees reflect off a still woodland pond.

Jordan Lake dam project. Today the only evidence of the old church and the "new" farmhouse, built in 1918, is a brick chimney adjacent to the Ebenezer Church site. Yet the naming of the recreation area for Ebenezer Church is an appropriate nod to the past.

Unfortunately, the log structure that was the original Ebenezer Church was damaged by vandals. Only the site remains. As time marched on, members of Ebenezer Church changed buildings twice, and thought they were settled for good in 1890, when their Gothic Revival–style building was constructed. Then, in the 1970s the church was moved to its present location on Beaver Creek Road, since its previous location was to be flooded by Jordan Lake. The 1890 Gothic Revival building was placed on the National Register of Historic Places in 1985. However, not only were the buildings displaced by the lake, but also many of the church members were moved from the land they loved. Many left the area, though others settled nearby. Sometimes we do not think about the cost of progress, such as a flood-controlling lake, to the people who came before us.

Today you are able to visit the original site of Ebenezer Church, see the long-standing chimney of the farm that was there, and view two old farm ponds of this former agricultural backwater. This excursion presents a good opportunity to reflect on how times have changed and how fast the pace of life is in the Triangle today. You will also walk quiet country lanes turned hiking trails, view wire fences that once contained livestock, and imagine crops growing in fields that are now protected forest, inhabited only by our fleeting visits.

GREEN TIP:
Avoid sensitive ecological areas. Hike, rest, and camp
at least 200 feet from streams, lakes, and rivers.

WHAT IS A WOLF TREE?

During this hike you will see what foresters call "wolf trees." These trees, obviously much larger than trees of the surrounding forest, were once "lone wolves"; for example, a white oak that once shaded a home, or a tree in a grazing pasture. These trees typically have thick trunks and horizontal or outward-protruding branches. Since the Ebenezer Church area has become part of Jordan Lake State Recreation Area, a forest has grown around these wolf trees and they are no longer alone, but they do still stand out.

However, those fleeting visits can be fun. Here at Ebenezer Church Recreation Area, you can not only hike the nature trails but enjoy the myriad picnic facilities, take a dip at the swim beach, play in the playground, fish along the shore, or launch your boat into Jordan Lake and tool around.

The two loops are short, not hilly, and great for families young and old. Do one loop or do both. Bring the whole clan. There is a lot to do here at Ebenezer Church Recreation Area.

Miles and Directions

0.0 Find the Ebenezer Church Trail in the southeast corner of the swim beach parking area, marked by a large sign. Join a gravel track in rich woods. Big trees line the trail. It is easy to see this trail was once a road.

0.1 Cross a little wooden bridge over a streambed. Willow oaks rise regal and tall.

0.2 Reach the loop portion of the Ebenezer Church Trail. Keep straight and quickly come to the Ebenezer Church site, marked by a sign and some rocks and metal relics. A short spur trail leads to a half-crumbled brick chimney. Contemplate all that has transpired here. After exploring, continue on the loop. Watch for a huge white oak, a "wolf tree," standing massive among younger trees.

0.4 Cross the road linking the main recreation area to the boat ramp. Ahead, come to then make a half circle around an old farm pond.

0.7 Cross the road linking the main recreation area to the boat ramp again. Rejoin another obvious wide, tree-lined former road. Ahead, complete the loop and begin backtracking.

0.9 Return to the swim beach area trailhead. Now head toward the main road and pick up the Connector Trail, leaving across the main road. Here it heads north then splits with a short path linking to Shelter #2. Stay right at the split. Cruise woods.

1.0 Cross a picnic area road then pass to the left of restrooms. Shortly cross a second picnic area road. The path is marked. Pass by picnic tables.

1.3 The Connector Trail emerges at a third picnic area road, at the official trailhead for the Old Oak Trail. The signed path starts across this last picnic area road. The Old Oak Trail quickly splits. Head left. Tree identification signs are posted along the path.

1.4 Stay straight after intersecting the Shortcut Trail. Wooden boardwalks cross potentially wet areas. An arm of Jordan Lake is visible through the trees to your left. Pass thick stands of nonnative bamboo to your left.

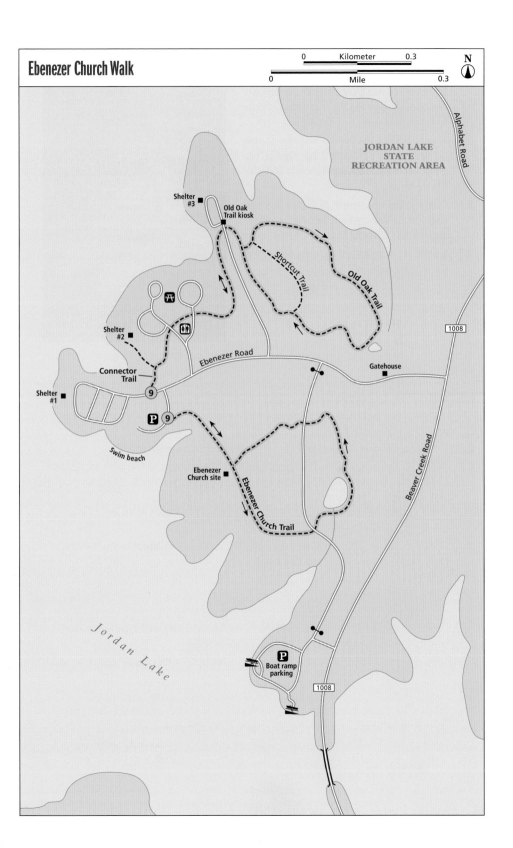

Ebenezer Church Walk

0 Kilometer 0.3
0 Mile 0.3

N

JORDAN LAKE
STATE
RECREATION AREA

Alphabet Road

Shelter #3

Old Oak Trail kiosk

Shortcut Trail

Old Oak Trail

1008

Shelter #2

Connector Trail

Ebenezer Road

Gatehouse

Shelter #1

9

P 9

Swim beach

Ebenezer Church site

Ebenezer Church Trail

Beaver Creek Road

Jordan Lake

P Boat ramp parking

1008

1.8 Walk near an old cattle pond to the left of the trail, more evidence of an agricultural past. Turn west into pines. Look for more evidence of homesteads—wire fencing, metal farm machinery parts, and more.

1.9 Keep straight on the Old Oak Trail after passing the other end of the Shortcut Trail. Pass an old pond that is now thick with sediment and only fills seasonally.

2.1 Complete the loop portion of the Old Oak Trail. Begin backtracking toward the beach parking area on the Connector Trail.

2.5 Emerge at the beach parking area, completing the two-part walk.

Trailside fungi add a touch of color to the woodscape.

10 American Tobacco Trail

A walk on the southernmost segment of this long rail trail will leave you wanting to explore the entire thing. This portion starts in southern Wake County and crosses the expansive wetlands of Beaver Creek, where marshy views stretch in the distance. Cross Olive Chapel Road then continue on to sandy Reedy Branch and a bridge. From there you can extend your hike another 20 miles if desired.

Start: South trailhead off New Hill-Olive Chapel Road
Distance: 2.8-mile there-and-back
Hiking time: About 1.5 hours
Difficulty: Easy
Trail surface: Pea gravel
Best season: Year-round
Other trail users: Bicyclers, joggers
Canine compatibility: Pets on 6-foot leash only

Land status: Jordan Lake Game Lands
Fees and permits: No fees or permits required
Schedule: 8 a.m. to 1 hour before sunset
Maps: American Tobacco Trail; USGS New Hill
Trail contacts: Wake County Parks, Recreation & Open Space, 1309 New Hill-Olive Chapel Rd., Apex, NC 27502; (919) 387-2117; www.wakegov.com/parks/att

Finding the trailhead: From the intersection of US 64 and NC 751 at the Wake-Chatham county line, southwest of Raleigh, take New Hill-Olive Chapel Road south for 2 miles to the trailhead entrance road on your left. Follow the entrance road to shortly dead-end at 0.4 mile. Official trailhead address: 1309 New Hill-Olive Chapel Road, Apex, NC 27502. *Note:* The trailhead gate is opened and closed strictly on schedule, so plan your outings accordingly. Trailhead GPS: N35 42.919', W78 56.604'

The Hike

The American Tobacco Trail is a 23-mile-long rail trail stretching from southern Wake County near Jordan Lake north into Chatham County and eventually into Durham County and the city of Durham. Hikers, bicyclers, and equestrians utilize this former railroad grade that a century back carried railcars full of tobacco brought up from both North and South Carolina to the American Tobacco factory, then a maker of several brands of cigarettes. It is this history that gave the trail its name.

Like many railroads, this branch of the old Norfolk Southern Railway fell out of use due to the rise of the automobile for personal travel and shipping via trucks. The rail line then lay dormant, but in 1990 the newly founded Triangle Rails to Trails Conservancy identified the Norfolk Southern Railroad corridor as a principal target for developing a rail trail in the capital region.

Back then rail trails were a relatively new concept, and it took many meetings—more government meetings than you would ever want to sit through—to get the ball rolling. However, local horseback riders were already using the abandoned railroad

This concrete post once kept engineers apprised of their mileages.

corridor and were also touting the possibility of this abandoned railroad line becoming an official trail open for not only equestrians but also hikers and bicyclers. Today we understand that rail trails can be self-transportation avenues, exercise venues, and just a way to simply stroll into nature.

Developing rail trails can be a complicated process. For example, the American Tobacco Trail spans three counties and multiple cities and towns, and crosses numerous roads, bridges multiple creeks, and even spans I-40 near Durham. Different government agencies maintain these parcels, roads, and waterways; therefore the trail and its crossings must be addressed individually. In addition, the American Tobacco Trail travels through Jordan Lake Game Lands, which are managed by the North Carolina Wildlife Resources Commission. And then there is developing trailheads, preparing the trail surface and informational kiosks and signage, and then maintaining it all. So you can imagine the bureaucratic red tape and nightmares that ensued. And we think going to get our driver's license renewed is a hassle!

The first portion of the trail in Wake County, 3.5 miles, was opened in August 2003. The rest of the Wake County segment was opened in 2005, including the trailhead where this hike starts. Meanwhile, Durham had already opened trail segments and Chatham County later followed suit. The pedestrian bridge over I-40, on the northern end of the trail, was a major costly challenge. However, the 270-foot, $11 million span was completed in February 2014 and provides a critical link in making the American Tobacco Trail contiguous from beginning to end, starting at the New Hill–Olive Chapel Road trailhead and going all the way to the Durham Bulls Athletic

Park. Other greenways and trails are linking to the American Tobacco Trail, creating a grand network of public pathways coursing through the Triangle. Speaking of grand pathways, the American Tobacco Trail is a designated portion of the East Coast Greenway, a partly built and planned 2,600-mile-long distance trail stretching from Key West, Florida, to Calais, Maine. Obviously, the East Coast Greenway is a long time in the making, but hopefully one day we can travel off roads from the Sunshine State all the way up the Eastern Seaboard to New England. And part of it will be on the American Tobacco Trail.

The American Tobacco Trail is surfaced in different ways, depending upon what stretch of trail you travel. This hike travels over what is known as compacted screenings, which means a hardened combination of gravel and clay. Other sections are asphalt with a parallel trail, or edge, of pea gravel. Still other sections have grass, clay, or are completely paved. Not all sections are open to equestrians, mostly the southern part of the trail in Chatham and Wake Counties, where it passes through rural areas more suitable for horses.

When starting this hike at the large New Hill–Olive Chapel Road trailhead, you wonder where the railroad grade is. Actually, you have to drop off a hill, entering Jordan Lake Game Lands, then make a turn and join the obvious railroad grade. What makes this segment alluring is the fact that it almost entirely travels through these wooded game lands, keeping the scenery natural. A corridor of trees provides shade over most of the track, except where it bridges Beaver Creek. But it is in this section along Beaver Creek where the most notable scenery stands. Here in the backwaters of Jordan Lake lies an expansive wetland, a place where craggy trees flooded from beaver activity stand naked over the landscape, providing perches for birds. Below, willows and other brush border the slow-moving stream, providing ideal conditions for wildlife from waterfowl to raptors to fish. Luckily for us the railroad corridor was built up over the wetlands, allowing dry passage yet good views. The bridge over Beaver Creek provides an ideal vantage point. Beyond here the American Tobacco Trail stays in woods before crossing Olive Chapel Road. It then comes to the bridge over Reedy Branch, a sandy, clear stream. The bridge here makes a good turnaround point, though trail travelers can continue another 2 miles, passing under US 64 then reaching another stretch of Jordan Lake Game Lands and the bridge over White Oak Creek, making for a nearly 7-mile there-and-back endeavor.

Miles and Directions

0.0 Leave the large parking area at the trailhead restrooms and kiosk, and descend a hill entering thick woods. Bridge a small streamlet. The wide track soon turns right.

0.1 Come to a four-way intersection. Here the undeveloped rail line enters from the right while a game lands access keeps straight. The American Tobacco Trail heads left here, joining the Norfolk Southern Railway right-of-way. The hiking is level on a wide, ditch-bordered track, though hills rise from the ditches. You are in thickly wooded North Carolina game lands, so consider the hunting seasons.

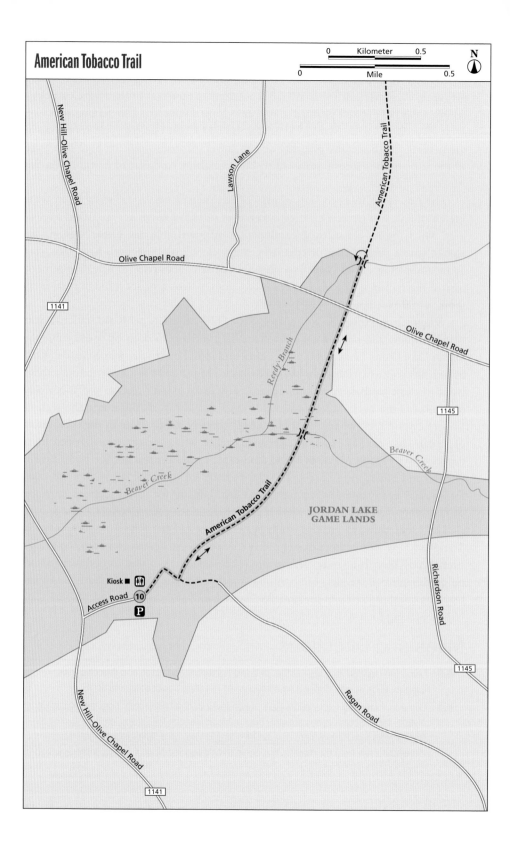

0.7 Enter the Beaver Creek wetlands. Forest falls away and marshes stretch on both sides of the elevated rail grade. In the summer frogs will be croaking loudly while in winter a skim of ice may cover the non-moving water surfaces.

0.8 Cross the bridge over Beaver Creek. This open area provides clear expanses of the wetlands, which stretch upstream to your right and downstream to your left toward Jordan Lake. The American Tobacco Trail continues traveling a high berm above the swamp. Forest continues after leaving the wetlands.

1.2 Pass an old concrete railroad line marker on the right-hand side of the trail just before reaching and crossing two-lane Olive Chapel Road. No parking is allowed here. Continue straight on the wide rail trail under a canopy of hardwoods and pines.

1.4 Come to the bridge over Reedy Branch. Here you can look down on the sandy water-way. This is a good place to turn around if just wanting to get a sample of the American Tobacco Trail. Just ahead, the path leaves the Jordan Lake Game Lands before continuing on to pass under US 64 via a tunnel. Backtrack from the Reedy Creek bridge if not continuing on.

2.8 Reach the trailhead, completing the hike.

11 Bond Park Hike

This loop sightsees throughout the entirety of Cary's Fred G. Bond Metro Park. The 310-acre park has multiple offerings for Triangle residents, including hiking trails integrated into the natural and man-made aspects of the preserve. The hike uses a mix of natural surface trails and paved greenways that link to Bond Park. Your adventure takes you through woods, along Bond Lake, atop wetlands, and more along the way.

Start: Bond Park Community Center trailhead
Distance: 3.2-mile balloon loop
Hiking time: 1.5–2.0 hours
Difficulty: Easy
Trail surface: Asphalt, natural
Best season: Early fall through late spring
Other trail users: Joggers, bicyclers on greenways

Canine compatibility: Leashed dogs allowed
Land status: City of Cary park
Fees and permits: None
Schedule: 7:30 a.m. to sunset
Maps: Fred G. Bond Metro Park; USGS Cary
Trail contacts: Fred G. Bond Metro Park, 801 High House Rd., Cary, NC 27512; (919) 462-3970; www.townofcary.org

Finding the trailhead: From exit 291 on I-40, west of Raleigh and east of Cary, take Cary Towne Boulevard 0.8 mile west to turn left on Maynard Road. Follow Maynard Road for 3.6 miles to turn left on High House Road. Follow High House Road for 0.8 mile to turn left on Maury Odell Place, the second entrance into Fred G. Bond Metro Park. Once in the park, follow Maury Odell Place a short distance to reach a T intersection. Turn left here and make another quick left to reach the Bond Park Community Center parking area. Trailhead GPS: N35 47.043', W78 49.491'

The Hike

Fred G. Bond Metro Park is a prototype millennial city park. Not only does it function as a greenspace for the town of Cary, the acreage also encompasses other community facilities such as the community center, senior center, and amphitheater. The park also presents a variety of outdoor pursuits, everything from baseball to fishing, self-propelled boating, even a ropes course, along with traditional picnic shelters and playgrounds. Furthermore, the park is a crossroads for Cary's greenways, adding more possibilities, including bicycling. There is something for everybody.

You will make an impromptu tour of the park on this hike, heading by nearly all the facilities. You will also see how the 310 acres are encircled by housing developments and business concerns, making it all the more valuable as a park. Start your hike on the Paw Paw Trail, initially circling the Bond Park Community Center and coming near the Senior Center then the Compost Education Center before turning to the base of Bond Lake, briefly joining White Oak Greenway, which leaves west, linking to other greenways.

This bridge spans a wetland/stream near Bond Lake.

Bond Lake, at 41 acres, offers a good opportunity for Triangle paddlers or anglers to ply their skill. Gasoline motors are prohibited, making for a serene experience. A boat ramp is available for park visitors, as long as their boats are 16 feet or under. There is a launch fee. During the warm season, park boats can be rented, from pedal boats to rowboats, canoes, kayaks, and even sailboats! Anglers take note that permanent underwater fish attractors have been placed in the lake. Catfish, bream, and bass are commonly caught.

Our hike wanders along much of the shoreline of Bond Lake, allowing you to scout out potential fishing spots and plan your paddle. Not only do you cruise the lakeshore, but also you get to circle around the wetlands of the upper lake, where Swift Creek and Crabtree Creek deliver their flows into Bond Lake. This blending of land and water, and these wildlife-rich wetlands, create another component of the

WHY THE FUNNY NAME?

The presence of pawpaw trees here at Bond Park inspires the name of the Paw Paw Trail. Pawpaws are a smallish understory tree growing in moist woods. They are often found together in groups since they reproduce by root sprouts. Pawpaws have large leaves, 6 to 12 inches in length, which droop like their tropical cousins farther south. Their yellow, banana-like fruit is favored by wildlife, especially raccoons and possums. Settlers made bread and puddings from pawpaw fruits, and attempts have been made to cultivate pawpaw as a fruit tree. Pawpaws range up the Eastern Seaboard to New England and down to north Florida. They are found all over North Carolina, save for the immediate Atlantic Coast and Outer Banks.

Lone waterfowl on Bond Lake

hike. Ahead, cross these tributaries by bridge, adding moving water panoramas to the still water overlooks of Bond Lake.

The hike then joins and leaves a pair of paved greenways, Oxford Hunt Greenway and Black Creek Greenway, both of which extend beyond the bounds of Bond Park and are important components of the Cary greenway network. Rejoin a natural surface path with the Pine Cone Trail. It leads through the eastern flank of the park then returns you to the trailhead, completing the hike. While you are here, save some time to engage in some of the other activities offered at this bountiful, modern park, whether it's picnicking, fishing, boating, or maybe even engaging the ropes course.

Miles and Directions

0.0   As you face the Bond Park Community Center, look right for the trailhead kiosk and asphalt path. Walk just a few feet on the asphalt path then head left on the natural sur-face Paw Paw Trail (another trail leads right toward Bond Lake, visible from the trailhead). The Paw Paw Trail stretches about 10 feet wide and is layered in wood chips in places. Roll under hardwoods and evergreens. Come near the Bond Park Community Center.

0.2   Reach a four-way trail junction. Here the Pine Cone Trail leaves right, an unnamed natural surface trail heads toward High House Road, and the Paw Paw Trail heads left, circling westerly between the community center and High House Road.

0.3   Come to another four-way intersection. Here a paved track leads left back toward the com-munity center parking lot, and another paved path leads right toward the senior center. Keep straight on the Paw Paw Trail, squeezing between the community center parking lot and Maury Odell Place. Pass another asphalt spur left to the parking area, then cross Maury Odell Place. Reenter woods.

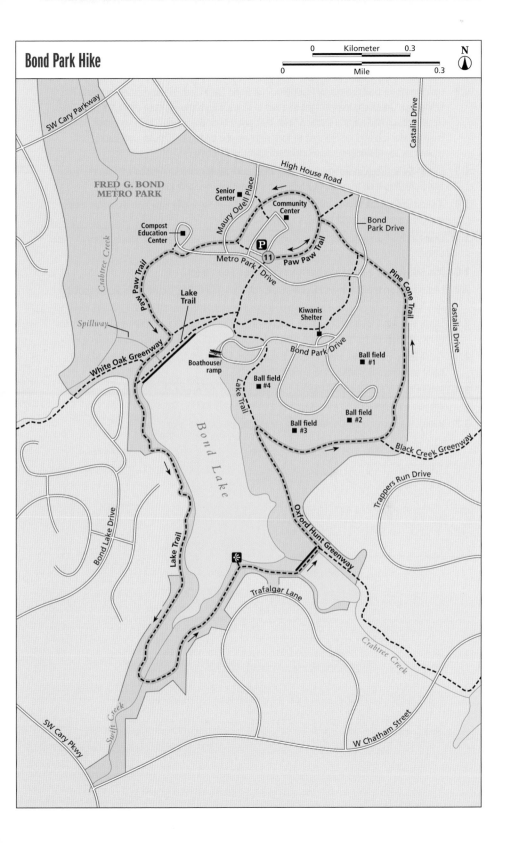

Bond Park Hike

SW Cary Parkway

Castalia Drive

High House Road

**FRED G. BOND
METRO PARK**

Senior
Center

Community
Center

Bond
Park Drive

Maury Odell Place

Compost
Education
Center

P
11

Metro Park Drive

Paw Paw Trail

Paw Paw Trail

Pine Cone Trail

Castalia Drive

Crabtree Creek

Lake
Trail

Kiwanis
Shelter

Spillway

White Oak Greenway

Lake Trail

Boathouse/
ramp

Ball field
#4

Ball field
#1

Ball field
#2

Bond Park Drive

Ball field
#3

Black Creek Greenway

Bond Lake

Trappers Run Drive

Bond Lake Drive

Lake Trail

Oxford Hunt Greenway

Crabtree Creek

Trafalgar Lane

SW Cary Pkwy

Swift Creek

W Chatham Street

0.5 Bisect Metro Park Drive on a well-marked and maintained pathway. Curve near the Compost Education Center.

0.7 Join the White Oak Greenway just below the Bond Lake Dam. Head right on asphalt. The White Oak Greenway leaves right at a set of stairs. Climb the stairs to meet the Lake Trail. Head right on the natural surface Lake Trail, southbound in woods. Now you have Bond Lake to your left and residences to your right as you tread an irregular undulating path broken by small bridges spanning intermittent streambeds.

1.5 Bridge Swift Creek in wooded wetland. The future Swift Creek Greenway will join the Lake Trail here. This hike turns back north, circling around the Swift Creek embayment.

1.8 A short spur leads to a point overlooking Bond Lake. Enjoy the view and then turn into a second, lesser arm of the lake.

1.9 Cross a small dam holding back a pond of Crabtree Creek. Watch for beaver signs in these parts.

2.0 Turn left, joining the Oxford Hunt Greenway. Head northwest.

2.3 Leave right on the Black Creek Greenway, still on asphalt. Begin curving in woods behind ball fields.

2.5 Leave left with the natural surface Pine Cone Trail as the Black Creek Greenway heads for points east. Hike north along the east boundary of Bond Park through gently rolling woods.

2.9 Cross Bond Park Drive. Just beyond, a spur path leaves left toward the Kiwanis Shelter. Keep straight, still on the Pine Cone Trail.

3.0 Return to the four-way intersection from the start of the hike. Leave left, backtracking on the Paw Paw Trail.

3.2 Reach the Community Center parking area, completing the hike.

12 Lake Crabtree County Park

This hike encompasses more than just this county park by Lake Crabtree. The trek actually leaves the park boundaries and makes a full 6-mile circuit around the entirety of Lake Crabtree using bridges, boardwalks, and narrow strips of land, meandering over wetlands, streams, along the shores of the impoundment, and over hills. Views are plentiful. The facilities at the county park enhance the experience.

Start: Westerly parking lot near the Old Beech Nature Trail

Distance: 6.0-mile loop

Hiking time: 3.0–4.0 hours

Difficulty: Moderate–difficult

Trail surface: Natural

Best season: Year-round

Other trail users: Mountain bikers on segments

Canine compatibility: Pets on leash only

Land status: Wake County park

Fees and permits: No fees or permits required

Schedule: 8 a.m. to sunset

Maps: Lake Crabtree County Park; USGS Cary

Trail contacts: Lake Crabtree County Park, 1400 Aviation Pkwy., Morrisville, NC 27560; (919) 460-3390; www.wakegov.com/parks/lakecrabtree

Finding the trailhead: From exit 285 on I-40, west of downtown Raleigh and southeast of Durham, take Aviation Parkway west for 0.2 mile to turn left into Lake Crabtree County Park; follow the main park road for 0.3 mile to the parking area on your right. The Old Beech Nature Trail starts from the parking area, but you will be taking the Lake Trail, which starts within sight of the parking area. Trailhead GPS: N35 50.533', W78 47.727'

The Hike

The emphasis is on recreation here at Lake Crabtree County Park. The 212-acre preserve is situated on the north shore of 512-acre Lake Crabtree, a lake built as part of the flood prevention effort in Wake County. Almost every square foot of this park is devoted to having a good time in the great outdoors. I-40 forms the north boundary of the park, and it is near the interstate where a 9-plus-mile vein-like network of mountain biking trails traverses wooded terrain. Closer to the lake you have aquatic outdoor activities such as fishing and boating. The park has a boat ramp for your own craft and also boat rentals for fishing, rowing, sailing, or simply paddling. Fishing here is catch and release only and is permitted only in designated areas. The park also has several picnic shelters and picnic sites as well as volleyball courts, horseshoe pits, and an elevated observation tower that is the park's signature building. You will see this tower while hiking the Lake Trail. The Lake Trail starts at Lake Crabtree County Park, beginning its 6-mile journey around Lake Crabtree. Most of the Lake Trail is hiker only, except for a portion where it intersects the Black Creek Greenway and near the main mountain biker parking area.

The development and layout of the Lake Trail is impressive in the way the trail uses finite shoreline property as well as going near roads, bridges, and businesses. But with adjacent woods and the open waters of Lake Crabtree always close by, the hike is certainly a natural experience. The adventure starts near the Old Beech Nature Trail, a worthy 0.6-mile walking experience in and of itself. To join the Lake Trail, walk across a wide, grassy floodplain area where park enthusiasts can often be seen tossing a disc or flying a kite next to the shores of Lake Crabtree. Join a marked, mown path and cruise wetlands along the shore of the impoundment, using boardwalks where the terrain is too sloppy. You enter a stand of pines then come alongside Aviation Parkway. Here the trail travels along a causeway directly next to the road. And yes, this is not the most pleasant portion of the Lake Trail, but to complete the loop around Lake Crabtree you have to compromise a little bit in certain locations. After leaving Aviation Parkway, the trail transforms, joining a boardwalk in beautiful forestland. Beyond here you find yourself at times along the shore soaking in views aplenty and at other times walking in the woods with business buildings in sight.

The Lake Trail then arcs around the wide floodplain and wetland of upper Crabtree Creek where it feeds Lake Crabtree. You cross Crabtree Creek on a hiker-only iron footbridge running parallel to Evans Road. Once again, come alongside cars for a brief period before turning away from Evans Road to again parallel the meandering shore. This section of trail is somewhat hilly, and hikers will experience ups and downs as well as fantastic views of Lake Crabtree County Park and its facilities. These views also give you an idea of how far you have to go to complete your 6-mile hike.

The Lake Trail bends into the Black Creek embayment. Black Creek is a tributary of Crabtree Creek. Here is another stream and wetland, and a trail intersection. This is where the Black Creek Greenway heads southeast, linking to other pathways in Wake County. The Lake Trail also becomes paved at this point and is open to bicycles. After curving out of the Black Creek embayment, the Lake Trail opens onto grassy shoreline with extensive views only to be topped by the better panoramas from the Lake Crabtree Dam, which you soon climb atop. From the dam, soak in commanding views of the lake and surrounding office buildings and Lake Crabtree County Park. This dam area offers an alternate access from Old Reedy Creek Road. From this point almost to the end, you will encounter mountain bikers, so be on the lookout, even though they are supposed to yield the right-of-way to hikers. In reality, many pedalers expect you to jump out of their way because they are going so fast. However, this section is quite scenic as it skirts the wooded shore, going by designated overlooks of the lake while intersecting part of the mountain bike trail network.

The last part takes you into the concentration of park facilities and parking lots. This area turns into a confusing maze of trails and roads under a forest canopy. My advice is if you get turned around, simply keep Lake Crabtree to your left and stick

This boardwalk leads you through piney, sometimes-wet woodlands. ▶

Overlooking Lake Crabtree and shoreline anglers

near the shoreline, and you will return to your car. On the other side is the main park road, and if you emerge along it, you can simply walk the road back to the parking area. Either way, your hike around the lake and the impromptu tour of the Lake Crabtree County Park facilities will bring you back to this outdoor jewel of the Triangle again.

Miles and Directions

0.0 From the Old Beech Nature Trail parking area, head northwest toward Lake Crabtree and look for the signed Lake Trail (do not take the Old Beech Nature Trail). Starting in a grassy area by the lake, immediately cross a small wooden bridge and then walk a mown path in open terrain. The lake stretches to your left. Boardwalks take you through wetter areas.

0.3 Enter pine-oak woods.

0.4 Come alongside Aviation Parkway. Turn southwest and parallel the road, crossing Lake Crabtree on a causeway. Willowy marsh stretches left.

0.8 Leave left from the road, enter woods, and join a boardwalk. Go on and off bridges and boardwalks between forested lands. Contemplation benches are scattered along the shore. Come off and on a sewer line right-of-way.

1.2 Curve into the marsh of Crabtree Creek. Connector trails link to businesses.

1.8 Come near Evans Road and cross Crabtree Creek on a hiker-only bridge. The trail continues to parallel Evans Road.

2.0 Turn left, away from Evans Road, joining a plank boardwalk in a forested wetland. Note the buttressed trees.

2.3 Skirt alongside a hill to your right with the lake to your left. Trail bridges, boardwalks, and plank walkways continue. Office buildings rise to your right.

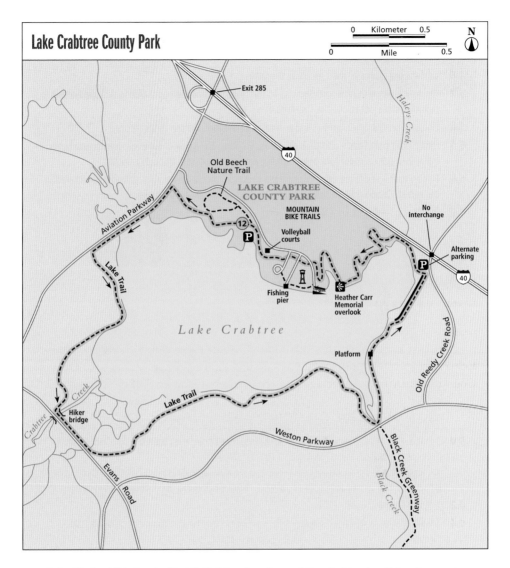

Lake Crabtree County Park

Exit 285

Old Beech
Nature Trail

LAKE CRABTREE
COUNTY PARK

MOUNTAIN
BIKE TRAILS

No
interchange

Aviation Parkway

Lake Trail

Volleyball
courts

Alternate
parking

Fishing
pier

Heather Carr
Memorial
overlook

Lake Crabtree

Platform

Old Reedy Creek Road

Lake Trail

Creek

Hiker
bridge

Crabtree

Weston Parkway

Black Creek Greenway

Black Creek

Evans
Road

Haleys Creek

2.6 Climb a hill below the MetLife Building then descend. The singletrack path heads on and off a hill and a sewer line right-of-way.

3.7 Cross the bridge over Black Creek after working around some hills. Here the Black Creek Greenway stretches southeast. The Lake Trail heads left, now as a paved track open to bicycles.

4.0 Pass an observation platform overlooking Lake Crabtree. The trail continues close to the shore. Pass through a fence line and the dam spillway. Climb the 45-foot dam.

4.4 Reach the end of the dam and the Old Reedy Creek Road alternate parking. Mountain bikers often use this trailhead to access the mountain bike trails of Lake Crabtree County Park; therefore be on the lookout for fast-pedaling mountain bikers. Return to natural surface trail.

4.5 Pass through a fence and come back alongside the lake, officially reentering Lake Crabtree County Park. Curve around the lake with noisy I-40 just to your right. Pass mountain bike trail intersections but stay on the Lake Trail.

4.8 Cross a dry drainage then return to the lake.

5.2 The trail splits with hiker-only access to the Heather Carr Memorial Overlook. Here a deck provides clear vistas of Lake Crabtree.

5.4 Bridge a branch after turning into a small embayment. Return to the shore.

5.5 Come near park roads and parking areas, entering the maze of facilities, roads, and paved trails. Turn past a mountain biker parking area then cut west through woods.

5.8 Return to the shoreline after passing playgrounds, picnic areas, and restrooms scattered in the forest. Cruise past volleyball courts in grassy flats along the shore.

6.0 Reach the trailhead, completing the loop.

13 Schenck Memorial Forest

This hike explores the woods of Schenck Memorial Forest, a North Carolina State University property. You first join the Francis L. Liles Trail then come alongside Richland Creek, following it to meet Reedy Creek Road and other potential trail connections. Next, backtrack a bit before continuing up Richland Creek. Explore richly wooded bottomlands before looping back to the trailhead via a gated forest road, passing the forest arboretum.

Start: Pole gate off Schenck farm road
Distance: 2.6-mile balloon loop
Hiking time: 1.0–2.0 hours
Difficulty: Moderate
Trail surface: Natural, gravel
Best season: Year-round
Other trail users: None
Canine compatibility: No pets allowed
Land status: North Carolina State University property

Fees and permits: No fees or permits required
Schedule: Sunrise to sunset
Maps: Schenck Forest Trail Map and Educational Signs; USGS Raleigh West
Trail contacts: College of Natural Resources, North Carolina State University, 2800 Faucette Dr., Raleigh, NC 27607; (919) 515-6191; http://cnr.ncsu.edu

Finding the trailhead: From exit 289 on I-40, west of downtown Raleigh and southeast of Durham, join Wade Avenue and go just a short distance before getting off at the Edwards Mill Road/PNC Arena exit. From there go left, away from the arena, northeast on Edwards Mill Road for 0.7 mile, then turn left on Reedy Creek Road. Follow Reedy Creek Road 0.1 mile to turn left into the Schenck Forest and go 0.2 mile. Park on your right on a dirt road. The hike starts at a pole gate, leaving right, off the dirt road. Trailhead GPS: N35 48.975', W78 43.231'

The Hike

So how does a German forester end up having a forest named after him in the Piedmont of North Carolina? It is called the story of Dr. Carl Alwin Schenck. Forestry was in the blood of this man born in Darmstadt, Germany, whose grandfather was a forester. At this time the scientific study of forestry was unknown and unpracticed in the United States. Nevertheless, in Germany Carl Alwin Schenck ran in the company of Sir Dietrich Brandis, the leading forester of his day. Schenck assisted Brandis while touring forests throughout Europe, gaining knowledge and learning the scientific process of forestry.

When George Vanderbilt established his massive Biltmore estate in western North Carolina, Schenck was hired as chief forester upon the recommendation of Mr. Brandis. This was 1894, and the twenty-six-year-old Schenck moved to the United States and became the father of American forestry. He even opened a forestry school—the first in the United States—in 1898. Schenck continued to manage the Biltmore

RIVER BIRCH ON RICHLAND CREEK

Richland Creek flows through the western edge of the Schenck Memorial Forest. It is here, in rich bottomlands, where river birches can be found. This is the only birch in the western hemisphere that grows at low altitudes. It is found throughout the Southeast and North Carolina as well as up the East Coast to southern New England and wetter parts of the Mississippi River Valley from Iowa down to Louisiana. River birches are easy to identify, and you had better get it right while in an educational forest like Schenck; otherwise you will have to pick up pine cones for two hours after your hike. First, look for the leaning tree in creek and river bottoms, with its silvery-gray, sometimes brownish, bark separating into papery scales. When bigger, river birch bark becomes thick, fissured, and shaggy. River birches regularly fork low to the ground and lean. Its often drooping leaves turn orange-yellow in autumn.

River birches can withstand occasional inundations that come with life in a floodplain. These high water events often shape the tree, to where it ends up facing downstream. However, this ability to live in the bottoms makes it an important plant to maintain stream bank integrity, cutting down on erosion and keeping streams like Richland Creek and forests like Schenck healthy and thriving.

Estate forest and the forestry school until 1914, when he felt the call to return home to defend his native Germany in World War I. Mr. Schenck served on the Russian front and was injured in battle.

After the war Mr. Schenck returned to forestry and became a world-renowned forester, speaking, lecturing, and leading forest tours in both Europe and the United States. In 1939 war again loomed in Germany, ending Schenck's travels. He stayed in his home country during the war, but his reputation grew such that by the 1950s Mr. Schenck came to the United States for a reunion tour of sorts. He was bestowed with honors that included forests and tree stands named for him. In 1952 North Carolina State honored him with a Doctor of Forest Science degree and ultimately named this 245-acre tract of forest for him. His papers are housed at North Carolina State University to this day.

The Schenck Forest is used by North Carolina State University as an outdoor training and study area for a number of outdoor-related programs in addition to forestry. You could say it is a gigantic outdoor classroom for the campus, standing 10 minutes east of Schenck. The forest is also open to the public and has a decent trail system that links to the Capital Area Greenway System.

The oldest and most popular trail here is the Francis L. Liles Trail, a path established in 1981 that includes interpretive signage along the way. It was named for an esteemed North Carolina State professor. Here you will learn that this area was once a farm and has undergone numerous changes and continues as an experimental

Planted pines shade the grassy forest floor.

forest. The path dips down a hollow, crisscrossing streamlets before making its way to Richland Creek. Here you can follow the Loblolly Trail downstream along Richland Creek to leave Schenck Memorial Forest and meet the Reedy Creek Trail, a paved path heading west to meet the trail system at Umstead State Park and right to link to the greater Capital Area Greenway. Here a portion of the Loblolly Trail also continues to meet the Loblolly Trail at Umstead State Park. These are additional options not detailed in this hike. The trek at Schenck Forest then backtracks, heading up Richland Creek and continuing up the creek drainage. At this point the trail has two names—Richland Creek Trail and Loblolly Trail. Names aside, the path comes near Wade Avenue, where this hike leaves the creek and joins a gated forest road crossing Schenck Forest. Here you pass a tree grove and arboretum as well as a maintenance area. The final part of the walk passes a welcome picnic area with a shelter.

Miles and Directions

0.0 From the gated road off the main entrance, leave right, westerly, walking 100 feet then splitting right on the signed Francis L. Liles Trail. Begin walking a singletrack pine needled path, enjoying a series of interpretive signs about the land and the forest.

0.2 A spur trail leads left to the forest picnic area. Stay right and descend into a hollow.

0.3 Cross a stream on a boardwalk bridge. Continue descending a ferny forested hollow. Big loblolly pines rise around you.

0.5 Bridge the main stream of the hollow again.

0.7 Reach a trail intersection. Here the Francis L. Liles Trail heads left and uphill, and has more interpretive signage from which to learn. Our hike, however, keeps right and descends a few feet to meet the Loblolly Trail. Head right on the Loblolly Trail, immediately bridging the

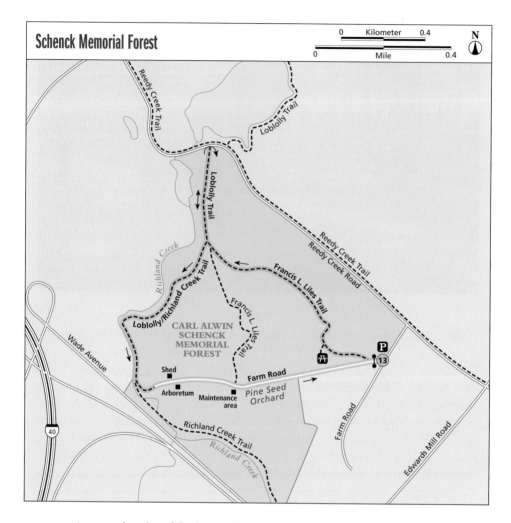

stream you have been following, northbound. Bottoms and wetlands of Richland Creek lie to your left as a hill rises to your right.

1.0 Come to Reedy Creek Road and extended hiking options, either continuing the natural surface Loblolly Trail or joining the paved Reedy Creek Trail. Both hikes leave the Schenck Memorial Forest. The Schenck hike, meanwhile, backtracks.

1.3 Return to the intersection where you just were, but this time pick up a new trail, heading along Richland Creek on the Loblolly/Richland Creek Trail. Walk flats alongside the creek, occasionally working around previously flooded areas. This can be a decent wildflower spot in spring. Richland Creek flows around sandbars, logjams, and vertical banks. Sycamores, river birch, and ash rise overhead.

1.9 Reach a trail intersection. Turn left, easterly up a hill, while the Richland Creek Trail keeps along Richland Creek and astride Wade Avenue. Soon rise to a gravel road. Keep straight here, shortly passing a shed on your left and the forest arboretum on your right. Stay straight with the doubletrack.

Hiker looks on Richland Creek.

2.2 Reach the maintenance area, to the right of the doubletrack. Here another doubletrack comes in on your left and is the end of the Francis L. Liles Trail. Stay straight to soon near the forest pine seed orchard.

2.5 Pass the forest picnic area, shaded by some large hardwoods. Keep straight.

2.6 Reach the forest road gate and the end of the hike.

14 Loblolly Trail

This loop combines one of the most scenic hiker-only paths in William B. Umstead State Park with a multiple-use trail to explore the south part of the park. First, pass a historic cemetery then drop to bottoms along Reedy Creek and a tributary stream before wandering hills and hollows to meet the multiuse trail. It takes you on high ridges then down to Reedy Creek Lake, a pretty impoundment. Finally, return to the trailhead using another multiuse trail and a quiet park road.

Start: Reedy Creek entrance to Umstead State Park
Distance: 4.0-mile balloon loop
Hiking time: 1.5–2.5 hours
Difficulty: Moderate
Trail surface: Natural, packed gravel and clay
Best season: Year-round
Other trail users: Hikers only on Loblolly Trail, bicyclers and equestrians on multiuse trails
Canine compatibility: Leashed dogs allowed

Land status: State park
Fees and permits: Seasonal entrance fee
Schedule: Reedy Creek entrance–Nov–Feb: 8 a.m.–6 p.m.; Mar, Apr, Sept, Oct: 8 a.m.–8 p.m.; May–Aug: 8 a.m.–9 p.m.; Nov: 7 a.m.–7 p.m.
Maps: William B. Umstead State Park
Trail contacts: William B. Umstead State Park, 8801 Glenwood Ave., Raleigh, NC 27617; (919) 571-4170; www.ncparks.gov

Finding the trailhead: From exit 287 on I-40, west of downtown Raleigh and southeast of Durham, take Harrison Avenue just a short distance east to the Reedy Creek entrance of Umstead State Park. Follow the main road to a large parking area at its end. Reedy Creek entrance official address: 2100 Harrison Ave., Cary, NC 27513. Trailhead GPS: N35 50.185', W78 45.564'

The Hike

William B. Umstead State Park has an extensive trail network. Some trails are hiker only and make multiple loops. Still other trails are multiuse and are open to bicyclers and equestrians. The Loblolly Trail, the main path on this hike, is a hiker-only track, but as an out-and-back path, it does not make a loop. However, also using the Reedy Creek Multiuse Trail, hikers can create a rewarding loop that visits not only moving streams but also still waters, not only narrow singletrack footpath where you watch your every step, but also wider foot-friendly trail that allows you to focus more on the surroundings instead of each footfall. To complete this circuit, you do have to follow a park road for a short distance, but the road is a dead-end road and is no busier than the multiuse trail.

The Loblolly Trail leaves from the northeast corner of the large parking area at the Reedy Creek entrance to Umstead near picnic shelter #2 and briefly follows an old road past the Young Cemetery, visible evidence that most of what became Umstead State Park was settled. Small subsistence farmers cobbled out a living here on the

A buckeye blooms beside the Loblolly Trail.

hilltops and down in the hollows, working the land and living for the next planting season. Of course, those days are long gone, but the simplicity of such a life sometimes seems welcome compared to our hectic, high-speed, electronic gadget–filled lives in the big city. Yet trails like this provide a welcome respite from the digital age and an opportunity to regenerate and reintegrate into nature.

The hike leaves the cemetery to cross a park road leading to a pair of ranger residences, as well as a couple of group campgrounds. You cruise along a ridge full of pines, perhaps the inspiration for the trail name. Loblolly pines grow primarily in the Southeast, from Texas up to Maryland and down to Florida. They thrive in a variety of habitats, from poorly drained floodplains like those along Reedy Creek to hilly uplands like this section of trail. Loblolly pines grow naturally throughout central and eastern North Carolina. It is also an important commercial pine, and is grown in plantations in the South and used for both pulpwood and lumber. Loblolly is a very fast-growing tree, which increases its commercial value. Loblolly pines can grow to huge dimensions along stream bottoms, which is the reason for its nickname as bull pine. Another secondary name is rosemary pine, from its fragrant resin-filled foliage.

This hike then drops down to Reedy Creek, one of the prettier waterways in the Piedmont. There has been a hiker bridge here in the past and there may be in the future, but at least there will be stabilized stepping-stones for crossing the creek. The wild water-flow fluctuations and urbanized streamshed of Reedy Creek create conditions that have blown out previous hiker bridges. Under flood conditions you may have to turn back. Beyond Reedy Creek the trail surmounts a ridge and dips to a feeder stream of Reedy Creek. Here the moist hollow recalls the mountains of the western part of the state. The hike then comes near Reedy Creek Lake but turns

A pre-park graveyard of former residents stands beside the trail.

away, climbing yet another hollow, ultimately rising to meet the Reedy Creek Multiuse Trail. The trailbed and atmosphere change as you walk a wide track atop a long ridge dividing Reedy Creek from Crabtree Creek. The walking is easy as you work your way down to the shores of Reedy Creek Lake. Here you join the Reedy Creek Lake Multiuse Trail, crossing Reedy Creek Lake Dam. A final climb leads to the infrequently driven road accessing the ranger residences and group camps. After completing the hike, I think you'll agree that the combination of singletrack and wide trails, high ridges, and deep hollows are an ideal mixture for a fine day hike.

REEDY CREEK STATE PARK?

The Reedy Creek entrance area of William B. Umstead State Park used to be its own entity under the name of Reedy Creek State Park. After the establishment of what is now Umstead State Park in the 1930s, the powers that be decided in 1950 to make a separate state park to be used only by African Americans. They portioned off 1,000 acres and created Reedy Creek State Park, which includes the area where this hike takes place and was the reason for this separate Reedy Creek entrance in the first place. Reedy Creek State Park was in existence for sixteen years until the entire park was integrated as one.

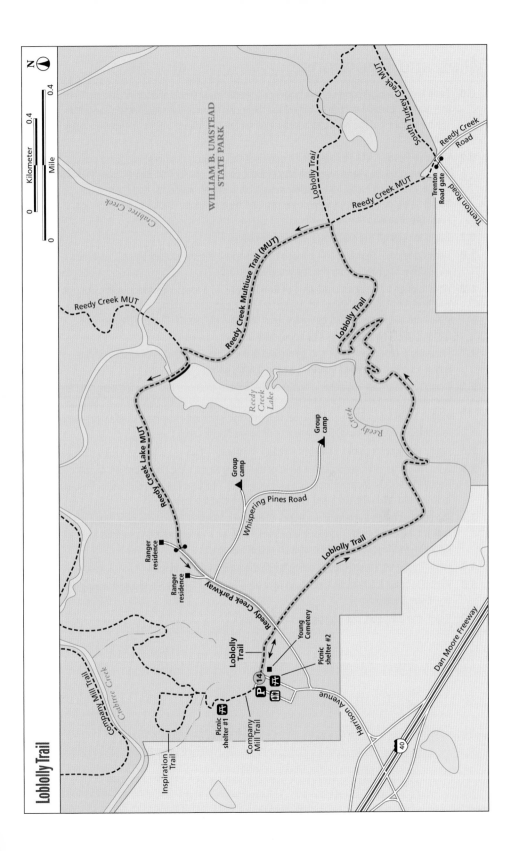

Loblolly Trail

Miles and Directions

0.0 From the back right corner of the large parking area, near picnic shelter #2, join the Loblolly Trail as it heads east to quickly reach the Young Cemetery. A rusted fence surrounds the headstones of the no longer used internment of the former cotton- and corn-farming family.

0.2 Come to Reedy Creek Parkway, which accesses the ranger residences and group camps. Cross the quiet, two-lane road and stay straight on the Loblolly Trail. Reedy Creek Parkway will be your return route. Immediately pass a homesite on your right, likely part of the Young family clan. Walk under a power line and reenter woods. Look for rock piles from when the area was farmland.

0.7 Begin to drop off the ridge you have been crossing.

1.0 Reach and cross Reedy Creek, shaded by sycamores and big loblolly pines. Cruise bottoms then climb away from the stream, entering hills.

1.2 After topping a hill, cross a tributary of Reedy Creek on a footbridge. Wander through hills and hollows. Pay close attention, as the trail has been rerouted over the years and some hikers are still using the old pathways. Stay with the trail blazes. Come within sight of upper Reedy Creek Lake before turning away.

1.7 Return to Reedy Creek Lake and its marshy regions, then turn away yet again, heading easterly up a steep-sided hollow. Rise into upland oaks.

2.1 Come to a four-way intersection and the Reedy Creek Multiuse Trail. Turn left here, heading northwest on the Reedy Creek Multiuse Trail, as the balance of the Loblolly Trail continues east to leave the state park. The wide multiuse trail, once a former road used by pre-park residents, is easy walking. Slowly descend toward Reedy Creek Lake.

2.6 Reedy Creek Lake comes into sight through the trees.

2.8 Come to a trail intersection within sight of the Reedy Creek Lake Dam. Turn left on the Reedy Creek Lake Multiuse Trail, as the Reedy Creek Multiuse Trail keeps straight. Descend to meet and cross the dam and spillway. Climb beyond the dam.

3.4 Top out and reach the end of the Reedy Creek Lake Multiuse Trail and a gate. Head left here on the ambitiously named Reedy Creek Parkway; a ranger residence stands to your right. Follow the road, passing a second ranger residence.

3.6 Pass Whispering Pines Road heading left to the park group camps.

3.8 Return to meet the Loblolly Trail. Head right here, rejoining footpath and backtracking. Pass the Young Cemetery.

4.0 Reach the trailhead, completing the circuit hike.

15 Company Mill Loop

This circuit hike leaves a busy trailhead then drops to a breached mill and scenic locale on Crabtree Creek. Beyond this popular spot the trek climbs a ridge then drops to visit Sycamore Creek before eventually returning to travel alongside Crabtree Creek again. The ample hills, alluring creeks, and tributary drainages all draped in woods keep beauty on the front burner the entire hike.

Start: Reedy Creek entrance to Umstead State Park

Distance: 5.8-mile balloon loop

Hiking time: 2.5–3.5 hours

Difficulty: Moderate–difficult

Trail surface: Natural

Best season: Spring for wildflowers, fall for color, winter for solitude

Other trail users: Joggers, dog walkers

Canine compatibility: Leashed dogs allowed

Land status: State park

Fees and permits: Seasonal entrance fee

Schedule: Reedy Creek entrance—Nov–Feb: 8 a.m.–6 p.m.; Mar, Apr, Sept, Oct: 8 a.m.–8 p.m.; May–Aug: 8 a.m.–9 p.m.

Maps: William B. Umstead State Park

Trail contacts: William B. Umstead State Park, 8801 Glenwood Ave., Raleigh, NC 27617; (919) 571-4170; www.ncparks.gov

Finding the trailhead: From exit 287 on I-40, west of downtown Raleigh and southeast of Durham, take Harrison Avenue just a short distance east to the Reedy Creek entrance of Umstead State Park. Follow the main road to a large parking area at its end. Reedy Creek entrance official address: 2100 Harrison Ave., Cary, NC 27513. Trailhead GPS: N35 50.194', W78 45.592'

The Hike

The Company Mill Trail starts at the Reedy Creek entrance to William B. Umstead State Park, conveniently located off I-40. Being an attention-grabbing trail with a combination of aquatic and upland habitats, as well as having local historical significance, makes it a popular path. However, many of the hikers who start the Company Mill Trail hike only the mile to the former Company Mill site on Crabtree Creek, and enjoy their time at this breached dam, rapids, pool, and rocks, rather than doing the entire circuit hike. Furthermore, multiple trails leave from this trailhead, making the parking area sometimes seem like a zoo. I think you will be surprised, though, how few people will be on the trail. Timing your hike for early morning, weekdays, and during winter will avail relative solitude.

Crabtree Creek is a fascinating waterway. Here inside the park, the waterway is one superlatively scenic stream, with rocky rapids, still pools, logs topped with sunning turtles, bluffs covered in mountain laurel, and, of course, a little history. The site of Company Mill is evident when you reach Crabtree Creek, as the breached stone dam forms a straight line. After crossing the creek on a bridge, you come to an

impressive millstone and plaque marking the site of the mill, operated by the Page family for about 120 years, starting in the early 1800s. In addition to the dam, various stoneworks, and the millstone, you will see other signs of the past, such as concrete forms whose purpose is lost to time. While searching for other clues of the past, you may also notice the rich forests that have regenerated throughout the park, providing a sea of green in the greater Triangle, with wildflower-rich flats lying below evergreen-clad bluffs. Outside the park, Crabtree Creek has its scenic spots but is looked upon by locals more as a flood danger than a wildlife corridor. That is why there are so many dams along it in the Raleigh metropolitan area. The establishment of a long greenway along Crabtree Creek is availing local residents a chance to view Crabtree Creek in a more favorable light, however.

After meandering through hollows and over a ridge, this hike also visits Sycamore Creek, itself a tributary of Crabtree Creek. Sycamore Creek is also alluring while flowing through the park, but the visit is brief as the hike takes you back through hills and upland woods before returning to Crabtree Creek for an encore stopover. Once again you return to the Company Mill site and the potential crowds. From here backtrack to the trailhead. If you are still feeling energetic, take the 0.4-mile-long Inspiration Trail, an interpretive path with informational signage located near the trailhead, which also has picnic shelters, restrooms, and a plethora of picnic tables.

◀ *A millstone from the Company Mill lies beside the trail.*

A dogwood stands out by Crabtree Creek.

Miles and Directions

0.0 From the back left corner of the large parking area, take the gravel Company Mill Trail north into woods. (Do not take the Loblolly Trail. It leaves from the back right corner of the same parking area.) Pass through an area with picnic tables scattered on either side of the trail.

0.1 Come to picnic shelter #1. Walk along the right side of the shelter then make a series of switchbacks, descending. Do not shortcut the switchbacks in this gravelly, erosive area. The path becomes natural surface, but has many rocks and roots exposed through heavy use.

0.2 Meet the Inspiration Trail after bridging a small tributary of Crabtree Creek. The Inspiration Trail leaves left to make a short loop featuring interpretive signage. The Company Mill Trail keeps straight, still working toward Crabtree Creek in pines and oaks rising amid exposed quartz.

0.5 Cross another drainage feeding Crabtree Creek. Scattered mountain laurel lies in the drainage.

1.0 Come to Crabtree Creek and the old breached Company Mill Dam. The intact stonework is still in place on the south side of the creek. The rapids, pool, and metal relics make for a scenic area. Upon reaching Crabtree Creek, head left, upstream a short distance, then cross Crabtree Creek on a sturdy bridge. Come to the loop portion of the hike. Head right, downstream along Crabtree Creek. Rock outcrops aplenty rise from the trail.

1.1 Reach the millstone and marker indicating the Company Mill site. This is a popular area and may have anglers, sunbathers, and water lovers about. Continue downstream in streamside flats, looking for irregular piles of rock, concrete forms, and other evidence of past use. Meanwhile, scenic mountain laurel–clad rocky bluffs rise across the creek, itself displaying an allure lesser seen outside of Umstead State Park.

1.4 Climb away from Crabtree Creek, bridging streamlets in gorgeous hollows scattered with relatively large trees.

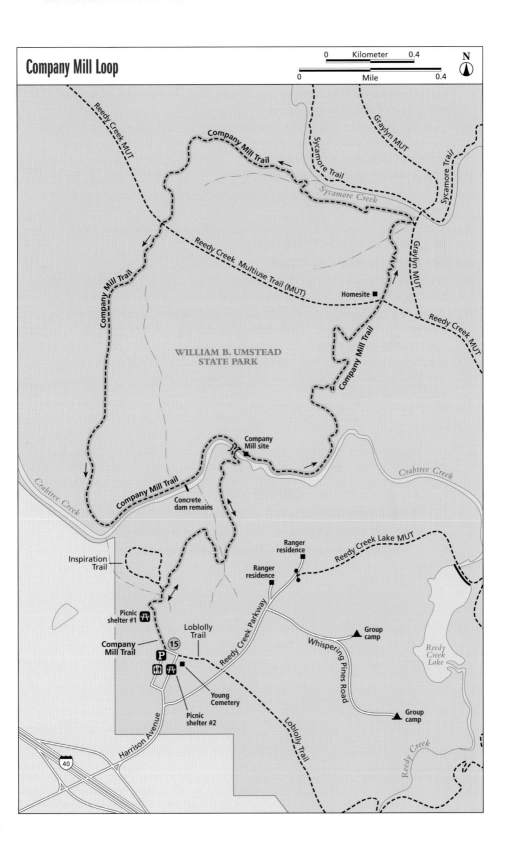

Company Mill Loop

0   Kilometer   0.4

0   Mile   0.4

N

Reedy Creek MUT

Company Mill Trail

Sycamore Trail

Graylyn MUT

Sycamore Trail

Sycamore Creek

Company Mill Trail

Reedy Creek Multiuse Trail (MUT)

Graylyn MUT

Homesite ■

Reedy Creek MUT

WILLIAM B. UMSTEAD
STATE PARK

Company Mill Trail

Company Mill
site ■

Crabtree Creek

Crabtree Creek

Company Mill Trail

Concrete
dam remains

Inspiration
Trail

Ranger
residence ■

Reedy Creek Lake MUT

Ranger
residence ■

Picnic
shelter #1 🏕

Loblolly
Trail

Company
Mill Trail

15

Group
camp ▲

Reedy
Creek
Lake

Whispering Pines Road

Reedy Creek Parkway

Young
Cemetery

Picnic
shelter #2

Group
camp ▲

Loblolly Trail

Harrison Avenue

Reedy Creek

40

2.1 Top out in oaks then reach the Reedy Creek Multiuse Trail. It follows old Reedy Creek Road across the state park. The Company Mill Trail descends north from a ridgeline, passing an old homesite marked with scattered bricks, tin roofing, and perennial planted flowers. A series of switchbacks takes you downhill.

2.4 Cross a small branch then come to a short spur leading right to the Graylyn Multiuse Trail. Sycamore Creek is within sight. Turn left here, still on the Company Mill Trail, upstream on an elevated berm along Sycamore Creek.

2.5 Climb a bluff well above Sycamore Creek.

2.8 Span a tributary of Sycamore Creek by footbridge. Trace the stream up through a wildflower area.

3.5 Reach and cross Reedy Creek Multiuse Trail. Keep south, walking a ridgeline on a level, tree-shaded path. The walking is easy under pines.

4.0 Start descending toward Crabtree Creek.

4.4 Return to Crabtree Creek and its sonorous shoals. Turn left, following it downstream in lush bottomland and some of the most glorious hiking of the loop.

4.7 Bridge a tributary flowing off the ridge you just crossed. Continue in bottomland. Just downstream, pass the remains of a concrete dam. This is a popular fishing area. Follow Crabtree Creek around a bend.

4.8 Return to the bridge over Crabtree Creek, having completed the loop portion of the Company Mill Trail. Backtrack toward the trailhead. Remember the Inspiration Trail should you want to extend your hike.

5.8 Reach the trailhead, completing the balloon loop.

GREEN TIP:
Be a happy land steward. Pick up after others who have left trash behind, so that those who come after you will enjoy a more natural hiking experience.

16 Sycamore Trail

This longer loop at Umstead State Park takes you into the relatively remote heart of the park, where miles of streamside scenery present beauty in every season. Start at a fine picnic area then cross Potts Branch, with beauty of its own. Roll over hilly, rich woods then drop into Sycamore Creek. Enjoy everywhere-you-look streamside splendor, from wildflowers to rocky bluffs, deep pools, and dancing rapids. Follow the stream for miles before looping up a tributary. The last part of the circuit is a backtrack.

Start: Picnic area at the end of Umstead Parkway
Distance: 7.2-mile balloon loop
Hiking time: About 3.5 hours
Difficulty: Moderate-difficult
Trail surface: Natural
Best season: Year-round, spring for wildflowers
Other trail users: None
Canine compatibility: Leashed dogs allowed

Land status: State park
Fees and permits: Seasonal entrance fee
Schedule: Nov–Feb: 7 a.m.–6 p.m.; Mar, Apr, Sept, Oct: 7 a.m.–8 p.m.; May–Aug: 7 a.m.–9 p.m.
Maps: William B. Umstead State Park
Trail contacts: William B. Umstead State Park, 8801 Glenwood Ave., Raleigh, NC 27617; (919) 571-4170; www.ncparks.gov

Finding the trailhead: From exit 4A on I-540, northwest of downtown Raleigh and southeast of Durham, take US 70 East/Glenwood Avenue for 1.3 miles to turn right into Umstead State Park. Stay straight on Umstead Parkway and follow it 1.7 miles to dead-end at a turnaround and picnic area. Trailhead GPS: N35 52.297', W78 45.655'

The Hike

Anybody who loves a moving woodland stream should enjoy this hike. It follows waterways of Umstead State Park for much of its length. The hike starts in a fine picnic area. Its only drawback is the maze of asphalt paths and natural surface trails that make getting your hike underway potentially confusing.

Each season brings a different side of Sycamore Creek. During spring you can see a chilly, frisky ribbon of clear water rolling through wildflower-laden flats spreading underneath budding trees. In summer Sycamore Creek becomes a lazy, warm stream, where water striders float atop still shallows. In fall the stream slows to a trickle, darkened by tannin from leaf litter, its ample pools reflecting golden leaves of sycamore and beech as well as other species. In winter a low, slanted sun reflects off its freshly recharged waters while fallen leaves stick together under a layer of frost.

After making it through the picnic area, you can gain your stride—and your first streamside trekking, albeit not on Sycamore Creek but Potts Branch, a smaller yet still alluring woodland creek nestled in the hills of Umstead. The path then abruptly

Sycamore Creek and the trail run beside one another.

leaves Potts Branch, meandering hills dividing Potts Branch from Sycamore Creek. At a high point the trail passes an old cemetery and old-growth trees that likely shaded old homesites. Eventually the path reaches its namesake stream, first clambering along bluffs before settling into bottomland, where you can really appreciate the valley, seeming light years distant from the state capital.

Thus ensues the best part of the hike. Here you follow Sycamore Creek downstream as the waterway and the adjacent valley reveal their many faces. Stop and walk out to a streamside outcrop. Peer into a deep pool. Watch rays of sunlight filter through smooth-trunked beech trees. Trace the curves of Sycamore Creek, morphing from shoal to pool and back again.

Sycamore Creek is eventually left behind, and the loop part of the trail heads up an unnamed tributary, exuding aquatic beauty of its own. Make your way to a hilltop before completing the loop. Now it is a simple backtrack to the trailhead. After passing through the elaborate picnic area a second time, you may wish you had brought something to grill out.

Miles and Directions

0.0 From the parking area turnaround, as you face easterly toward the parking area, take steps up to a circular asphalt trail. Head right, circling around the asphalt loop, passing the natural surface Potts Branch Trail. After making a half circle, continue east, passing picnic shelter #2 on your left, then picnic shelter #1. Just past picnic shelter #1, the Sycamore Trail becomes a natural surface path. Make a long loping switchback downhill through rocky woods.

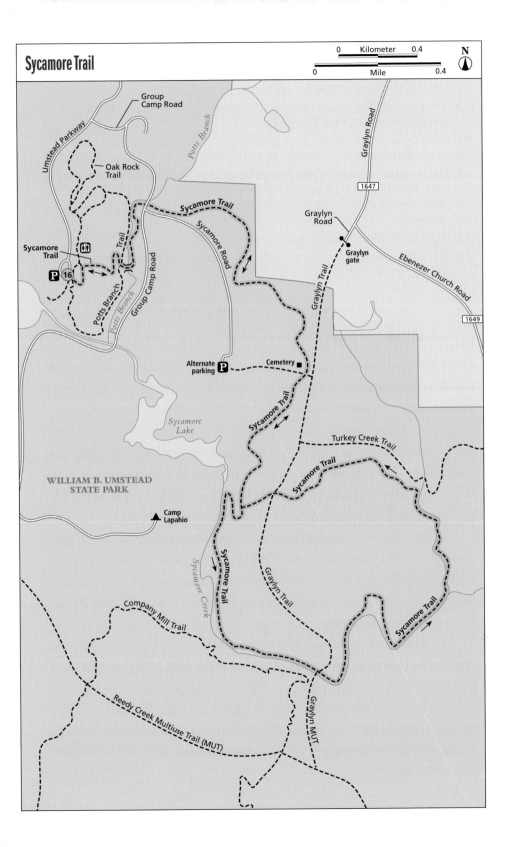

0.3 Intersect the Potts Branch Trail. Stay straight here, bridging Potts Branch, then turn left, northerly, upstream along Potts Branch. Rock outcrops abound under beech, hornbeam, and tulip tree woodland. Potts Branch Trail is across the creek.

0.5 Come very near Group Camp Road as you bridge a feeder branch. Ahead, reach the confluence of Potts Branch and Sals Branch.

0.6 Cross Group Camp Road, now heading easterly, into hilly terrain and away from water, under tall loblolly pines.

1.6 Reach a hilltop sprinkled with big, old trees from pre-park days. Note the cemetery to the west side of the trail. Just ahead, a connector linking the Graylyn Trail to a parking area on Sycamore Road crosses the Sycamore Trail. Stay straight here, heading south on a downgrade.

2.0 Cross an intermittent stream on a footbridge. Climb a hill.

2.2 Reach the loop portion of the Sycamore Trail. You will return here later. For now, stay straight, switchbacking off a hill.

THE RELIABLE SYCAMORES

Along aptly named Sycamore Creek, you will see many large sycamores. These hardwoods thrive in bottomlands and prefer deep, rich, moist soils such as found along Sycamore Creek. They also will grow in old fields and disturbed sites. Their intertwining roots help stabilize stream banks, cutting down on erosion. Sycamores range throughout the state of North Carolina. The state record sycamore is found in Northampton County. It is 115 feet high and 228 inches—19 feet—in circumference! Sycamores are known for having the biggest circumference of all native hardwoods. Beyond the Tar Heel State, sycamores stretch northeast to New England, west to Iowa, south to East Texas, and east to northern Florida.

Sycamore wood is fairly lightweight, somewhat hard, stiff, and of average strength. Sycamore is used inside other pieces of wooden furniture as drawer slides, but rarely as a piece of furniture itself. Other uses include lesser wood products such as boxes and crates. Sycamore does make fine firewood. Live sycamores are used in landscaping since they grow fast and spread out, providing good shade.

Even the most novice student of trees can identify the sycamore. Its bark is unlike any other tree. On older specimens the bark is plated like other trees, but higher up the trunk the mottled white skin is a dead giveaway. Sometimes the bark looks like it is peeling, hence the saying to help you remember the name, "sycamores look sick." The leaves of the tree are large and have three to five points. In fall the leaves turn a golden brown. The fruit is a roundish, brown, smooth-edged ball about an inch in diameter. Birds enjoy the sycamore seeds in the fruit.

2.3   Come to big Sycamore Creek and turn left, tracing it downstream. Immediately pass under a power line.

2.6   Rise to a steep bluff above the stream. Note the mountain laurel in this part of the drainage. Stroll the bluff among rock outcrops, mosses, and views.

2.8   Descend to bottomland scattered with ferns, beech, and big loblolly pines. A bluff rises across Sycamore Creek.

3.3   Intersect and cross the Graylyn Trail. Note the arched stone bridge over Sycamore Creek, a relic from the park's development in the 1930s. Continue downstream along Sycamore Creek. The creek and trail curve left, against a big bluff.

3.4   Pass under a power line then span a tributary on a footbridge. Climb a bluff above Sycamore Creek.

3.7   Return to the creek just as it makes a sharp bend to the left. Saunter through a vast bottomland, bridging a high water channel of Sycamore Creek.

4.0   Bridge another tributary of Sycamore Creek. Walk through former fields. Turn north up this unnamed perennial feeder of Sycamore Creek.

4.2   Cross the tributary on a footbridge. Cross the creek a second time. You are now back on the left-hand bank, hiking up an intimate valley.

4.3   The Sycamore Trail turns left, westerly, up a still smaller valley. The Turkey Creek Trail is visible to the right.

4.9   Top out on a hill and meet the Graylyn Trail again. Descend.

5.0   Complete the loop portion of the Sycamore Trail. Turn right and begin backtracking toward the trailhead.

5.6   Cross the connector linking the Graylyn Trail with the Sycamore Road trailhead. Keep straight, still backtracking.

6.6   Cross Group Camp Road. Turn left here, heading downstream along Potts Branch.

6.9   Bridge Potts Branch. Climb away from the stream on a loping switchback.

7.2   Reach the trailhead after passing through the picnic area, completing the hike.

GREEN TIP:

When hiking in a group, walk single file on established trails to avoid widening them. If you come upon a sensitive area, spread out so you don't cut one path through the landscape. Do not create new trails where there were none before.

17 Sals Branch Loop

Soak in some varied water features on this triple-loop hike at conveniently located Umstead State Park. First, the Sals Branch Trail leads across its namesake creek then through big woods to emerge astride Big Lake. Next, cruise along the rocky shoals of Sycamore Creek and Potts Branch on the Potts Branch Trail. Visit odd Oak Rock on the Oak Rock Trail then return to Sals Branch Trail before finishing this triple play.

Start: Umstead State Park Visitor Center
Distance: 4.8-mile triple loop
Hiking time: About 2.5 hours
Difficulty: Moderate
Trail surface: Natural
Best season: Year-round
Other trail users: None
Canine compatibility: Leashed dogs allowed
Land status: State park

Fees and permits: Seasonal entrance fee
Schedule: Nov–Feb: 7 a.m.–6 p.m.; Mar, Apr, Sept, Oct: 7 a.m.–8 p.m.; May–Aug: 7 a.m.–9 p.m.
Maps: William B. Umstead State Park
Trail contacts: William B. Umstead State Park, 8801 Glenwood Ave., Raleigh, NC 27617; (919) 471-4170; www.ncparks.gov

Finding the trailhead: From exit 4A on I-540, northwest of downtown Raleigh and southeast of Durham, take US 70 East/Glenwood Avenue for 1.3 miles to turn right into Umstead State Park. Stay straight on Umstead Parkway and follow it 0.8 mile to the visitor center and trailhead on your right. Trailhead GPS: N35 52.856', W78 45.509'

The Hike

What once was an outlier of Raleigh and well away from Durham and Chapel Hill is now an oasis of nature enveloped in the urbanization of the Research Triangle. Way back in the 1930s, the Civilian Conservation Corps (CCC), a government entity, developed agriculturally abused lands in the Crabtree Creek valley, west of the state capital, into a park. The CCC built roads, trails, picnic facilities, and more. Later, what was then known as Crabtree Recreation Area was sold to the state of North Carolina for a dollar. Finally, another parcel was added, and in 1966 Umstead State Park came to be.

What a fortunate stroke for today's capital area residents! Umstead State Park comes in at a whopping 5,579 acres and is easily accessible for most Triangle residents. Umstead features over 20 miles of hiking-only trails, plus more mountain biking and bridle paths, three lakes, a campground, numerous picnic areas, and two major entrances. Residents near and far hike park paths as part of their daily exercise routine.

This particular hike explores the northwest parcel of the park, using three connected loop trails. Therefore you can easily alter your hike by taking only one or two of the loops. However, I recommend all three circuits, since they each add something

Autumn leaves color Sals Branch.

to the adventure. Furthermore, the total hike mileage is only 4.8 miles, making the entire hike doable in a half day.

The triple loop leaves the visitor center, crosses Sals Branch then rambles south in the wooded expanse for which Umstead State Park is known. You will also become familiar with one of the disadvantages of having civilization nearby—the close proximity of Raleigh-Durham Airport. You can hear the planes roar on part of the hike.

The heavily used hiker-only trail journeys along Sals Branch, then turns south under a canopy of beech, pine, white oak, and tulip trees. Ferns add a green touch to the forest floor. Undulate over hills divided by moist hollows, some with footbridges over intermittent streambeds. Note the gullied areas, relics of when this area was overfarmed, primarily growing cotton. Today's dense growth has arrested further erosion, however.

The hike pops out at Big Lake, where you soak in still water aquatic views before joining the Potts Branch Trail. Come to a popular picnic area before returning to the water along Sycamore Creek then up Potts Branch, both scenic streams with serene pools, rocky shoals, sheer bluffs, and wildflowers along their banks in season. This is one of the best parts of the hike. The trail then passes an old dam, perhaps once used to power turbines to grind corn. Potts Branch is graced with rocky rapids and rock outcrops along its banks. Ahead you reach the confluence of Potts Branch and Sals Branch. The hike then turns up Sals Branch, passing another dam. This one is intact but silted in on its upstream side.

Next you join the Oak Rock Trail, named for the unusual oak tree growing atop a linear rock outcrop. In addition to this strange tree, the trail also presents interpretive information about the landscape, and another small dam. You then wander through

The serenity of the trails at Raleigh's Umstead State Park can amaze.

a picnic area, working your way back to Big Lake. From here rejoin the Sals Branch Trail as it climbs over a hill then returns to the visitor center and the trailhead.

Miles and Directions

0.0 As you face the visitor center, walk around the right-hand side of the building and pick up Sals Branch Trail on the wood's edge. Descend to emerge at a lower parking area. Bisect the parking area then reenter forest. Immediately cross Sals Branch on a footbridge. Turn up along Sals Branch as it snakes a convoluted course in deep woods.

0.3 Sals Branch Trail abruptly turns left, westerly.

0.4 Stay straight as a spur trail heads right to the park campground. Ahead, turn left, south, for Big Lake. Begin the part of the hike where planes can be loud.

1.0 Pass a big rock pile on your right after rising up a hill. Its former purpose is now lost to time.

1.2 Cross a closed gravel road. Walk past smaller rock piles and crumbled-down stone fences, agricultural remnants of the past.

1.4 Walk through an area with many scattered stone picnic grills. This was formerly an auto-accessible picnic area from the park's early days, now an anomaly in the woods. Begin gaining glimpses of Big Lake off to your right.

1.6 Emerge at a power line that has been running parallel to the trail. Walk down to the asphalt path beside Big Lake. The park boathouse is to your right. Do not turn left into the woods on Sals Branch Trail. You will return here later to finish your loop, but for now walk about 100 feet along the asphalt path then turn left back into woods, now on the Potts Branch Trail. Meanwhile the asphalt path continues along Big Lake to cross its dam and end at Group Camp Road. Climb away from Big Lake on the Potts Branch Trail.

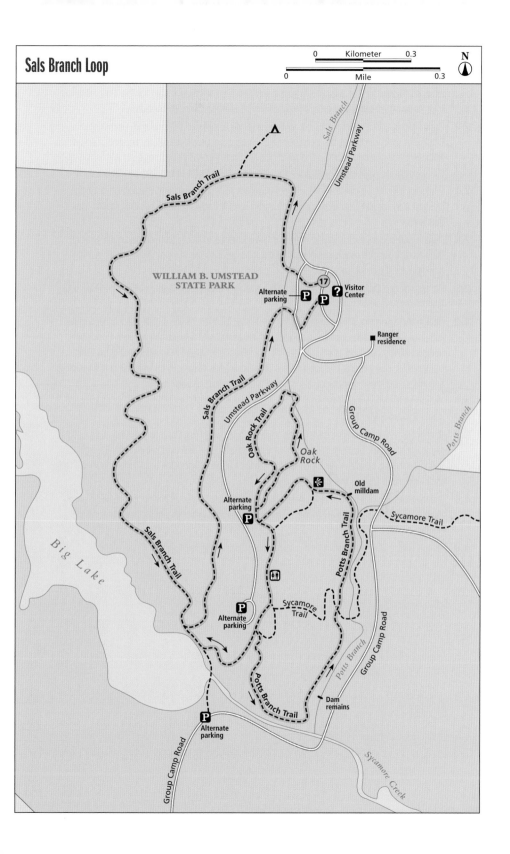

Sals Branch Loop

0   Kilometer   0.3

0   Mile   0.3

N

Sals Branch

Umstead Parkway

Sals Branch Trail

WILLIAM B. UMSTEAD
STATE PARK

Alternate
parking   P   P   17   ?   Visitor
Center

Ranger
residence

Sals Branch Trail

Umstead Parkway

Oak Rock Trail

Oak
Rock

Group Camp Road

Potts Branch

Alternate
parking   P

Old
milldam

Sycamore Trail

Potts Branch Trail

Sals Branch Trail

Big Lake

P
Alternate
parking

Sycamore
Trail

Potts Branch

Group Camp Road

Potts Branch Trail

Dam
remains

P
Alternate
parking

Group Camp Road

Sycamore Creek

1.7 Emerge at a picnic and parking area and the Sycamore Trail trailhead. This can be a confusing area. Walk up steps to a circular asphalt trail looping through a picnic area. Head right, southerly, on the asphalt. In just a few feet, you will see a sign for the Potts Branch Trail. Leave the asphalt track and join a natural surface path, descending.

2.0 Come alongside Sycamore Creek. Walk along the stream in bottomland. Come near an old CCC-built road bridge at the confluence of Sycamore Creek and Potts Branch. Turn left up Potts Branch before reaching the road bridge. Pass the stone remnants of a washed-away dam. Continue upstream in a rocky mini gorge, where Potts Branch noisily flows.

2.4 Intersect the Sycamore Trail. Here the Sycamore Trail crosses Potts Branch on a bridge, but you stay straight, continuing upstream in beech flats bordered by streamside rock outcrops.

2.6 Pass a silted-over milldam just above the confluence of Potts Branch and Sals Branch. Turn away from the creek, passing a wheelchair-accessible stream overlook. Stay right here, passing through a picnic area.

2.8 Emerge at the Oak Rock Trail and a parking area. Turn acutely right, joining the Oak Rock Trail. It soon splits; stay right.

3.0 Reach the short spur heading right to Oak Rock. Turn left beyond Oak Rock, cruising the valley of Sals Branch. Join an old roadbed, bridging Sals Branch via culvert. Come very near Umstead Parkway then cross back over Sals Branch on a small stone dam. Turn back south, completing the loop of the Oak Rock Trail. Now join an asphalt path heading southbound. Pass a restroom. Umstead Parkway is just to your right.

3.7 Return to the picnic and parking area at the south end of Umstead Parkway. Backtrack down toward Big Lake.

3.9 Reach Big Lake. Turn right here on an asphalt path, with Big Lake to your left. Just before reaching the park boathouse, turn right under the power line and rejoin Sals Branch Trail. Begin climbing up a hollow on a natural surface track. Surmount a hill under tall oak trees that were here before the area was a park.

4.6 Bridge Sals Branch a final time. Ahead, open onto the lower visitor center parking area. Walk right in the parking area, then leave left on a foot trail. Ascend toward the visitor center.

4.8 Reach the rear of the park visitor center, completing the hike.

18 Shelley Lake Loop

This city of Raleigh greenway adventure explores still and moving water. First, trace Bent Creek downstream to meet Mine Creek, then follow Mine Creek to pretty Shelley Lake. Loop around the impoundment, using boardwalk part of the time and gaining views from a high dam. Spur trails present additional hiking opportunities.

Start: Corner of Longstreet Drive and Bent Creek Drive
Distance: 4.0-mile balloon loop
Hiking time: 2.0–2.5 hours
Difficulty: Moderate
Trail surface: Asphalt
Best season: Year-round
Other trail users: Joggers, bicyclers

Canine compatibility: Leashed dogs allowed
Land status: Raleigh city park
Fees and permits: No fees or permits required
Schedule: Sunrise to sunset
Maps: Capital Area Greenway System
Trail contacts: Shelley Lake Park, 1400 W. Millbrook Rd., Raleigh, NC 27614; (919) 996-3285; www.raleighnc.gov/parks/

Finding the trailhead: From exit 11 on I-540, north of downtown Raleigh, take Six Forks Road south for 2.5 miles to turn right on Longstreet Drive. Follow Longstreet Drive for 0.1 mile to the intersection with Bent Creek Drive. Parking is available on either street. The Bent Creek Trail starts at the southwest corner of Bent Creek Drive and Longstreet Drive. Trailhead GPS: N35 52.455', W78 38.847'

The Hike

The city of Raleigh has stepped up and developed their greenways. The network of pathways is known as the Capital Area Greenway System. The mostly interconnected set of trails follows drainages flowing through Raleigh and Wake County. The still-growing system currently totals over 100 miles. No matter the time of year, the streams and the woods that surround them present a slice of nature amid the capital city.

This hike utilizes part of this greenway mileage to make a scenic loop. First, you join the Bent Creek Trail and cruise along this waterway to meet bigger Mine Creek and the natural surface Mine Creek Trail, an alternate path for added mileage. Keep downstream along the wooded Mine Creek valley, bordered by neighborhoods. Head under Lynn Road then follow the asphalt ribbon south in forest to tunnel under North Hills Drive. You enter a wetland near the confluence of Snelling Creek and Mine Creek. Begin making your 2-mile loop around Shelley Lake, the most popular part of the hike. The trail crosses a boardwalk that offers excellent views of Shelley Lake Park, centered by the lake. Another spur trail heads to the Sertoma Arts Center and up to Lake Park Drive.

Shelley Lake as seen from a trailside overlook

Keep looping around the lake. Climb to the dam and gaze north up the impound-ment, with its brushy wetlands in the distance. Head up the east side of the lake, undulating a hilly shoreline. Meet the Snelling Branch Trail, which travels east along Snelling Branch to Optimist Park. It is just a short distance back to the Mine Creek Trail, where you backtrack a mile to the trailhead.

Be apprised the parking at the hike's beginning is on streets. There is no official parking lot. However, the on-street parking is ample.

Miles and Directions

0.0 From the intersection of Longstreet Drive and Bent Creek Drive, just west of Six Forks Road, join the Bent Creek Trail as it drops from the southwest side of the road intersection. Quickly sidle alongside Bent Creek in a wooded valley. A big pool lies just below the culvert running under Longstreet Drive.

0.2 Cross a bridge over Bent Creek. The green corridor widens. Sweetgums, oaks, and tulip trees shade the shoal-filled stream.

0.5 Natural surface Mine Creek Trail enters on your right and is marked by a post with a hiker symbol. Come alongside then bridge Mine Creek. Follow a much bigger stream.

0.6 The greenway passes under Lynn Road. Asphalt connector paths lead up to both sides of the street. Keep straight beyond Lynn Road. Ahead, an alternate natural surface hiking trail stays close to Mine Creek, while the asphalt greenway curves away.

0.8 The natural surface alternate returns to meet the asphalt path.

0.9 Use a narrow pedestrian tunnel to pass under North Hills Drive.

Parts of the Shelley Lake Trail are very level.

GREENWAYS SERVE CITIZENS IN MULTIPLE WAYS

The average city park of the 1950s, with a metal swing set, a seesaw, a few picnic tables with peeling paint, and a dusty baseball diamond, is now as passé as a rotary dial phone compared to the smart phones we live by today. City dwellers of the twenty-first century are demanding more than just a little park for their neighborhoods. In addition to traditional ball field parks, they want greenways upon which to bicycle, hike, and even roller blade through a strip of nature connecting those neighborhoods.

The past few decades have seen phenomenal growth in greenways. Exactly what is a greenway? We have all heard this buzzword. Specifically, a greenway is a linear park, a corridor of protected land overlain with a trail that travels along or through specific natural features.

These paths can be asphalt, gravel, or mulch. Greenways often follow along creeks or lakes. Greenways can utilize former railroad right-of-ways, utility right-of-ways, or already established park lands to connect two parks together. New land is sometimes purchased; other times easements are granted across private land.

While most often linear, greenways can be a loop confined to one city park, as is the Shelley Lake Trail. Greenways are primarily used for recreational travel, but can also be used by commuters and other citizens simply trying to get from point A to point B.

Greenways have broad appeal. You can see mothers with strollers pushing their newborns, runners huffing and puffing, couples strolling hand in hand, dogs walking their masters, or birders with binoculars pushed against their eyeballs. Bicyclers use greenways for exercise and travel. Any reason and venue for exercise helps cut down on North Carolina's sky-high obesity rate.

More than family recreation venues, these oases of nature amid the city provide homes to urban wildlife. Critters use greenways to travel from one larger greenspace to another—wildlife corridors if you will. Animal health is improved since gene pools aren't isolated, and wildlife corridors allow overall larger territories for wildlife to exist. Shaded streams make for richer aquatic habitat, further improving stream quality.

Greenways have practical benefits too. Wooded streamsheds cut down on urban flooding, reducing erosion for property owners. Wooded streams also absorb water and filter pollutants from urban runoff. Greenway forests help keep cities cooler, reducing the urban heat island effect, and cut down on summertime electric bills. Trees also filter air, improving air quality.

And the property values of adjacent lands are improved by the existence of greenways. Residents realize greenways are more likely to carry alert citizens on the lookout for criminals rather than criminals themselves.

(continued on p. 96)

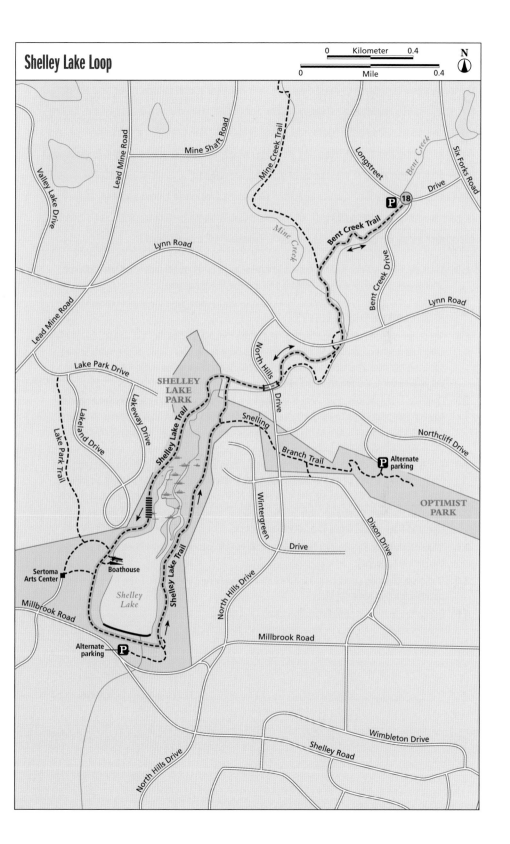

Shelley Lake Loop

0   Kilometer   0.4

0   Mile   0.4

N

Mine Shaft Road

Lead Mine Road

Valley Lake Drive

Mine Creek Trail

Longstreet

Bent Creek

Six Forks Road

Drive

18

Bent Creek Trail

Lynn Road

Mine Creek

Bent Creek Drive

Lead Mine Road

Lynn Road

North Hills Drive

SHELLEY LAKE PARK

Lake Park Drive

Lakeway Drive

Shelley Lake Trail

Snelling

Northcliff Drive

Lakeland Drive

Branch Trail

Alternate parking

Lake Park Trail

OPTIMIST PARK

Wintergreen

Drive

Dixon Drive

Sertoma Arts Center

Boathouse

Shelley Lake Trail

North Hills Drive

Shelley Lake

Millbrook Road

Millbrook Road

Alternate parking

Wimbleton Drive

North Hills Drive

Shelley Road

What does the future hold? Greenways are being adapted into overall urban planning. Developers and city planners must deal with ever-increasing regulations regarding stormwater runoff, public health and safety, resource protection, and resource management. Adding greenways to developments addresses many questions. For example, a greenway can cut down on stormwater runoff, reducing flooding, which addresses public safety. A greenway helps protect the natural resources of an area. Developing a greenway enhances overall aesthetics, improving the "quality of place." The whole process is known as integration. That is government-speak for putting it all together. The Triangle is growing fast. Let's develop greenways as we develop new areas of town. Everyone will benefit from it.

1.0 Meet the Shelley Lake Trail. Keep straight here, beginning your counterclockwise loop of Shelley Lake. Enter Shelley Lake Park and a wider forest corridor.

1.2 Shelley Lake appears through the trees. Shortly come alongside the impoundment. The 53-acre lake was created in 1975.

1.6 Reach an elevated view perch to the right of the trail. Keep straight; just ahead, the Shelley Lake Trail opens onto the lake and becomes a boardwalk. This is one of the more scenic spots on the hike. The lake boathouse is visible down the way, as is the lake dam. Span the embayment and return to dry land.

1.8 Come to a trail intersection. Here the Lake Park Trail leads right to Lake Park Drive, and a spur of that path turns to the Sertoma Arts Center. Keep straight on the Shelley Lake Trail, intersecting a pair of spurs to the lake boathouse then passing an additional connector to the Sertoma Arts Center.

1.9 Climb to the lake dam above Millbrook Road. Cross the 1,155-foot earthen dike then turn north, passing a pair of connectors linking the Shelley Lake Trail to the parking on Millbrook Road. Keep north along the east shore of Shelley Lake in a mix of field and woods.

2.4 Span an intermittent stream. You are now walking alongside a wooded wetland on one side and hills on the other. The lake is left behind.

2.8 Intersect the Snelling Branch Trail. It leaves right 0.8 mile to Optimist Park. Keep straight on Shelley Lake Trail.

3.0 Complete the loop portion of the hike just after bridging Mine Creek. From here turn right, backtracking up Mine Creek.

4.0 Reach the trailhead, completing the hike.

19 Lake Lynn Loop

This Raleigh park trek circles a pretty impoundment. Start at Lake Lynn Community Center then drop through a transitional wetland. Begin circling Lake Lynn. As an added plus, much of the loop traverses boardwalk that runs atop the water. Grab long views from atop the lake dam, then continue walking shoreline and more long stretches of boardwalk before returning to the community center.

Start: Lake Lynn Community Center
Distance: 2.6-mile balloon loop
Hiking time: 1.0-1.5 hours
Difficulty: Easy
Trail surface: Asphalt, boardwalk
Best season: Year-round
Other trail users: Joggers, a few bicyclers
Canine compatibility: Leashed dogs allowed

Land status: Raleigh city park
Fees and permits: No fees or permits required
Schedule: Sunrise to sunset
Maps: Capital Area Greenway System
Trail contacts: Lake Lynn Park, 7921 Ray Rd., Raleigh, NC 27613; (919) 996-2911; www .raleighnc.gov/parks/

Finding the trailhead: From exit 4A on I-540, northwest of downtown Raleigh and southeast of Durham, take US 70 East/Glenwood Avenue for 3.3 miles to turn left on Lynn Road and follow it for 1.9 miles. Turn left on Ray Road and follow it for 1.3 miles then turn left into Lake Lynn Park and Community Center. Follow the main road to the community center; the greenway trail is just past the center on the left. Trailhead GPS: N35 53.243', W78 41.890'

The Hike

The Lake Lynn Greenway is an exemplary city park and presents the best of what a city greenway can be. Encircling the shores of Lake Lynn, the greenway delivers excellent lake views while traveling a surprisingly large portion of its circuit on boardwalk elevated above the lake. The impoundment was created in 1976 for flood control, when Hare Snipe Creek was dammed. Quixotically named Hare Snipe Creek is a tributary of Crabtree Creek, which flows through the heart of Raleigh. Lake Lynn Dam is but one of many flood control measures taken to keep Crabtree Creek from wreaking havoc on capital area citizens.

Though Lake Lynn Park comes in at only 75 acres, most of that land is stretched along the shores of Lake Lynn. However, before you imagine a wilderness in the heart of Raleigh, realize that apartments and houses come right to the park border, and on your hike you will see adjacent dwellings more often than not. Several spur trails lead to these complexes. These spur trails are so well integrated into the Lake Lynn Greenway that it may prove temporarily confusing. The loop hike is quite popular not only for those adjacent residents but also for those who want to soak in the lake scenery and enjoy those waterside boardwalks. The lake itself stretches 55 acres in a long, narrow fashion, broken with small inlets.

DAMMING HARE SNIPE CREEK

So why dam seemingly small and insignificant Hare Snipe Creek here in the Triangle? Hare Snipe Creek flows from well-populated hills south of I-540 near Leesville. But dammed Hare Snipe Creek was, back in 1976, and the Triangle population was even much smaller then. Previously, repeated floodings of Crabtree Creek, into which Hare Snipe Creek flows, had already occurred as Crabtree Creek coursed through Raleigh north of downtown. Tropical storms had caused the biggest problems, dumping inches of rain at a time on Piedmont streams. And as Raleigh has grown, more and more impervious surfaces (read: asphalt parking lots, roads, concrete patios, and roofs) push rain faster into streams, making waters rise quicker than streams flowing through forested lands.

So Hare Snipe Creek, Mine Creek—another tributary of Crabtree Creek—and Crabtree Creek itself were dammed in places to slow this runoff. Other tributaries of Crabtree Creek that flow through the greater Raleigh urban area have also been dammed: Turkey Creek, Sycamore Creek, and Richland Creek. Together these smaller dams help mitigate runoff during storms.

Even at that, floods have occurred and will occur in the future. The parking lots at Crabtree Valley Mall are notorious for flooding. So what can we do to help? Make your home less impervious to rain by creating green spaces to absorb rainwater. Plant trees along streams and around wetlands to cut down on erosion. Store roof rainwater for reuse. The city of Raleigh has added storm-water collection ponds along Crabtree Creek, places where overflows fill, then slowly seep back into the earth.

If you are interested in following the flow of Crabtree Creek, please visit the US Geological Survey website (www.usgs.gov). Look for real-time flow for the gauge "Crabtree Creek at Anderson Drive at Raleigh, NC." This is one of five stream gauges in Wake County for Crabtree Creek. Following this gauge will help you understand the highs and lows of Crabtree Creek and why a little ol' tributary like Hare Snipe Creek is dammed, helping to minimize flooding in the Triangle.

But there is more. Avian life congregates on the lake, so bird watching is popular. The view from atop Lake Lynn Dam is a pleasant surprise as well. On the other end of the lake, a wetland and concentration of woods is home to deer and other critters. While Lake Lynn isn't wilderness, it is an oasis of green enveloped by urbanization that makes for a fun, eye-pleasing hike.

The community center at Lake Lynn Park draws in area residents. City-sponsored programs are held there regularly, and the fitness center is a big attraction. The building

One of the greenway's many long boardwalks shines in the morning sun.

features a large gymnasium, art room, and dance studio. Outside facilities include tennis courts, bocce courts, and a baseball field. The Lake Lynn Greenway complements these varied facilities.

After leaving the community center parking area, the hike descends to Hare Snipe Creek. This lowland floodplain is periodically inundated, and therefore was designed for such occurrences. At high water you may have trouble getting across the stream dry shod. The trail heads south through and along a richly vegetated wetland before opening onto Lake Lynn. Join a boardwalk and you are immediately rewarded with long-reaching southerly views of the impoundment and its wooded shoreline. After returning to dry land, an asphalt track leads through a wooded ribbon with the shoreline on one side and apartments on the other. Joggers will be enjoying the trail alongside you. Since the greenway is busy with walkers, hikers, and joggers, bicyclers are few. The trail bridges an embayment on another boardwalk and continues south to eventually reach Lake Lynn Dam. The loop takes you across the 620-foot barrier, presenting views up lake and down to an alternate parking area off Lynn Road. Don't be surprised to see paddlers plying canoes and kayaks on the no-motors-allowed lake.

The second half of the hike turns back north, tracing the west shore of Lake Lynn.

Geese stand atop the dam above Lake Lynn.

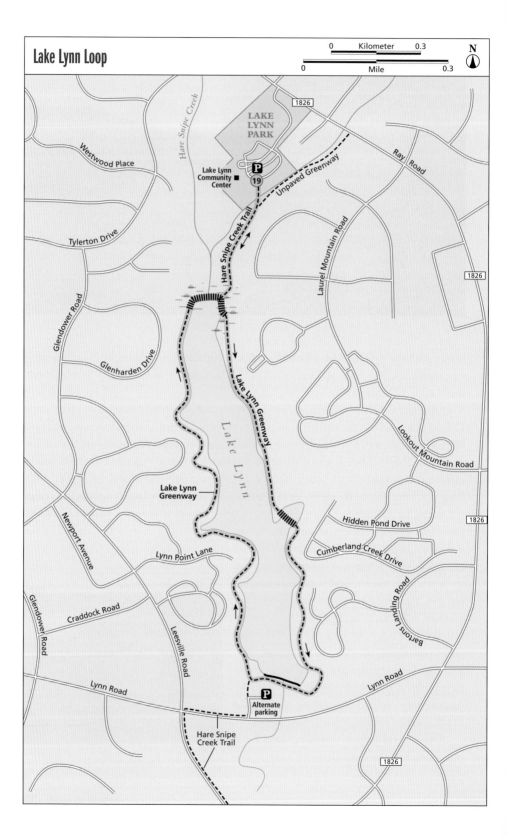

Lake Lynn Loop

0 — Kilometer — 0.3

0 — Mile — 0.3

N

1826

LAKE LYNN PARK

Ray Road

Westwood Place

Lake Lynn Community Center

19

P

Unpaved Greenway

Tylerton Drive

Hare Snipe Creek Trail

Laurel Mountain Road

1826

Glendower Road

Glenharden Drive

Lake Lynn Greenway

Lake Lynn

Lookout Mountain Road

Lake Lynn Greenway

Hidden Pond Drive

Newport Avenue

Cumberland Creek Drive

1826

Lynn Point Lane

Bartons Landing Road

Glendower Road

Craddock Road

Leesville Road

Lynn Road

Lynn Road

P

Alternate parking

Hare Snipe Creek Trail

1826

Aquatic panoramas continue as you wind along the main shore and around other small coves. The last part of the trek utilizes another long boardwalk that puts an exclamation mark on the loop. Enjoy the wetland a second time before returning to the park community center.

Miles and Directions

0.0　From the southwest end of the community center parking area, pick up the asphalt Lake Lynn Greenway. Descend into woods and quickly reach Hare Snipe Creek. It is but a small stream, and during normal flows you will be able to walk over it dry footed. Just beyond the stream an unnamed natural surface trail leaves left to Ray Road, up Hare Snipe Creek. Continue in seasonally inundated wetland. Loblolly pines and tulip trees border the path.

0.2　Come to the first boardwalk of the loop. It stretches over a wetland then opens onto Lake Lynn. Ahead, the long and impressive boardwalk splits. You have reached the loop portion of the hike. Keep straight here, soaking in excellent down lake views. Return to land. Walk in woodland with Lake Lynn to your right. Pass spur trails to apartment complexes.

0.5　Cross a short boardwalk and quickly rejoin dry land, still heading south.

0.7　The Lake Lynn Greenway again morphs to boardwalk and crosses a small cove of the lake then returns to terra firma.

1.2　Circle around a small cove before rising to meet the Lake Lynn Dam. Turn right here and walk westerly. Peer out on good lake views. The Lynn Road alternate trail access is visible downstream of the dam. Here the Hare Snipe Creek Trail heads across Lynn Road 2 miles to Wooten Meadow Park. Our hike turns right and heads north up the west side of Lake Lynn. Walk a wooded asphalt path with apartment complexes bordering the trail.

1.7　Cross another boardwalk. Walk under a power line.

1.8　Bisect another small cove of Lake Lynn.

2.1　Join one of the longest boardwalks of the entire greenway. Pass a short spur left on dry land then quickly link to another boardwalk.

2.3　The boardwalk curves right, easterly, then works through willow thickets. Note the planted cypress trees in the wetland.

2.4　Complete the loop portion of the hike. Turn left, backtracking toward the Lake Lynn Community Center.

2.6　Reach the Lake Lynn Community Center trailhead, finishing the hike.

20 Eagle Spur Trail

Take a walk on the Piedmont's forgotten rail trail. Set in the southernmost reaches of New Hope Creek, the trail follows the old Eagle Spur train line through game lands its entire distance. Traverse wide, wildlife-rich bottoms while slowly curving to the shore of Jordan Lake, where the causeway of the old rail line reaches into the lake and delivers fine views.

Start: Trailhead on Stagecoach Road
Distance: 4.6-mile there-and-back
Hiking time: About 2.5 hours
Difficulty: Easy-moderate
Trail surface: Natural
Best season: Fall through spring
Other trail users: Occasional bicycler, hunters in season
Canine compatibility: Pets on 6-foot leash only

Land status: Jordan Lake Game Lands
Fees and permits: No fees or permits required
Schedule: Sunrise to sunset
Maps: Eagle Spur Trail; USGS Southwest Durham, Green Level
Trail contacts: Triangle Rails to Trails Conservancy, PO Box 61091, Durham, NC 27715, www.triangletrails.org

Finding the trailhead: From exit 274 on I-40, east of Chapel Hill, south of Durham, and west of Raleigh, take NC 751 south for 1 mile to Stagecoach Road. Turn right on Stagecoach Road and follow it 0.2 mile to a gated entrance into the Jordan Lake Game Lands. You will see a sign indicating the North Carolina Wildlife Resources Commission. Limited parking is on the south shoulder of Stagecoach Road, west of the trail entrance gate. Trailhead GPS: N35 53.172', W78 57.624'

The Hike

The Eagle Spur Trail is a former railroad line turned path that runs south from Stagecoach Road in Durham County and into Chatham County. It roughly parallels the lowermost, still-flowing portion of New Hope Creek before it enters Jordan Lake. From its beginning the path passes through Jordan Lake Game Lands, keeping the setting wild (check the North Carolina Wildlife Resources Commission website for seasonal hunting dates in the Jordan Lake Game Lands before starting your trek). Lying within the game lands is part of the reason that the railroad line is still intact as a transportation corridor for hikers, bicyclers, and hunters in season.

The Eagle Spur Trail has not developed the way its nearby cousin rail trail, the American Tobacco Trail, has—with good walking surfaces, trailside kiosks, and parking areas. Arguably its biggest asset—being inside the Jordan Lake Game Lands—has also been the Eagle Spur Trail's biggest liability. Simply put, the North Carolina Wildlife Resources Commission, which manages the game lands, is "not in the trail business," though the trail is now managed by the Triangle Rails to Trails Conservancy, and has thus improved. Yet, hikers will notice that some parts of the pathway

Peering out over Jordan Lake from trail's end.

have been washed out due to compromised culverts. However, at the same time, the unkempt condition of the path adds wildness to it.

In my opinion the Eagle Spur Trail is a delight to hike and an underutilized resource for Triangle trail trekkers. First off, solitude is there for the taking. Secondly, unlike other rail trails in the area, it passes through an entirely forested and natural venue. Moreover, much of this is through bottoms of New Hope Creek, where wetlands and tall hardwood forests lie next to hilly pine woods. In places hikers can spot New Hope Creek and its many braids that course through trailside flats. Finally, there is the overlook of Jordan Lake. This spot lies where the railroad berm extended over the bottom of formerly free-flowing New Hope Creek then used a bridge to cross the waterway. Before Jordan Lake was flooded, the railroad bridge was dismantled; thus the former railroad line simply stops, surrounded on three sides by water. It is my favorite place on Jordan Lake, a place where you can peer into the uppermost embayment of the impoundment. Ironically, this spot, although the closest lake locale to Chapel Hill and Durham, exudes a wilder nature than seen at many other places on the impoundment.

Upon arriving at the trailhead, you will experience one of the disadvantages of the Eagle Spur Trail—limited shoulder parking. After getting your car settled, head south on the former rail trail and quickly reach a surprise as the former railroad grade gives way to a dip and lowhead dam, where a tributary of New Hope Creek crosses the former trail. This is a small waterfowl impoundment added by the US Army Corps of Engineers when developing Jordan Lake. Soon rejoin the grade. Vegetation is thick, with willows and other trees closing in on the path. Bottomland stretches far to your right. The trail gradient is nearly level as you continue walking closer to

RAILROAD RIGHT-OF-WAYS IN NORTH CAROLINA

The state of North Carolina was once laced with over 5,200 miles of railroad lines. Like many other areas, North Carolina now has far fewer miles of rail lines than in its peak in the late 1940s. This abandonment of rail lines was caused by changing transportation patterns, primarily the rise of the automobile for personal transportation and the truck for product movement.

While rail use has declined in nearly every state, North Carolina is different from other states in respect to the railroad right-of-ways after they have been abandoned. In most other states the railroad right-of-way is treated as a linear property and can be bought and sold, and it continues to function as a linear transportation line. This is the way that so many rail trails throughout the country have been established. Typically, a public entity such as a city, county, the US Forest Service, and others purchase a railroad right-of-way then turn it into a trail. Conversely, in North Carolina if a railroad line is abandoned, adjacent property owners can claim the corridor through which the railroad ran, closing it off for use as an auto road, railroad, or a rail trail.

North Carolina is down to 3,200 miles of active railroad line. That means 2,000 miles of railroad right-of-ways could have been turned into rail trails. Some have, but others have reverted to the adjacent landowners. This is good for the landowner's peace of mind, but current law precludes building a rail trail or banking a railroad corridor in case it needs to be used in the future.

These railroad right-of-ways, when preserved, also function as greenbelts, strips of nature passing through urban areas. Furthermore, it is much easier to preserve an old railroad right-of-way than it is to establish a new railroad right-of-way. Since many communities in the Triangle were established along rail lines, these railroad right-of-ways link communities and can provide alternative transportation connections and bank railroad lines for the future. Finally, when rail trails are established, they offer convenient exercise venues for nearby residents. The Eagle Spur Trail, for example, provides not only a convenient and scenic place to walk, but also a place to reconnect with nature in the Triangle, using a railroad right-of-way.

the lake. Your final reward is reaching the part of Jordan Lake with the largest summertime concentration of bald eagles on the entire body of water. On your return trip, enjoy the trail again, considering how much better the experience if the Eagle Spur Trail got as much attention as its next-door cousin, the American Tobacco Trail.

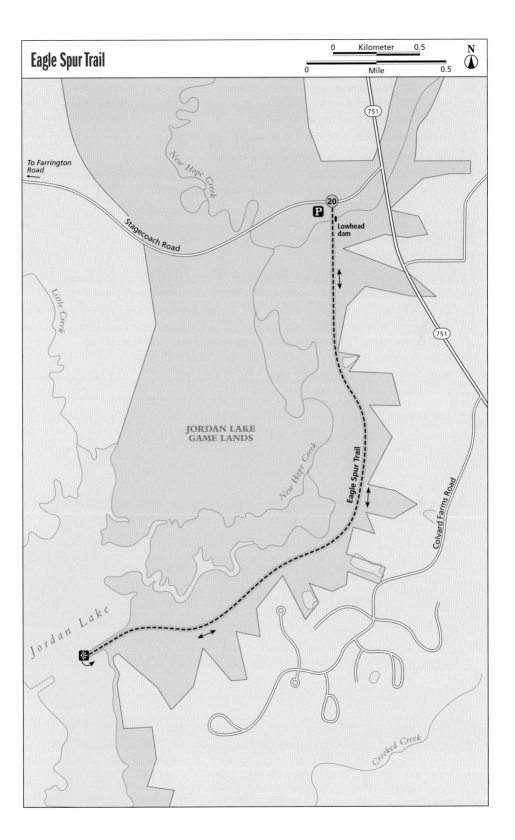

Eagle Spur Trail

Kilometer
0   0.5

Mile
0   0.5

N

To Farrington Road

New Hope Creek

Stagecoach Road

751

20

P

Lowhead dam

751

Little Creek

JORDAN LAKE GAME LANDS

New Hope Creek

Eagle Spur Trail

Colvard Farms Road

Jordan Lake

Crooked Creek

Miles and Directions

0.0 Leave south from Stagecoach Road after passing around a pole gate. Shortly come to a dam slowing an unnamed tributary of New Hope Creek. Cross the lowhead dam then resume the railroad grade through game lands.

0.5 The trail curves slightly southeast. A large wetland opens to your right.

0.8 The trail curves southwest in a completely dense forest.

1.0 Pass a concrete marker from the former rail line emblazoned with the number "9." Traverse sections of trail where tributaries of New Hope Creek are undermining the trailbed. The path continues arcing southwest.

1.4 A user-created trail leaves left for private property.

1.8 Cross a streambed via a still-functional culvert.

1.9 Continue curving westerly.

2.2 Pass the foundation of an old water tank and tower formerly used by the rail line. Ahead, emerge onto the man-made causeway entering what is now Jordan Lake. Views open of Jordan Lake.

2.3 The trail and the causeway end. You are overlooking the upper New Hope Creek embayment of Jordan Lake. This is a good place to observe raptors and waterfowl and look across to where a rail bridge once spanned New Hope Creek. Backtrack.

4.6 Reach the trailhead, completing the hike.

Greater Durham, Chapel Hill, and Hillsborough Area

This swinging bridge crosses the Eno River (hike 26).

21 Rhododendron Bluff Hike

This loop penetrates one of the deepest valleys in the Triangle area. Here New Hope Creek cuts a mini gorge, flowing as a rocky, rapid-filled waterway beneath steep Piney Mountain. Start your hike on wide fire roads leading to New Hope Creek, where the New Hope Creek South Trail provides a challenging singletrack path. Hike along the rugged and stony stream with bordering rocky flats that resemble watersheds of the Southern Appalachians. Come upon the base of Rhododendron Bluff, a steep, evergreen-cloaked hill and sheer rock cliff towering over New Hope Creek. Leave the creek using a combination of forest roads and trails to complete the loop.

Start: Gate 26 on Laurel Hill Road
Distance: 3.1-mile balloon loop
Hiking time: 2.0–2.5 hours
Difficulty: Moderate, difficult in sections
Trail surface: Natural
Best season: Year-round
Other trail users: None
Canine compatibility: Leashed dogs allowed

Land status: Duke Forest
Fees and permits: No fees or permits required
Schedule: Sunrise to sunset
Maps: Duke Forest Korstian Division; USGS Chapel Hill
Trail contacts: Office of the Duke Forest, Duke University, PO Box 90332, Durham, NC 27708; (919) 613-8013; http://dukeforest.duke.edu

Finding the trailhead: From exit 270 on I-40, east of Chapel Hill, take US 15/US 501 north toward Duke/Durham. Drive 0.5 mile then turn left on Mount Moriah Road. Drive 1.4 miles then turn right on Erwin Road. Follow Erwin Road 0.5 mile then turn left on Whitfield Road. Follow Whitfield Road for 0.6 mile to Gate 26, on your right. There is road shoulder parking where designated only. Trailhead GPS: N35 58.670', W79 0.988'

The Hike

Despite the fact that hiking in the various divisions of Duke Forest is not highly touted or advertised in any way, Triangle area hikers seem to make their way to the trails open to the public. The Korstian Division of Duke Forest contains within it the arguably most exhilarating gorge in the area, and thus is one of the more popular parcels of Duke Forest. Although using the word *gorge* may be a stretch, New Hope Creek has cut a valley that drops off 200 feet from its hilltops in places. This vertical variety adds biodiversity to the watershed, especially when you consider that the winding stream creates multiple exposures, resulting in bluffs where Catawba rhododendron colors the hillsides, and in other places microclimates where wildflowers thrive. Additionally, the large amount of exposed rock enhances the hilly terrain and recalls the rocky Appalachians in the western part of North Carolina.

Make no mistake, the amount of rock, while geologically alluring, adds a challenging element to the hike in some places. The footbed can be very irregular for these

RHODODENDRON AND MOUNTAIN LAUREL

Both mountain laurel and rhododendron grow here. Rhododendron, with bigger, leathery evergreen leaves, prefers shaded ravines and being near streams, but will also grow along moist slopes and on high-elevation, well-watered ridges. Mountain laurel, with smaller evergreen leaves, prefers dry, south-facing ridges amid pine-oak forests. That being said, the two overlap habitats, as is the case here. To add to the confusion are the historical names. Many pioneers called mountain laurel, ivy. They called rhododendron, laurel, as well as calling hemlock trees, spruce (and there are hemlock trees here). Botanists of the last century, while cataloging the vast array of plants in the South, must have been confounded by all the names the locals had given their flora.

Just to confuse things further, there are two types of native rhododendron growing in North Carolina. Catawba rhododendron is what cloaks the slopes of the New Hope Creek gorge and is the namesake for Rhododendron Bluff. Rosebay is the other native rhododendron. Interestingly, rosebay rhododendron grows in mountainous North Carolina and easterly to about Hanging Rock State Park and Pilot Mountain State Park, then peters out. However, Catawba rhododendron grows in the highest elevations of the Carolina mountains (we are talking above 6,000 feet!) and also in scattered lower, disjunct areas of the Piedmont, elevations that are simply too hot and dry for rosebay rhododendron.

To provide further contrast, Catawba rhododendron blooms in mid-spring here in the Piedmont but later spring in the mountains. Rosebay rhododendron blooms in mid- to late summer in the western highlands of the state, where it is found in huge numbers, providing a whitish flower that is easily distinguished from the deep pink flowers of the Catawba rhododendron. Rosebay blooms vary year to year in the mountains, where they grow in massive patches along mountain streams. Some years rosebay rhododendron stands can look like a sea of white, and other years just a few bushes will bloom. The leaves of Catawba rhododendron are much smaller than those of rosebay rhododendron, but both share a commonality of having dark green, leathery leaves with a light underside.

A note of caution: Rosebay rhododendron is poisonous if ingested, though I see no reason why anyone would even try to eat any portion of the plant. However, a popular campfire tale relates that smoke from the rosebay rhododendron's limbs and branches will make you sick if inhaled, though I can't verify this for a fact. And I hope I never do. . . .

Water rushes through the New Hope Creek gorge.

parts. Wear sturdy shoes with gripping soles. However, the walk starts out innocuous enough, tracing gated doubletrack forest roads (closed to public vehicles) through upland oak forests. After dropping off Slick Hill, the hike reaches noisy New Hope Creek, with a concentration of rocky rapids within the Korstian Division that also recalls the mountains. Over the approximately 5-mile stretch between Turkey Farm Road at the west end of Korstian and Erwin Road on the east end, New Hope Creek drops 20 feet per mile, with some stretches approaching 40 feet per mile!

Piney Mountain, elevation 452 feet, rises just across from your meeting point with New Hope Creek. Then you turn upstream, working your way over periodically inundated flats as well as stone-pocked slopes. The trail also cuts across sporadic intermittent streambeds. Views of the creek are nearly constant and reveal an everywhere-you-look beauty.

The streamside trekking culminates in the stretch underneath Rhododendron Bluff. Here the sheer rock wall bordered with the lesser-seen evergreen combined with the challenging walking among boulders make for a true highlight. You can also walk up to the top of Rhododendron Bluff to gain an elevated view up New Hope Creek. Enjoy more intimate streamside trekking, much of it rocky, until you gratefully emerge onto Concrete Bridge Road. The walking is easy now as this doubletrack leads you up and away from New Hope Creek.

Next, a foot trail winds through a restored pine/wiregrass forest that once covered much of the Piedmont but is seldom seen today. Here you can see the lay of the land mostly covered in high grasses and brush mixed with sporadic tall pines. Finally, enjoy a final bit of easy hiker trail through oaks to complete the adventure.

Rhododendron Bluff Hike

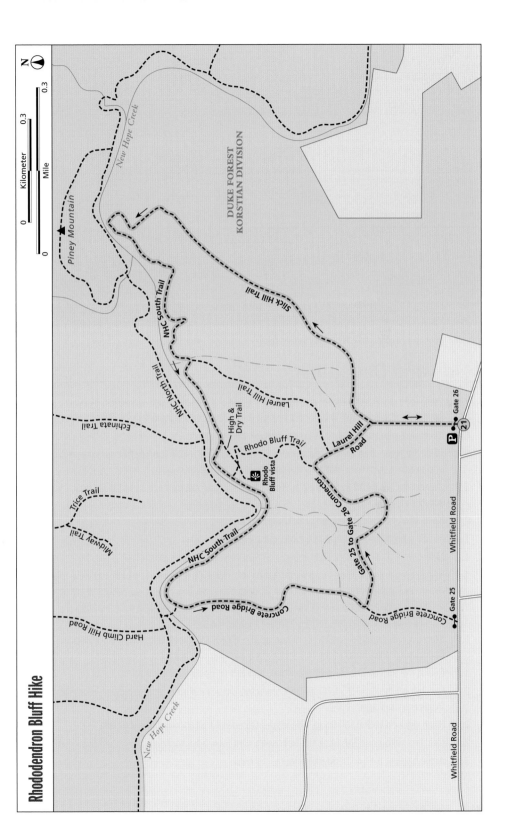

Hikers have to squeeze past Rhododendron Bluff—or walk atop it.

Miles and Directions

0.0 Head north from Gate 26 on gravel Laurel Hill Road under Piedmont pine/oak woods.

0.2 Split right with Slick Hill Trail, a doubletrack path. Descend northeasterly.

0.7 Reach an auto turnaround. The path morphs to singletrack.

0.9 Meet the New Hope Creek South Trail. Stay right, making a little loop before turning west and heading upstream along New Hope Creek, which delivers quite a splash as it flows.

1.2 Come near an island in the stream. Keep west, bridging intermittent streambeds flowing into New Hope Creek.

1.3 Keep straight after intersecting the Laurel Hill Trail.

1.4 Reach a prominent outcrop overlooking the creek.

1.5 Meet the High & Dry Trail. Stay straight on the New Hope Creek South Trail.

1.6 Keep straight as the Creek Connector heads left. However, if you want a bluff-top view, take the Creek Connector to the Rhodo Bluff Spur to the vista. This hike stays along the creek on the New Hope Creek South Trail. Work upstream amid boulders and over outcrops, directly beside the stream, below hemlock and rhododendron.

1.7 Step over an unnamed creek. Continue up the New Hope Creek valley in a rocky, wooded floodplain. Pass an old stone fence from long-ago farming days.

1.9 Reach the ford at Concrete Bridge Road. Turn left on doubletrack, climbing.

2.4 Turn left on the Gate 25 to Gate 26 Connector. Enter a restored pine/wiregrass ecosystem. Cross two drainages.

2.8 Head right on Laurel Hill Road. Ahead, the Laurel Hill Trail comes in on your left.

2.9 Reach a hilltop and the Slick Hill Trail. Keep right, now backtracking.

3.1 Arrive back at the trailhead, completing the hike.

22 Piney Mountain Double Loop

This hike explores the highs and lows of the Duke Forest's Korstian Division. Start your hike on the Piney Mountain Road to reach the crest of Piney Mountain, standing 200 feet above New Hope Creek below. Drop to the water's edge and squeeze past rocky bluffs. The trail then crosses Piney Mountain Creek and pinches past still more bluffs before opening to richly forested bottomland. Downstream, find sheer bluffs across the water and two milldams. Your return route wanders woods before returning to New Hope Creek and a backtrack. Finally, climb back to the top of Piney Mountain and on to the trailhead.

Start: Gate 21 on Mount Sinai Road
Distance: 3.8-mile double loop
Hiking time: 2.5–3.0 hours
Difficulty: Moderate, difficult in spots
Trail surface: Natural
Best season: Year-round
Other trail users: None
Canine compatibility: Leashed dogs allowed

Land status: Duke Forest
Fees and permits: No fees or permits required
Schedule: Sunrise to sunset
Maps: Duke Forest Korstian Division; USGS Chapel Hill
Trail contacts: Office of the Duke Forest, Duke University, PO Box 90332, Durham, NC 27708; (919) 613-8013; http://dukeforest.duke.edu

Finding the trailhead: From exit 270 on I-40, east of Chapel Hill, take US 15/US 501 north toward Duke/Durham. Drive 0.5 mile then turn left on Mount Moriah Road. Drive 1.4 miles then turn right on Erwin Road. Follow Erwin Road for 1.2 miles then turn left on Kerley Road. Follow Kerley Road for 0.2 mile then turn left on Mount Sinai Road and follow it for 0.9 mile to Gate 21 on your left, across the street from Mount Sinai Baptist Church. There is road shoulder parking just past the church. Do not park in the church lot. Trailhead GPS: N35 59.693', W79 0.516'

The Hike

Yes, there are some named mountains in the Piedmont. However, it takes more than a name for a mountain to be a mountain. It also takes a little elevation, and Piney Mountain has that. Rising to a height of 452 proud feet above sea level, Piney Mountain stands on the edge of a gorge overlooking New Hope Creek nearly 200 declivitous feet below. And when you stand on the edge of Piney Mountain, it seems a long way down.

The hike starts on a ridgeline stretching south from Mount Sinai Road. A doubletrack leads to the crest of Piney Mountain, where you can look down into the abyss of New Hope Creek. Luckily, foot trails link to New Hope Creek, allowing a sane descent. The hike then squeezes downstream between Pine Mountain and New Hope Creek, where you will be dancing over rocks and between leaning trees bent from previous flooding.

The remains of Breached Dam Mill

By the way, do not take this hike during flood conditions, as this section of trail might be inundated. The nearest streamflow monitoring gauge is New Hope Creek near Blands, North Carolina. The gauge is located where New Hope Creek flows under the Stagecoach Road Bridge. Though the gauge is downstream of this hike, check this gauge to see if New Hope Creek is flowing at normal levels for any given time. Add "USGS" to your search. If it is near normal, then you should have no problem getting down the trail. This part of the hike really does squeeze over rocks and even around a couple of outcrops penetrating into the stream.

Next comes the unbridged crossing of Piney Mountain Creek. Again, this should be no problem under normal flows, and even at higher flows you can simply take off your shoes and ford the stream. From there the hike squeezes past a couple more rocky bluff areas bordered by rapids, all making for a scenic albeit more challenging trail. Then the path opens onto richly wooded bottoms and the going is easy, for the steep, rough bluffs are now on the other side of the creek. Look for overhangs amid the rock. Pass an old milldam backed against a bluff, known as the Breached Dam Mill.

Just when you've had all the waterside walking you can stand, the hike comes near Erwin Road and a gristmill site known as the Mann Patterson Mill. The dam and millrace are evident here. After checking this out, cut through woods on Mrs. Browns Trail. Squeeze back upstream on New Hope Creek. Finally, it is time to climb Piney Mountain. After your ascent you may think it really does deserve to be called a mountain.

MILL LIFE ON THE PIEDMONT

During this hike you will pass two mills. When Piedmont North Carolina was becoming settled, entrepreneurial types were establishing mills along waterways, places where waterpower could convert raw materials into usable products, such as turning corn and wheat into meal, or logs into lumber or paper, or metal slabs into usable shapes. Breached Dam Mill was apparently an early paper mill, while the Patterson Mill primarily ground wheat and corn. Mills were built along creeks and were dammed using local stone, hopefully built in an area along a given waterway with a solid geological foundation to hold the dam up on each side of the creek. Then a waterwheel was built to turn a turbine that created power. Other mechanical devices were added, depending upon the product being made, but often it was simply a millstone used to grind meal. Millers took a toll of what they ground, anywhere from one-eighth to one-twelfth of the product, then resold it for a profit or used some of it for themselves. Most mills were owner operated, though bigger, busier ones did have employees. Before the Civil War, slaves were used to operate mills.

Wages were factored into the cost of running a mill, but simply keeping the mill running could be expensive, for there was constant adjustment of water intake, the mill wheel, gearing, and other concerns.

However, floods were what mill owners feared the most. Naturally, mills were set directly alongside waterways such as New Hope Creek, in this instance, as well as other streams in the area like Crabtree Creek, Reedy Creek, and the Eno River. A man could build a milling empire and have it washed away in one big flood. The story of Piedmont area mills is one of rising and falling with the waters of these streams. Repairs and rebuilding of mills and their dams was expensive work and often portended the selling of a mill to a new owner.

Since local residents came regularly to mills to have their wheat and corn ground, logs sawn, cotton ginned, and other services provided, it was only natural that mills developed into community and social centers. For some farm families a trip to the mill was the big social experience, in addition to the weekly church service. Other businesses naturally located near the mills, for customers of yesteryear enjoyed one-stop shopping as much as we do today. Of course others enjoyed visiting with—and gossiping about—their neighbors. In contrast to today, mills brought people together to interact personally rather than talking on the phone, texting, or trolling social websites. So when hiking by Breached Dam Mill and the Mann Patterson Mill, think of all the passersby who gathered here to do a little business—and a little socializing. It was all part of mill life on the Piedmont.

Miles and Directions

0.0 Head south from Gate 21 on gravel Piney Mountain Road, bordered by pines.

0.5 Reach the top of Piney Mountain and a trail junction. The drop-off is evident to the south. Leave right on a stony footpath. Descend sharply to flats with rock piles from former fields. Come alongside a tributary of New Hope Creek under tulip and sycamore trees. Watch for a stone fence.

A sand beach lies across an evergreen-cloaked bluff.

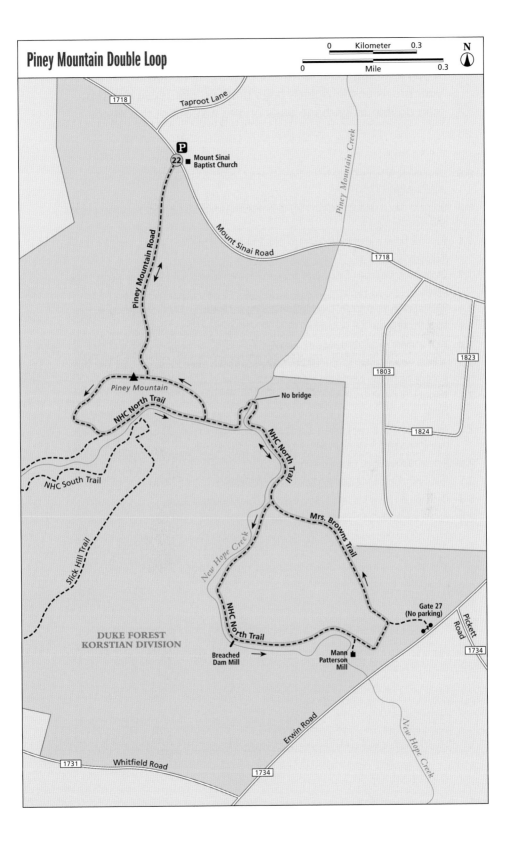

Piney Mountain Double Loop

0 Kilometer 0.3

0 Mile 0.3

N

1718
Taproot Lane

P
22 ■ Mount Sinai Baptist Church

Mount Sinai Road

Piney Mountain Creek

1718

Piney Mountain Road

1803

1823

Piney Mountain

No bridge

NHC North Trail

NHC North Trail

1824

NHC South Trail

Mrs. Browns Trail

Stick Hill Trail

New Hope Creek

NHC North Trail

Gate 27 (No parking)

Pickett Road

DUKE FOREST KORSTIAN DIVISION

Breached Dam Mill

Mann Patterson Mill

1734

Erwin Road

New Hope Creek

1731

Whitfield Road

1734

0.8 Meet the New Hope Creek North Trail. Head left, downstream, paralleling the rocky, rooty water's edge.

0.9 Squeeze over a sloped, ferny, mossy bluff reaching toward the waters. The stream bends and slows in a pool.

1.1 Pass the other end of the Piney Mountain Trail. Keep along New Hope Creek then turn up Piney Mountain Creek.

1.2 Cross Piney Mountain Creek. Turn downstream then keep downstream along New Hope Creek.

1.4 Work around a prominent outcrop overlooking the creek.

1.6 Pass Mrs. Browns Trail, your return route. Stay along New Hope Creek.

1.8 View a sheer rock bluff across the creek.

1.9 Walk in view of a partial milldam stretching across the creek, Breached Dam Mill. Overhanging bluffs rise across the water. Cross a big flat.

2.1 The spur to the Mann Patterson Mill leaves right. The loop soon turns left, away from the creek.

2.2 Turn left at Mrs. Browns Trail. It is a short distance right to Gate 27 on Erwin Road. Roll through woods.

2.6 Return to New Hope Creek; backtrack.

3.1 Join new trail, leaving right to climb Piney Mountain.

3.3 Crest out on Piney Mountain. Backtrack on Piney Mountain Road.

3.8 Reach the trailhead, completing the hike.

23 Johnston Mill Nature Preserve

This hike explores a protected parcel of the upper New Hope Creek watershed. Follow New Hope Creek downstream past two former mill sites, then make a loop around a tributary—Old Field Creek—walking hilly bluffs and streamside flats. These watercourses deliver beauty in each season, luring you to return for multiple visits.

Start: Mount Sinai Road parking area
Distance: 3.5-mile balloon loop
Hiking time: 1.5-2.5 hours
Difficulty: Moderate
Trail surface: Natural
Best season: Spring for wildflowers
Other trail users: None
Canine compatibility: Leashed dogs allowed

Land status: Nature preserve
Fees and permits: No fees or permits required
Schedule: Sunrise to sunset
Maps: Johnston Mill Nature Preserve
Trail contacts: Triangle Land Conservancy, 514 S. Duke St., Durham, NC 27701; (919) 908-8809; www.triangleland.org

Finding the trailhead: From exit 266 on I-40, north of Chapel Hill, take NC 86 north for 1.8 miles to turn right on Mount Sinai Road. Follow it for 1.1 miles to the parking area on the right just before the bridge over New Hope Creek. Trailhead GPS: N35 59.730', W79 3.249'

The Hike

Sometimes while driving, we roll on bridges right over creeks and never give them much thought. However, many creeks in the Triangle area harbor natural beauty and a glimpse of the area's past. New Hope Creek and its tributary Old Field Creek are two such waterways, streams that once hosted mills where local farmers ground their corn into meal, streams now functioning as wildlife corridors, valleys where trees rise regally to cool the waters below them, and where wildflowers from trout lilies to jack-in-the-pulpit color the woodland floor.

Johnston Mill Nature Preserve comes in at 296 acres and protects a segment of New Hope Creek in Orange County. New Hope Creek has its headwaters not far west from here, where the stream flows off a low ridge then picks up several east-running tributaries. New Hope Creek cuts steep bluffs as it meanders through hills then curves south, carving a valley dividing Chapel Hill from Durham. It is dammed upon entering Chatham County, and the waters of Jordan Lake flood the lowermost New Hope Creek valley. It is in this lake that New Hope Creek meets its mother stream, the Haw River.

Since New Hope Creek is deep in the Triangle, it has been under continuous development pressure, making this preserve even more valuable. This pressure was recognized by the North Carolina Natural Heritage Program, as well as it being "one of Orange County's most important natural areas." Fortunately for local hikers and

A trail bridge crosses upper Old Field Creek.

nature enthusiasts, the Triangle Land Conservancy purchased and protected this and several other such preserves. The 296 acres that comprise Johnston Mill Nature Preserve was bought in the late 1990s for over $3 million. Imagine how much this land would cost today! Consider that when you enjoy this conserved tract.

The hike leaves the Mount Sinai trailhead and immediately drops to meet New Hope Creek. Follow the perennial waterway downstream as it bends in nearly continuous arcs, showing gravel bars in summer and fall when flowing low, but also sporting evidence of winter floods—downstream-bent tree trunks, logs piled against rocks, brush hanging in trees. With increased urbanization, having a natural floodplain helps absorb fast runoff from asphalt roads and parking lots. The trail clambers around rock outcrops. Ahead you see scattered stone remains of a gristmill located across the creek in Hogans Bottom. Look for remnant rock walls and the old tailrace. Continue following New Hope Creek downstream to reach its confluence with Old Field Creek. The New Hope Creek valley has been cultivated for centuries, and logged too. Old Field Creek likely got its name from its bottomland being cultivated. The land has since healed from its time with the plow and the axe.

Before heading that way, our hike continues down New Hope Creek as it makes a dramatic bend. You reach the site of Johnston Mill. A portion of the milldam is still intact and easily visible. The hike then heads to Old Field Creek. Here you wander through a stand of impressive gray beech trees on a bluff above Old Field Creek. Stay above the stream in rich woods then turn up smaller Johnston Branch. The Johnstons first settled this land in the early 1700s, so it is no surprise that more than just a mill is named for them.

THE MIGHTY BEECH

Part of this hike travels through a mature beech forest. Beech trees are among the easiest trees to identify. The smooth, gray trunk makes it stand out in the forest, as the carved trees along this trail testify. Many woodland walkers simply cannot resist the flat surface of the beech—it seems a tablet for a handy pocketknife—but fight the urge.

Pick up a beech leaf from the forest floor. They are generally 2 to 4 inches long with sharply toothed edges, dark green on top and lighter underneath. In fall they turn a yellowish golden brown. After the leaves fall from the beech, notice the buds of next year's leaves. The half-inch buds resemble a mini cigar. Come spring these buds will unfurl, becoming next year's leaves.

Beechnuts are an important food for wildlife, from mice to deer, and birds from ducks to blue jays. Critters break apart the burr-covered shell to reach the nutrient-rich treat. For man the wood of beech trees is used for everything from flooring to railroad ties to charcoal—and, of course, as a carving tablet.

The hike bridges Johnston Branch then spans Old Field Creek, comfortably ensconced in woods, completely belying its name. The Old Field Bluff Trail meanders through bucolic rolling woods, a perfect place to soak in fall color. Finally, you return to New Hope Creek, backtracking to the trailhead.

Miles and Directions

0.0 From the parking area off Mount Sinai Road, join the singletrack Robins Trail. Drop off a rise, bisect a flat, and shortly come upon New Hope Creek. Turn right, downstream. New Hope Creek alternates in singing shoals and lazy pools. Tall hardwoods rise in the ferny floodplain.

0.2 The trail comes to a bluff. Take the wooden steps right, ascending above the sheer rock outcrop.

0.3 Pass under a power line. Note the rugged rock formations below, through which New Hope Creek flows. Just ahead, reach a trail intersection. Here the Bluebird Trail leaves right and roughly follows the power line clearing. Stay straight with the Robins Trail, hiking under tall tulip trees.

0.4 Pass beside an old unnamed mill site. It almost looks like a rapid, with lots of stones strewn into the creek. Look for remnants of the old tailrace.

0.6 Come to an intersection. Here the Old Field Bluff Trail leaves right. This will be your return route. For now stay straight and immediately span Old Field Creek on a bridge, then come to a four-way trail intersection with the Beech Loop. Here stay left with the Robins Trail toward Johnston Mill. Course through richly vegetated flats that are alive with wildflowers in spring.

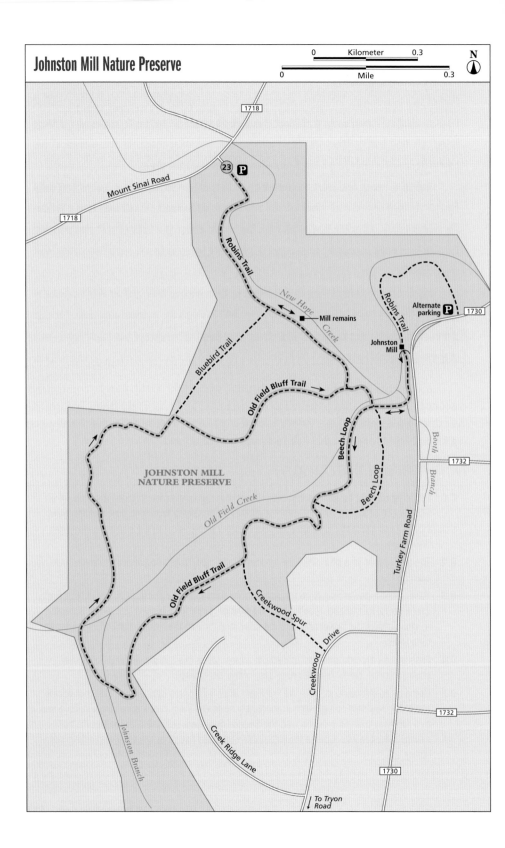

Johnston Mill Nature Preserve

0   Kilometer   0.3

0   Mile   0.3

N

1718

1718

Mount Sinai Road

23 **P**

Robins Trail

New Hope Creek

Mill remains

Robins Trail

Alternate parking **P**   1730

Johnston Mill

Bluebird Trail

Old Field Bluff Trail

Beech Loop

Beech Loop

Booth Branch

1732

JOHNSTON MILL NATURE PRESERVE

Old Field Creek

Turkey Farm Road

Old Field Bluff Trail

Creekwood Spur

Creekwood Drive

Johnston Branch

Creek Ridge Lane

1732

1730

To Tryon Road

0.7 Bridge Booth Branch very near Turkey Farm Road. The trail then squeezes between Turkey Farm Road and New Hope Creek.

0.8 Reach the old Johnston Mill site. Drop to New Hope Creek. Look upstream at the remains of the milldam. Imagine the activity that went on here, the locals gathering to visit and swap stories, then imagine the flood that took away the mill. Robins Trail continues curving through bottoms, but you backtrack toward the Beech Loop.

1.0 Return to the four-way intersection and the Beech Loop. Stay straight here. Come directly alongside Old Field Creek. This is another favorable wildflower area. Look for twisted hornbeam trees in the flats. Rise above the river and enter a stand of mature, gray-trunked beech trees on this northwest-facing slope.

1.2 Meet the other end of the Beech Loop. Stay straight here, joining the Old Field Bluff Trail. Turn in and out of small hollows with boardwalk bridges amid more regal beeches.

1.5 Reach the Creekwood Spur, leading left to a neighborhood. Stay right here, still on the Old Field Bluff Trail. Climb well above the creek, at the top end of a steep slope.

1.9 Drop to Johnston Branch, to cross it on a bridge. Descend toward Old Field Creek.

2.0 Bridge Old Field Creek then climb into hilly woods.

2.2 Open onto a mown meadow. Next, turn left, passing under a power line. Reenter woods.

2.4 Bridge an intermittent tributary.

2.5 Reach the power line again. Head left, following the power line about 50 yards. Here the Bluebird Trail keeps straight under the power line, but you turn right, reentering woods on the Old Field Bluff Trail.

2.9 Reach a trail intersection after descending through woods. Here you turn left on Robins Trail and backtrack.

3.5 Arrive back at the Mount Sinai Road trailhead, finishing the hike.

24 Occoneechee Mountain State Natural Area

This hike takes place at one of the most significant plant and animal communities in the greater Triangle. The trek circles Occoneechee Mountain, first exploring its vast oak stands on the south slope. Next, visit the Eno River and its aquatic splendor. Make a side trip to a quarry then ascend the north slope to a vista. Pass by rare butterfly habitat before descending past fishing ponds and returning to the trailhead.

Start: Occoneechee Mountain State Natural Area parking area
Distance: 2.6-mile loop
Hiking time: About 1.5 hours
Difficulty: Moderate
Trail surface: Natural
Best season: Year-round
Other trail users: None
Canine compatibility: Leashed dogs allowed
Land status: State natural area

Fees and permits: No fees or permits required
Schedule: Nov–Feb: 8 a.m.–6 p.m.; Mar, Apr, Sept, Oct: 8 a.m.–8 p.m.; May–Aug: 8 a.m.–9 p.m.; closed Christmas Day
Maps: Occoneechee Mountain State Natural Area
Trail contacts: Eno River State Park, 6101 Cole Mill Rd., Durham, NC 27705; (919) 383-1686; www.ncparks.gov

Finding the trailhead: From exit 164 on I-85, north of Chapel Hill, turn right, north, on Churton Street and follow it for 0.1 mile to turn left at a traffic light on Mayo Street. Follow Mayo Street for 0.3 mile then turn left on Orange Grove Road and follow it for 0.3 mile. Turn right on Virginia Cates Road. Follow it into the state natural area then turn left into the parking area at 0.3 mile. Official address: 625 Virginia Cates Road, Hillsborough, NC 27278. Trailhead GPS: N36 3.638', W79 7.017'

The Hike

Occoneechee Mountain is purportedly the highest place in North Carolina between its location near Hillsborough east all the way to the Atlantic Ocean. However, it has more significance than just its height, for the 867-foot peak also harbors mountain species such as Catawba rhododendron, galax, and ferns such as mountain spleenwort. Not only is it home to disjunct populations of plants, but it is also home to the brown elfin butterfly, one of the few places in the Piedmont where this insect lives. Though its highest point is capped with communication towers, and a rock quarry was dug into its side, the 190-acre plot of protected land remains an outpost for exemplary oak forests, as well as a wide variety of plant species along its north slope all the way down to the Eno River, which adds still more biodiversity. Occoneechee Mountain rises more than 350 feet from the Eno River, creating conditions for biodiversity unmatched in the greater Triangle.

Occoneechee Mountain was once a landmark for settlers heading to and from the capital in Raleigh. Later, simple farmers lived in its shadow. The town of Hillsborough grew to its north. Today Occoneechee Mountain is bounded by Hillsborough and on the south by I-85. Despite the nearness of civilization, area citizens saw the importance of preserving the peak and its flora and fauna. In the early 1960s a mine began operations extracting pyrophyllite, a flaky silica. Known for thermal stability, it is used in combination with other elements for making everything from bricks to chemicals. Orange County, North Carolina, is one of the major regions where it is found. Nevertheless, this mining activity signaled a couple, Allen and Pauline Lloyd, to purchase 66 acres on the mountain. Subsequently, more mountain acreage was donated for a Hillsborough city park, but the park was never opened due to lack of public access. The Eno River Association then bought out a logger and petitioned North Carolina State Parks to include Occoneechee Mountain as an add-on to Eno River State Park. Occoneechee Mountain was established as a state natural area in 1997.

The preserve includes over 3 miles of hiking trails, a picnic area, and two ponds where anglers can vie for largemouth bass and bream. The north side of the park is bounded by the Eno River, which also provides angling opportunities. This hike leaves the picnic parking area and skirts the south slope of Occoneechee Mountain. Here you experience the downside of this state natural area—the proximity to the interstate on the mountain's south side leaves your ears ringing with passing trucks and cars. However, if it is good enough for the deer you will likely see here, then it is good enough for Triangle area hikers.

A sloped, rocky oak forest provides a visual reward as you curve around Occoneechee Mountain. The north side provides not only a quieter experience but also increased biodiversity. The route takes you alongside the Eno River, where sheer bluffs contrast with flatter bottomlands. The hike then leaves the river and travels to a now closed mine that once extracted pyrophyllite. It is interesting to see the pines and other trees taking hold in the former barren area. From the lowlands the hike climbs along a power line then curves to the top of the mine area and a surprisingly far-reaching vista. Here you can look northwest up the Eno River Valley. From there rise to the main crest of Occoneechee Mountain. The high point of the mountain is closed because of communication towers; however, do not let that deter you from enjoying the experience.

Take the Brown Elfin Knob Trail, so named for the rare Piedmont population of this butterfly. Though rarely dense anywhere in North Carolina, brown elfin butterflies reach surprisingly high populations here at Occoneechee Mountain State

Natural Area, despite the fact that the nearest other population is 100 miles distant. Most Tar Heel State mountain counties harbor the brown elfin butterfly, though a few populations are found in the sandhills near the South Carolina border. The hike leads through the brown elfin habitat then drops to the lowlands. Here you find a pair of fishing ponds. Grassy trails connect to the ponds from the main loop. Finally, the hike leads to the on-site ranger residence before returning to the picnic parking area and hike's end.

Miles and Directions

0.0   From the parking area, head west from a trailside kiosk beyond the shaded picnic area, entering full-blown woods on the Occoneechee Mountain Loop Trail. The interstate roars nearby as you wander underneath oaks and pines. When curving around the southwest side of the mountain, chestnut oaks become more prevalent.

0.2   Walk under a power line.

0.4   Reach a trail intersection. Here the Chestnut Oak Trail turns right, north, up Occoneechee Mountain. You stay straight on the Occoneechee Mountain Loop Trail, still westbound on a rocky, piney slope. Ample rock outcrops rise in the woods.

0.8   Begin dropping off the mountain by switchbacks. Next, curve east above a floodplain of an unnamed tributary of the Eno River.

1.0   Bridge a ravine then come alongside the Eno River above a huge riverside boulder. You are on the edge of the preserve property. Please do not head into private property. Cruise along the Eno, cloaked in mountain laurel, which blooms in May. The river is the preserve boundary here. Contemplation benches are situated alongside the trail.

1.2   Hike along the base of a sheer bluff. Cut across more ravines ahead.

1.4   Take the spur trail leading right to the old pyrophyllite mine. Here you can see a former rock and gravel wasteland returning to life, being colonized primarily by scrub pines. Back-track to the main loop. From here the Occoneechee Mountain Loop Trail climbs rock steps uphill under a power line.

1.6   Turn right back into woods after passing directly under a power line tower. Climb to reach an intersection. Turn right here, joining the Overlook Trail.

1.7   Arrive at a surprisingly far-reaching overlook. You are standing atop the old quarry. The clearing below combined with the elevation allows a vista northwesterly up the Eno River. This is one of the best views in the entire Triangle area. From this view continue on the Overlook Trail southbound.

1.8   Come to another trail intersection. Head left, joining the doubletrack Chestnut Oak Trail. Descend.

1.9   Leave left from the wide Chestnut Oak Trail, joining the singletrack Brown Elfin Knob Trail. Angle up a knob flanked in mountain laurel. Begin dropping again.

2.1   Rejoin the Occoneechee Mountain Loop Trail, turning right and descending.

◄ *The view from Occoneechee Mountain*

Occoneechee Mountain State Natural Area

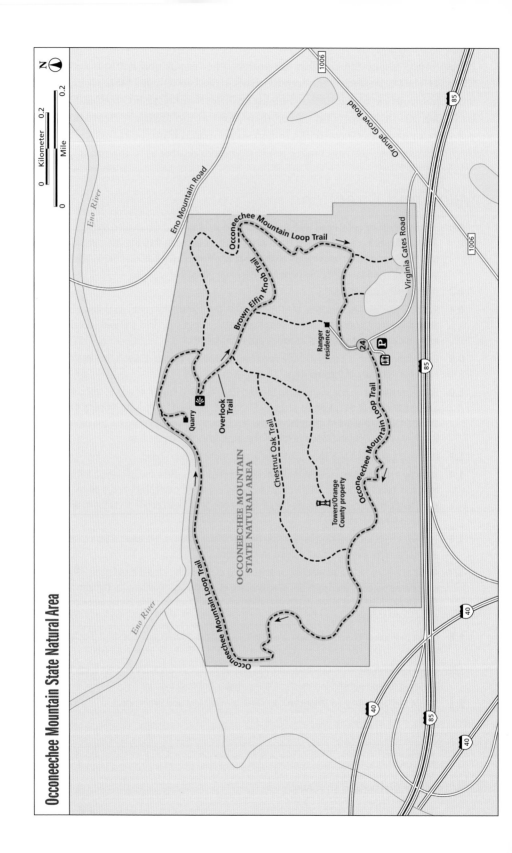

2.3 Reach the flatlands. Here a spur trail keeps straight toward the lowermost natural area pond, while our hike turns right, westerly. This is an opportunity to visit the ponds.

2.4 Open onto a grassy area with easy access to the upper pond. Turn right here to soon emerge on a gravel road below the ranger residence. Turn left here.

2.6 Reach the parking area, finishing the hike.

GREEN TIP:

Wildflowers are best appreciated when captured by your phone or camera rather than being picked or dug up.

25 Historic Occoneechee Speedway Hike

This is perhaps the most unusual hike in this book. Here you can walk the only original speedway left from the inaugural 1949 NASCAR racing circuit, now on the National Register of Historic Places. This locale on the banks of the Eno River still features parts of the original track and facilities, from the ticket booth to the built-in stands to the banked turns, now all set in tall shady woods. Additional trails on this historical hike take you through hills and along riverside flats.

Start: Elizabeth Brady Road trailhead
Distance: 2.7-mile multi-loop
Hiking time: About 1.5 hours
Difficulty: Easy–moderate
Trail surface: Natural
Best season: Year-round
Other trail users: Joggers
Canine compatibility: Leashed dogs allowed
Land status: Preservation trust
Fees and permits: No fees or permits required

Schedule: Jan, Feb, Nov, Dec: 8 a.m.–5 p.m.; Mar and Oct: 8 a.m.–6 p.m.; Apr, May, Aug, Sept: 7 a.m.–7 p.m.; June and July: 7 a.m.–8 p.m.
Maps: Occoneechee Speedway & Ayr Mount
Trail contacts: Classical American Homes Preservation Trust, 69 E. 93rd St., New York, NY 10128; (212) 369-4460; http://classical americanhomes.org

Finding the trailhead: From exit 165 on I-85, east of Hillsborough and west of Durham, take NC 86 north for 0.6 mile to a traffic light and US 70. Keep straight at the traffic light and join Elizabeth Brady Road north for 0.3 mile to reach the trailhead on your right. Official trailhead address: 320 Elizabeth Brady Road, Hillsborough, NC 27278 Trailhead GPS: N36 4.213', W79 5.092'

The Hike

Back in 1947 NASCAR founder Bill France was flying his plane over the Carolina Piedmont when a farmer's oval horse track caught his eye. Upon landing he contacted Occoneechee Farm owner Julian Carr about building a stock car racetrack in the very same spot, situated in a flat on the banks of the Eno River. The land lay just south of Ayr Mount, the historic 1815 home that still stands today and is partly the reason for this hike being possible.

By September of that year, Julian Carr's oval horse venue was expanded and altered into a dirt racetrack for the budding stock car racing circuit that was founded a little over two months later. France eventually bought the former Occoneechee Farm, a long-standing holding, named for the Occoneechee Indians who once roamed the Eno River Valley. Viewing stands were built into adjacent hills. A ticket booth, restrooms, and refreshment stand as well as spectator parking were put together around the track and adjacent fields. Occoneechee Speedway came to life. The first competition was held June 27, 1948.

Snow melts away from the old stands at historic Occoneechee Speedway.

The venue was one of the original stops on the NASCAR tour. Racing legends Richard Petty and Junior Johnson, among others, plied their trade here. The speedway was renamed Orange Speedway in 1954 (likely due to the difficulty of spelling Occoneechee, in this writer's opinion). The crowds grew, as did the prize money for the dirt track winners. In 1965 movie star Jayne Mansfield came to inaugurate the race. However, the speedway's days were numbered as local preachers pressured Bill France to cease his Sunday racing, to keep with the Sabbath as a day of rest. As a result, Mr. France found another venue in Alabama, the now famous Talladega Speedway. Stock car racing in the shadow of the Eno River became a thing of the past. Sweetgums, pines, and oaks slowly reclaimed the once noisy race venue, leaving it to the birds, squirrels, and occasional deer that passed through. The tin fencing, stands, and outbuildings were left to serve no one.

Just across the river, historic Ayr Mount, an 1815 historic-preserved home run by the Classical American Homes Preservation Trust, enlarged its bounds and purchased 44 acres that encompassed the old speedway. The trust worked to preserve the track infrastructure then developed a trail system on the now wooded banks of the Eno River. The track was added to the National Register of Historic Places in 2003. Today you can hike to the old track, make a loop (much slower than those NASCAR boys did), and explore its outlying areas, combining history and nature in this most unusual park, home to one of the most unique hikes in the United States, much less North Carolina.

First you follow the old access road then drop down to a flat and join the actual racetrack. Here, make a loop of your own, just inside the banked turns, tracing where early stock cars skidded, slid, and streaked their way through the 0.9-mile oval.

Strangely, trees rise throughout the once open track and add an almost eerie aspect to the walk. You will wonder if stock cars ever ran off the racecourse into the Eno River. After tracing where horses then cars raced and where hikers and joggers now each make their own paces, take the Spectator Trace Trail to the hilltop stands, where you can imagine watching the races from this elevated vantage, though some fans did observe from inside the track.

Walk by the old ticket booth, enter the spectator gates, and take a seat in the stands, imagining a place roaring with excitement, where Pepsi-drinking fans chomped hot dogs and soaked in the competition. Next, an interconnected set of short pathways lead you to the banks of the Eno River, where in winter Ayr Mount stands through the trees, as does the Poets Walk Trail (not linked to the Occoneechee Speedway trails) as it loops through the grounds of the home and along the river. Cruise bottomlands on the Big Bend Trail before returning to the trailhead using the short pathways. If the hike is too short, you can join a segment of the Mountains-to-Sea Trail that heads downstream along the Eno River to US 70.

Miles and Directions

0.0 From the parking area kiosk, head easterly on a doubletrack gated path. It is a level walk flanked by cedars and pines.

0.3 Reach a four-way trail intersection. There is a trailside kiosk here as well. The Spectator Trace Trail leaves left. The Mountains-to-Sea Trail leaves right. Keep straight, passing through original tin fencing from the old days, then descend the hill to reach the former Occoneechee Speedway, now the Speedway Trace Trail. Turn right here on what was Turn #1. Imagine the driver's perspective as you make your counterclockwise loop of the track. Turn north at Turn #2. The Eno River flows to your right.

0.7 Veer left into Turn #3. Most of the trail and old track is now shaded by hardwoods and evergreens.

0.8 Pass a short spur linking to the Big Bend Trail.

1.0 Walk astride the stands embedded in the hill to your right. This was the starting line. Visualize excited drivers revving their engines, ready to start racing.

1.2 Return to the four-way intersection after completing the actual racetrack part of the hike and walk uphill, back through the old tin fence. Turn right, joining the Spectator Trace Trail in thick pines.

1.3 Pass the ticket booth and through the old tin fence once again. You are now in the grandstand area. Turn right here, joining the Terrace Trace Trail.

1.4 Leave right from the Terrace Trace Trail and join a singletrack path still heading north in woods, now in the mix of short pathways.

1.5 Join the Beech Bluff Trail. Descend from a hill to the Eno River and a trail intersection. The Beech Bluff Trail leaves left. Stay straight along the Eno River, now on the Big Bend Trail. Look across the river for the Poets Walk Trail and historic Ayr Mount through the trees. Pass a shortcut to the Speedway Trace Trail.

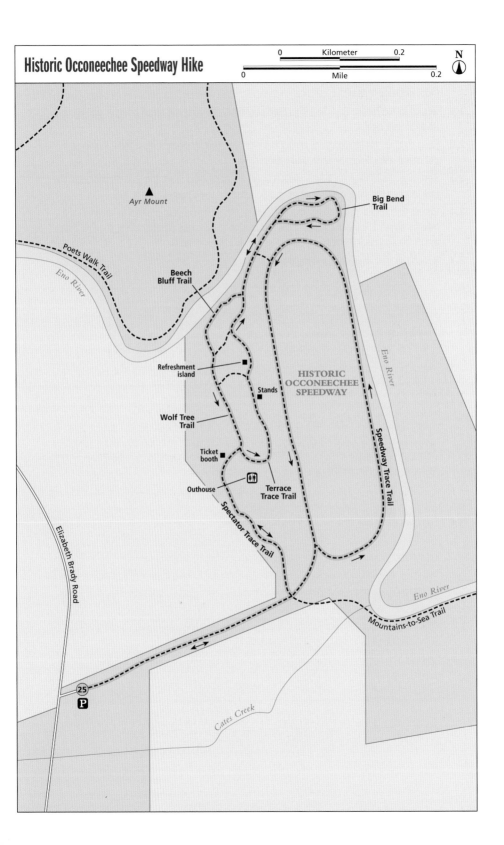

Historic Occoneechee Speedway Hike

0   Kilometer   0.2

0   Mile   0.2

N

Ayr Mount

Big Bend Trail

Poets Walk Trail

Eno River

Beech Bluff Trail

Eno River

Refreshment island

HISTORIC OCCONEECHEE SPEEDWAY

Stands

Wolf Tree Trail

Ticket booth

Outhouse

Terrace Trace Trail

Speedway Trace Trail

Spectator Trace Trail

Eno River

Elizabeth Brady Road

Mountains-to-Sea Trail

25

P

Cates Creek

1.6 Stay left, joining the loop portion of the Big Bend Trail. Cruise alongside the Eno River, gaining downstream aquatic views. Observe the bluffs across the Eno. After making the loop, head upstream.

1.9 Return to the Beech Bluff Trail. This time stay right, climbing the slope of a hill with the Eno River to your right.

2.0 Keep right at the intersection, joining the Wolf Tree Trail. Walk through woods, looking for old metal relics from the farm and racing days.

2.1 Return to the Terrace Trace Trail. Walk a short distance then leave the grandstand area, cutting through the tin fence a final time. Backtrack on the Spectator Trace Trail.

2.4 Return to the four-way trail intersection a final time. Here is your chance to lengthen the hike by about 1.5 miles by taking the Mountains-to-Sea Trail easterly along the Eno River to US 70 and back. Otherwise, backtrack toward the trailhead.

2.7 Reach the parking area, finishing the hike.

26 Cox Mountain Hike

This fun loop at the Fews Ford area of Eno River State Park takes you through lands high and low. Leave the main parking area and dip to a swinging bridge and the effervescent Eno River. Work up and over the regal forests of Cox Mountain before returning to the Eno River. Walk this history-filled and pretty river valley. Visit Fannys Ford and pass a backpacker campground before returning to the trailhead. Elevation changes range over 250 feet in this hilly part of the Triangle.

Start: Picnic parking area of Fews Ford
Distance: 4.6-mile balloon loop
Hiking time: About 2.5 hours
Difficulty: Moderate
Trail surface: Natural
Best season: Year-round, spring for wildflowers
Other trail users: None
Canine compatibility: Leashed dogs allowed
Land status: State park

Fees and permits: No fees or permits required
Schedule: May–Sept: 7 a.m.–10 p.m.; Mar, Apr, Oct: 7 a.m.–9 p.m.; Nov: 7 a.m.–8 p.m.; Dec–Feb: 7 a.m.–7 p.m.
Maps: Eno River State Park
Trail contacts: Eno River State Park, 6101 Cole Mill Rd., Durham, NC 27705; (919) 383-1686; www.ncparks.gov

Finding the trailhead: From exit 173 on I-85, west of downtown Durham, join Cole Mill Road northbound. Follow it 5.1 miles to enter the Fews Ford area of Eno River State Park. Continue past the ranger station and follow the main road to dead-end at the trailhead at 0.5 mile. Trailhead GPS: N36 4.427', W79 0.372'

The Hike

The story of Eno River State Park starts with the growing city of Durham desiring an additional water supply for its citizens. City fathers eyed the Eno River. They wanted to not only use the water of the Eno River but also dam the river and create a water storage impoundment in order to have a reliable water supply. This reservoir was to be situated west of Durham. Turns out, though, thousands of area residents enjoyed and appreciated the Eno River as it was, the way it wound through wooded Piedmont hills. Some locals even called these hills mountains, though they are not quite those of western North Carolina.

The Eno then was still pretty wild in places. If it wasn't forest, it was farmland. The big cities seemed distant then, and weren't connected by buzzing interstates and a maze of roads. It was 1965, and a group of citizens banded together, rallying to keep the Eno wild and free, aiming to thwart Durham's dam plan. They formed a group called Association for the Preservation of the Eno River Valley. They not only wanted Durham's dam stopped but also desired the Eno River Valley protected in perpetuity as a state park. Eventually more people wanted that park than they did the dam! And

GREEN TIP:

Don't take souvenirs home with you. This means natural materials such as plants, rocks, shells, and driftwood as well as historical artifacts such as fossils and arrowheads.

in 1975 Eno River State Park came to be, preserving over 1,000 acres of the river valley. More properties were added. Today Eno River State Park covers more than 3,900 acres, roughly bounded by Hillsborough to the west and Durham to the east.

The park is literally a wildlife corridor. Beavers have made a real comeback here too. A century back, the toothy varmints were trapped nearly to extinction in North Carolina. You probably won't see one swimming in the water or building a dam, but you will likely see their handiwork in the form of gnawed-off tree stumps and bark-stripped limbs. Beavers are primarily nocturnal, but you may see one around dusk or dawn. You will likely see deer here any time of the year. Wild turkeys are becoming more common as well.

While much of the park is limited to a narrow strip along the Eno River, the Fews Ford area, where this hike takes place, encloses not only the river corridor but also some big hills—dare we say mountains—well back from the waterway.

Therefore, this hike not only soaks in the Eno River but also Cox Mountain, a hillock rising to 688 feet, overlooking a bend of the Eno River. The hike actually starts across the river from Cox Mountain. Here, drop past a hilltop picnic area then make your way down to the Eno River. A picturesque and practical swinging bridge takes you across the Eno River. The trail then uses settler roads before breaking off to surmount Cox Mountain.

What goes up must come down, so down you go, returning to the Eno River near old Holden Mill. The Cox Mountain Trail next turns downstream, tracing the Eno River through bottoms, allowing easy river access for fishing, swimming, or playing in the rocks and rapids. However, parts of the trail climb above the bluffs. Later you find yourself in bottomland and following the old road to Fannys Ford, a crossing from pre-park days. You do not ford, though; instead follow the flowing Eno around a curve and past a backpacker campground. Overnight camping is allowed at this designated spot. Accommodations are primitive, just a tent pad, fire ring, and privy. Preregistration is required.

The hike curves south beyond the campground and comes to Fannys Ford. This is a historic spot, site of a stream crossing and mill. A homesite is nearby. Eventually you leave the Eno before completing the loop. A little backtracking is in order to get you back across the Eno River and to the trailhead.

Looking across the swinging bridge over the Eno River ▶

Miles and Directions

0.0 From the main parking area, take the concrete Cox Mountain Trail through a developed picnic area with water, restrooms, picnic tables, and shelter. The path quickly evolves to natural surface.

0.1 Reach the Eno Trace Trail. It leads left and heads down to the river before looping back. Our hike stays right on the Cox Mountain Trail, curving right along a bluff beside a fence. Come to earth-and-wood stairs and the spur trail to the backpacker parking area. Stay left here, descending toward the Eno River.

0.3 Come to the suspension bridge over the Eno River. Carefully cross the span, noting the water levels of the Eno during 1989's Hurricane Fran. A trail leads left just after the span to a cabin. Climb away from the Eno River on the Cox Mountain Trail. Pass a second access to the cabin. Dogwood, cedar, oaks, and other hardwoods shade the track.

0.6 A power line access road leaves left. Stay right on the Cox Mountain Trail.

0.7 Reach the loop portion of the hike. Turn left here, staying with the Cox Mountain Trail. Begin climbing westerly on the slope of Cox Mountain.

0.9 Open onto a power line that allows a view of wooded hills to the west.

1.0 Look for rock piles and old rock fences from the days when Cox Mountain was cultivated. Back in those days farmers pushed rocks around fields. Today we push buttons on a computer screen. The mountain remains rocky to this day.

1.3 Begin dropping off Cox Mountain.

1.5 Enter a hollow that opens to tulip tree– and sycamore-studded bottomland.

1.6 Sidle alongside the Eno River, with ironwood and sycamore and alder flanking the waterway. Beardcane forms thickets. Notice how the riverside trees bend downstream, a result of occasional yet certain floods that sweep through the Eno River Valley. Begin heading downstream. Look for a wing dam on this side of the stream and for Holden Mill across the water. Rock outcrops are plentiful in this wildflower-rich locale.

2.0 The trail and river turn east. Here the path joins a wide former settler road. Rise above the river.

2.2 Pass under a power line then reenter woods. Descend. Stroll through a huge bottomland.

2.7 Come to a trail intersection. One path heads to the backcountry campground while another heads right toward the swinging bridge. Join a third path, Fannys Ford Trail, left to enter a grove of tulip trees.

3.0 Return to the Eno River. Turn downstream. Buckquarter Creek enters the Eno River across the water. The Eno River widens with the additional flow from Buckquarter Creek.

3.2 A spur trail leads right to the backcountry campground. Stay straight on the Fannys Ford Trail. Begin curving south.

3.3 Pass a second spur to the backcountry campground. Buckquarter Creek Trail is visible across the river.

3.4 Walk near a particularly rock-strewn, rapid-laden stretch of river. It makes a fun river play area.

3.5 Come to the actual Fannys Ford and an old mill site. Park vehicles still drive across this ford. This hike stays on this side of the river and turns away from the water.

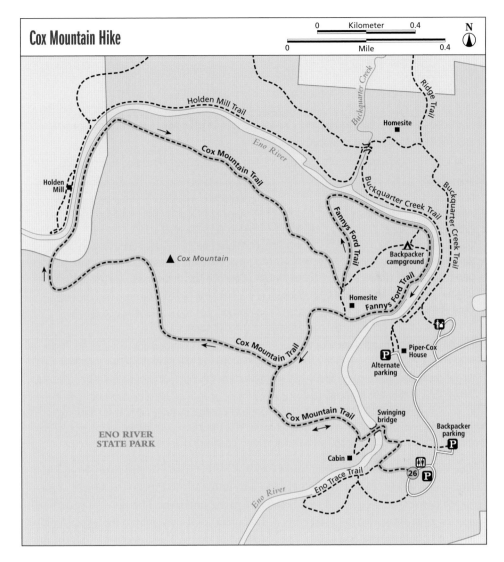

Cox Mountain Hike

0 Kilometer 0.4

0 Mile 0.4

N

Holden Mill Trail

Buckquarter Creek

Ridge Trail

Homesite ■

Eno River

Cox Mountain Trail

Holden Mill ■

Buckquarter Creek Trail

Fannys Ford Trail

Buckquarter Creek Trail

▲ Cox Mountain

Backpacker campground ⛺

Fannys Ford Trail

Homesite ■

Fannys Ford

Cox Mountain Trail

Piper-Cox House

P Alternate parking

Cox Mountain Trail

Swinging bridge

Backpacker parking P

ENO RIVER STATE PARK

Cabin ■

🚻

Eno Trace Trail

26 P

Eno River

3.6 Pass an old homesite on the right. You can still see the crumbled stone chimney. Just ahead, the Cox Mountain Trail comes in on your right. Keep straight, resuming the Cox Mountain Trail. Cruise in woods above the river.

3.9 Complete the loop portion of the hike. Begin backtracking toward the swinging bridge and the picnic area trailhead.

4.6 Reach the trailhead after passing through the picnic area, completing the hike.

27 Holden Mill Circuit

This hike starts at the historic Piper-Cox House of Eno River State Park. Leave the homestead then traverse an aquatic wonderland en route to a former mill, much of which is intact. Your return trip navigates high bluffs above the river, giving a different perspective to the water below, where you will also pass another old homestead, adding more history to this scenic jaunt.

Start: Piper-Cox House
Distance: 4.0-mile double loop
Hiking time: 2.0–2.5 hours
Difficulty: Moderate
Trail surface: Natural
Best season: Year-round
Other trail users: None
Canine compatibility: Leashed dogs allowed
Land status: State park

Fees and permits: No fees or permits required
Schedule: May–Sept: 7 a.m.–10 p.m.; Mar, Apr, Oct: 7 a.m.–9 p.m.; Nov: 7 a.m.–8 p.m.; Dec–Feb: 7 a.m.–7 p.m.
Maps: Eno River State Park
Trail contacts: Eno River State Park, 6101 Cole Mill Rd., Durham, NC 27705; (919) 383-1686; www.ncparks.gov

Finding the trailhead: From exit 173 on I-85, west of downtown Durham, join Cole Mill Road northbound. Follow it 5.1 miles to enter the Fews Ford area of Eno River State Park. Continue past the ranger station and take the first right, shortly reaching the Piper-Cox House and a parking area. Trailhead GPS: N36 4.686', W79 0.409'

The Hike

The Eno River is chock-full of history, so it is no surprise that this hike through the river valley is historical as well. Start this adventure at the Piper-Cox House, a preserved homestead established well before the park came to be. The house is really two houses joined together by a breezeway. The older log cabin, where the Piper family lived, was built in the late 1700s. They worked at the mill just down the hill on the Eno River. The clapboard house was added in the 1870s by a man named Wiley Cox, who lived here until 1908. The house was restored to its 1870s appearance. You can tour the grounds of the house any time. The park seasonally holds tours of the inside.

From the Piper-Cox house, descend to quickly reach the Eno River and notable Fews Ford. In 1758 a mill was located just below the shallow crossing. William Few had moved down here from Maryland. He operated his mill for six years before selling out. A mill of one type or another operated here for a long time thereafter.

This was one of over thirty mills eventually set up along the Eno River. There were several types of mills, the most common being a gristmill, where large circular stones were turned by waterpower to grind corn and wheat into meal for consumption. Oil mills squeezed linseed oil from flaxseeds. At one time our destination—Holden

A relic home from the days before this was parkland

Mill—was an oil mill. Sawmills turned trees into usable lumber. Paper mills transformed pulpwood into paper. A forge mill ran a hammer to bang and pressed metal into shape. A textile mill used waterpower to spin cotton and wool into yarn and run looms to weave the yarn into fabric.

The original mill operating at Fews Ford was a sawmill and gristmill. Beyond here you pass around a large rock formation protruding into the Eno River. This locale also has rapids aplenty. The hike then rambles along the river, where you can appreciate the continuous beauty this preserved waterway has to offer. In some places steep, rocky bluffs push to the water's edge, whereas in others the extensive seasonally inundated flats stretch along the water.

A footbridge allows you to cross Buckquarter Creek, a tributary of the Eno River. From there continue upstream along the Eno. The hike then makes a loop around Holden Mill, built in 1811 by Isaac Holden. Note where he altered the river with wing dams to force the water toward the mill then dug a channel to power the turbine. The mill, constructed of native rocks, is still partially intact. The milldam, channel, and turbine's location are easily discernable.

The mill originally ground flour and corn as well as cut lumber. The enterprise grew when Isaac's son Thomas inherited the mill from his father in 1820. Thomas Holden added an oil mill, a cotton gin, and threshing machines. A regular community grew around the mill. At one point ten men were employed at the mill, and a schoolhouse was built to educate the children of the families who worked at and lived near Holden Mill. Later, Thomas Holden passed on ownership of the mill to his son-in-law John F. Lyon. Lyon operated the mill from 1851 to 1868, when he lost it through financial mismanagement. A fellow named Samuel Cole operated the mill

The Eno River in autumn can be low and rocky.

for eleven years until he died in 1893. Interestingly, the road used to access this area of Eno River State Park was named during this period and attributed to Mr. Cole.

Beyond the mill the trail loops through bottomland then curves back above the mill. From this point the hike climbs a steep and rugged bluff rising above the Eno. You ascend over 200 feet into rocky hardwoods. The hike presents views down into the valley before dropping to bridge Buckquarter Creek again. It passes within sight of a wooden house from pre-park days then climbs another bluff above the Eno River, where more top-down views await. The final part of the walk leads back from the river to the Piper-Cox House.

Miles and Directions

0.0   From the Piper-Cox House, you can see a wide, road-like canoe carry path and the single-track Buckquarter Creek Trail to the left of the house. Take the Buckquarter Creek Trail down toward Fews Ford.

0.1   Reach Fews Ford and the site of the Eno River's first mill. Head right, downstream. Stay along the river. The Buckquarter Creek Trail splits. Stay left, closest to the water. Ahead, climb over a rock crag above river rapids via wooden stairs. Quickly return to the Eno. Walk a stabilized stone trail beneath rocky bluffs where cedars cling to precipices. Excellent river vistas open.

0.4   Turn away from the bluff to enter a sycamore, river birch, and tulip tree flat. The Eno flows slowly as one big pool.

0.6   Come along much smaller Buckquarter Creek. Turn upstream.

0.7   Reach and cross the wooden footbridge over Buckquarter Creek. Later you will return here to finish the loop. For now stay left beyond the bridge, joining the Holden Mill Trail and turning downstream along Buckquarter Creek.

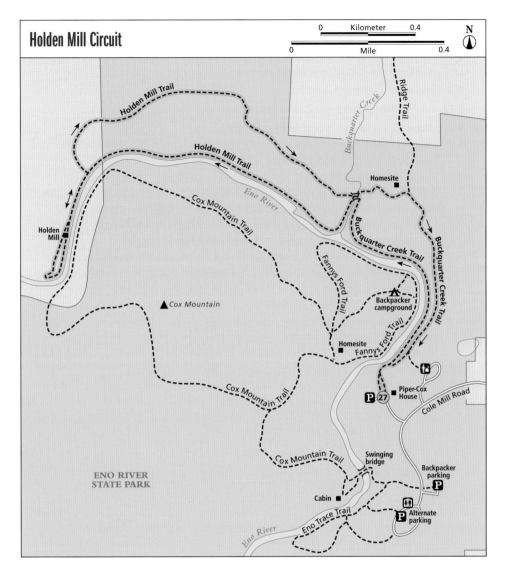

Holden Mill Circuit

0   Kilometer   0.4

0   Mile   0.4

N

Holden Mill Trail

Holden Mill Trail

Cox Mountain Trail

Eno River

Homesite

Buckquarter Creek

Ridge Trail

Holden Mill

Buckquarter Creek Trail

Buckquarter Creek Trail

Fannys Ford Trail

▲ Cox Mountain

Backpacker campground

Homesite

Fannys Ford Trail

Cox Mountain Trail

Piper-Cox House

P 27

Cole Mill Road

ENO RIVER STATE PARK

Cox Mountain Trail

Swinging bridge

Backpacker parking

P

Cabin

Eno Trace Trail

P Alternate parking

Eno River

0.8   Return to the now smaller Eno River, heading upstream in seasonally inundated bottoms.

1.2   Work through a waterside boulder garden.

1.3   Pass under a power line.

1.4   Squeeze through more boulders and circumvent a large, open rock slab.

1.6   Reach a trail intersection. Keep straight for Holden Mill.

1.7   Come to a sub-loop of the Holden Mill Trail, just after crossing a normally dry branch. Stay left with the river. Come to the tailrace of the mill and its intact stone remains.

1.8   Pass by what remains of the old milldam. Keep forward in bottomland then loop back away from the river. Wooden posts help you find your abrupt right turn. Climb a hill above the river.

2.1 Pass above the mill tailrace then complete this sub-loop. Backtrack toward the main loop of Holden Mill Trail.

2.2 Rejoin the main loop of the Holden Mill Trail, heading left. Ascend a draw then curve right, climbing a rocky hill, rich with hickory, cedar, and oak.

2.6 Pass under a power line, still climbing.

2.7 Top out on the hill after your 220-foot climb. Now begin a prolonged downgrade.

3.1 Pass some old farmer's rock piles. Drop steeply.

3.2 Cross the footbridge over Buckquarter Creek. Stay left, rejoining the Buckquarter Creek Trail. Quickly turn away from the stream.

3.3 Pass an old homesite on the left, standing in a fast-disappearing clearing. This former farmhouse is currently in disrepair. It is worth a look but stay out of the house, since much of it is rotten and full of nail-laden boards. Ahead, meet the Ridge Trail. It leaves left and offers an additional side loop, using it along with the Shakori Trail. Our hike stays straight with the Buckquarter Creek Trail. Roll through hills back from the Eno River.

3.5 The Buckquarter Creek Trail splits right from the old settler road it has been tracing. Edge closer to the Eno River on a bluff scattered with mountain laurel. River views open below. The hike remains challenging as it undulates on the bluff using wood, earth, and stone steps.

3.8 Pass the connector trail leaving left to the park ranger station. Stay straight, soon returning to Fews Ford. For new trail, take the wide canoe carry path back toward the Piper-Cox House trailhead.

4.0 Reach the parking area after climbing from Fews Ford, finishing the hike.

28 Eno Quarry Hike

This trek starts at a riverside trailhead and uses the Laurel Bluffs Trail to climb bluffs above the Eno River. From there descend to river bottoms and reach Eno Quarry. Here you can explore three bodies of water simultaneously—the Eno River, Rhodes Creek, and the clear waters of Eno Quarry. Loop around the quarry then return to the trailhead.

Start: Pleasant Green parking area
Distance: 3.2-mile balloon loop
Hiking time: 1.5-2.5 hours
Difficulty: Easy-moderate
Trail surface: Natural
Best season: Year-round
Other trail users: Anglers, swimmers
Canine compatibility: Leashed dogs allowed
Land status: State park

Fees and permits: No fees or permits required
Schedule: May-Sept: 8:30 a.m.-8:30 p.m.; Mar, Apr, Oct: 8:30 a.m.-7:30 p.m.; Nov: 8:30 a.m.-6:30 p.m.; Dec-Feb: 8:30 a.m.-5:30 p.m.
Maps: Eno River State Park
Trail contacts: Eno River State Park, 6101 Cole Mill Rd., Durham, NC 27705; (919) 383-1686; www.ncparks.gov

Finding the trailhead: From exit 170 on I-85, west of downtown Durham, take US 70 west a short distance to Pleasant Green Road. Turn right and follow Pleasant Green Road 0.4 mile to the trailhead on your left, just before the bridge over the Eno River. Trailhead GPS: N36 2.817', W79 0.683'

The Hike

Much of this hike traverses an important tract of Eno River State Park that was acquired back in 2004. Known as the Coile Estate, the land included 1.3 miles of riverbank on the south side of the Eno. It provided a link from Pleasant Green Road to the Cabelands, and made for a contiguous protected section of riverway. Comprising 159 acres, the Coile Estate tract also included Eno Quarry. The Coiles had owned this piece of land since the 1930s, running cattle on what was then pastureland, as well as doing a little farming. Dr. Coile's primary occupation was as a forestry professor at Duke University.

They built their house next to one of the high bluffs overlooking the Eno River and enjoyed the property for decades. Mr. Coile passed away, leaving his wife, Margaret, to manage the property. In 1973, with momentum building for the establishment of Eno River State Park, Mrs. Coile partnered with The Nature Conservancy and the Eno River Association to protect a slice of her property along the river as state park lands, which would make it that much harder to build a proposed dam that would flood the Eno River Valley. Three decades later the entirety of the estate was added to the state park. The former pastures have now grown over or were otherwise planted

Gazing across Eno Quarry

in pines, which you will walk through on your hike. Efforts have been under way also to pare back invasive species that were on the property. You will also pass one of the Coiles' houses on the hike, now the home of a park ranger.

When I-85 was being built through the Triangle, the Coiles leased some of their property to acquire stone for building the road. The Eno Quarry was worked by the Superior Stone Company from 1961 to 1964. After, the quarry was abandoned and the land returned to the Coiles. Water slowly filled the void, mostly from underground, and created a 60-foot-deep, 4-acre pond, separated from Rhodes Creek by a man-made berm and from the Eno River by a narrow neck of land. (There is very little runoff from the quarry into the Eno.)

It was not long until the first teenager found the quarry and saw a ready-made swimming hole. Despite being fenced, it was a simple matter of working around the fence and having a ball in the former worksite. This went on for decades. In 1993 a drowning occurred in Eno Quarry, upsetting Mrs. Coile mightily. She wanted the trespassing and swimming stopped. In strode a man of strong disposition named Ron Schores, who patrolled the quarry for Mrs. Coile, apparently cutting down on illegal dips. Mr. Schores moved away in 1998.

By the time Eno River State Park acquired the property in 2004, a beaten-down path had been created by swimmers visiting the quarry from Howe Street. Today the park has official trails and two ways to reach Eno Quarry. It is still a magnet for swimmers, despite drownings in 2007, 2015, and in 2019. Around a dozen medical calls per year originate from the quarry. The park has established a ranger road reaching directly to the quarry, for management and rescue purposes. The fact is, swimming is not illegal but is officially discouraged due to the chilly waters, imposing depth, and sheer banks. There is very little sloping shoreline, prohibiting easy egress from the water. Moreover, do not tempt fate by skinny-dipping. Word is out that the rangers will ticket naked swimmers, and not all your fellow quarry visitors want to see you "nekkid," as we Southerners say.

As with any endeavor, use common sense and you will have a good time. Rowdy behavior and carelessness endanger not only yourself but also other hikers and park personnel who have to come out and patrol and/or rescue drunken swimmers and showoffs. It also costs a lot of taxpayer money. Stop accidents before they happen, and let your conscience be your guide before you do what you know you should not do.

You should execute this hike, however. It leaves east from Pleasant Green Road, often used as an Eno River paddler access, joining the Laurel Bluffs Trail. The path curves past a stream flowing into one of the sharper bends on the Eno. It then climbs to impressive rock bluffs cloaked in laurel. Come very near a ranger residence and continue in woods, formerly Coile pasturage. Cut through a dark copse of planted pines before dropping to hardwood flats along the Eno, returning to a riverine environment. Ahead, you will reach a line of huge stones and Eno Quarry. The land looks manipulated, and it was. Trace the margin of terra firma between the Eno and the quarry, then come upon Rhodes Creek. Here you are astride three bodies of water simultaneously. The hike then loops around the quarry, where a berm separates you from Rhodes Creek. Anglers may be bank fishing at waterside clearings. Continue curving along the banks then reach the ranger access road. From there pass through irregular, now vegetated hills, piles of spoil from the quarry. Soon you are back at the Laurel Bluffs Trail, backtracking to the trailhead.

Miles and Directions

0.0 From the parking area on the west side of Pleasant Green Road, head east on the Laurel Bluffs Trail. Pass under Pleasant Green Road and through a power line clearing, looking for old bridge pilings, before turning south along the road.

0.1 Reenter woods shaded by tulip trees, oaks, and pines.

0.3 Turn up and cross a rocky tributary that forms a cascade at higher flows. Soon bridge a second stream in a steep, narrow hollow. Climb to a high bluff above the Eno, traipsing among mountain laurel. Pass behind a ranger residence. Tunnel through laurel in places. This area is scenic and seems a slice of the Carolina mountains to the west. The Eno bends away from the trail.

1.0 Cut through a stand of straight rows of pines, an obvious plantation. Descend.

1.2 Reach bottoms along the Eno River. Walk among hardwoods and wildflowers in season, especially spring beauties by the thousands in April.

1.3 Come to a line of huge stones, a relic of the quarry. Curve around the line of stones. Old roads and manipulated terrain seem out of place at first.

1.4 Reach the Eno Quarry Trail and the loop portion of the hike. Keep straight on the Laurel Bluffs Trail. Come alongside the still quarry to your right and the moving river to your left.

1.5 Curve up Rhodes Creek, turning away from the Eno River.

Eno Quarry Hike

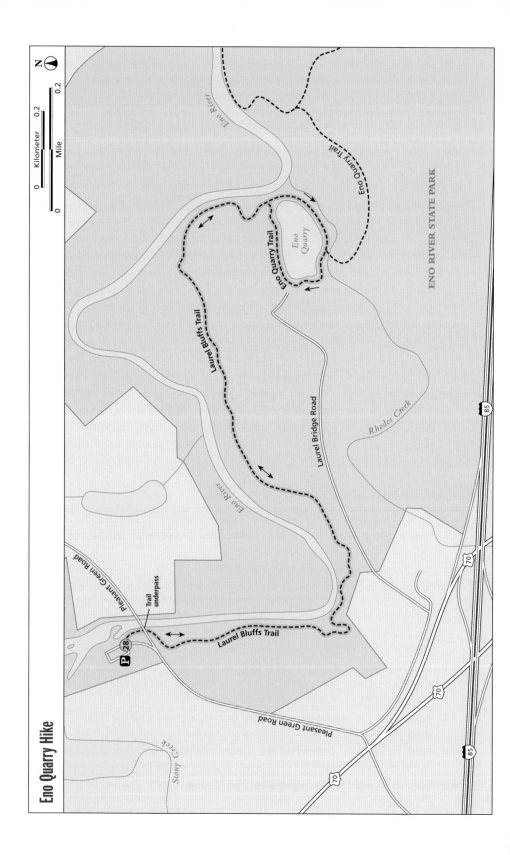

ENO RIVER STATE PARK

Eno River

Eno Quarry Trail

Eno Quarry

Eno Quarry Trail

Laurel Bluffs Trail

Laurel Bridge Road

Rhodes Creek

Eno River

Pleasant Green Road

Trail underpass

P 28

Laurel Bluffs Trail

Pleasant Green Road

Stony Creek

N

0   Kilometer   0.2

0   Mile   0.2

70

85

70

70

85

1.6   Come to a trail junction. Here the Eno Quarry Trail leaves left across Rhodes Creek 0.8 mile to the Howe Street trailhead, which is the most popular access for Eno Quarry. This hike keeps straight and continues circling around Eno Quarry. Ahead, the berm becomes very narrow. Skirt by a wetland on the west shore of the quarry.

1.7   Come along the ranger emergency access road. Walk astride the north shore of the quarry, slaloming among irregular spoil mounds, covered in trees. Pass beside rock cliffs created from the quarry cuts.

1.8   Complete the loop around Eno Quarry. Backtrack along the Eno River on the Laurel Bluffs Trail.

3.2   Reach the Pleasant Green trailhead, completing the hike.

29 Cole Mill Loop

This trek starts at the Cole Mill area of Eno River State Park. Wander upland hills before dropping to the river at the Bobbitt Hole, a large pool. Next, head downriver, enjoying miles of riverside grandeur. Turn back into hills after viewing Durham's old water pump station. Pass an old homesite and cemetery. Return to the Cole Mill area with its excellent picnicking facilities. Additionally, a backcountry campground is located along the circuit, creating overnight possibilities.

Start: Upper part of Cole Mill parking area
Distance: 5.6-mile double loop
Hiking time: 3.0–3.5 hours
Difficulty: Moderate
Trail surface: Natural
Best season: Year-round
Other trail users: None
Canine compatibility: Leashed dogs allowed
Land status: State park

Fees and permits: No fees or permits required
Schedule: May–Sept: 7:30 a.m.–9:30 p.m.; Mar, Apr, Oct: 7:30 a.m.–8:30 p.m.; Nov: 7:30 a.m.–7:30 p.m.; Dec–Feb: 7:30 a.m.–6:30 p.m.
Maps: Eno River State Park
Trail contacts: Eno River State Park, 6101 Cole Mill Rd., Durham, NC 27705; (919) 383-1686; www.ncparks.gov

Finding the trailhead: From exit 173 on I-85, west of downtown Durham, join Cole Mill Road northbound. Follow it 3.4 miles to reach a traffic light just after bridging the Eno River. Turn left at the traffic light onto Old Cole Mill Road and follow it to enter the park. The Cole Mill Trail starts in the upper parking area on the right, near the restrooms. Trailhead GPS: N36 3.515', W78 58.813'

The Hike

This is one of my favorite hikes in the Triangle. The adventure travels a formerly well-settled portion of the Eno River Valley. Along the way you cruise through hills down to a place known as the Bobbitt Hole, where a man of that name purportedly drowned. Just upstream is the site of the old Alpha Woolen Mills, though not much remains. Heading back downstream, you come near the crossing at old Cole Mill Road, site of the former McCown/Cole Mill. Continuing downstream, you see natural beauty as well—high, rocky bluffs clad in mountain laurel and other natural scenes—before reaching the site of the old Durham pump station. From there, climb into hills, passing a pair of old homesites, one of which is the Dunnagan Place, for which a hiking trail is named. Keep your eyes peeled while undertaking this walk, looking for clues of the past as well as the ample natural beauty contained within this naturally regenerated area, now protected as a state park.

The trailhead can be a popular and busy place, with its picnic shelter, shaded picnic sites, canoe/kayak launch, and easy access to the river along which families play.

The Eno River is a highlight of the Cole Mill Loop.

It is also an important trailhead for hikers and is the primary parking area for those using the backcountry campground situated along the Bobbitt Hole Trail.

After making your way west through hills and drainages, reach Piper Creek Campground. Designated campsites are available for a fee and must be reserved in advance. Each site has a tent pad, fire ring, and bench. It is recommended you pack in your own water. A spigot is provided at the trailhead. Take note that Piper Creek is dry in late summer and early fall. This is a great route for someone to break into backpacking.

Cruise through flats to reach a spur heading to the Bobbitt Hole. This wide, still water spot on the Eno is supposedly one of the deepest locations on the river, and is renowned as a swimming spot. Alpha Woolen Mill was located just upstream of the Bobbitt Hole. Nothing remains of the site built in 1852 and operated until the 1860s, when both partners were killed in the Civil War.

The hike then undertakes its long run down the Eno. The pathway alternates in bottoms and along occasional bluffs. The closer you get to the Cole Mill trailhead, the more people you will see. However, once you pass the trailhead and get downstream of Cole Mill Road, the crowds decrease. An underpass makes getting beyond Cole Mill Road a breeze.

Near Cole Mill Road and across the river stands the old McCown/Cole Mill site. This mill, started in 1813, was a tilt hammer mill, which used a giant hammer to forge metal. It was later a gristmill for wheat and corn. Moses McCown built a house on a bluff above his mill. In 1874 John Cole bought the mill. He and members of his family ran the mill until 1908, when it was destroyed by flood. Later a man named Sparger bought the property and the old McCown house as a country home. Sparger constructed the stone pump house and springhouse still visible near the old dam site. Nearby Sparger Road is named for him.

The hike crosses Pea Creek and continues downstream along the Eno River to find the Durham pump station site. The hike then turns into hills away from the river, meeting the old Dunnagan homesite and graveyard. The small cemetery has but a few graves, and only one of them is marked. This is the grave of Catherine Dunnagan, who was born March 7, 1826, and died January 6, 1914. The homesite is nearby and is marked with a pile of chimney stones and perennial flowers still coming up. This is where Catherine and her husband, Norman, lived on their 250 acres. Oddly, Norman is buried at Mount Lebanon Primitive Baptist Church in the Little River area. Beyond the homesite, the hike returns to Pea Creek and the Eno. Finally, trace the Eno back to the spur leading to the lower parking area, then walk the road back to the trailhead.

Miles and Directions

0.0 From the picnic shelter and restroom parking area, join the Cole Mill Trail heading west into woods as a footpath. Walk just a short distance then come to another intersection. Turn right here, still on the Cole Mill Trail as the other end of the Cole Mill Trail heads down to the river. Shortly pass under a power line clearing then bridge a little branch.

0.3 Come to a trail intersection. Here the Cole Mill Trail leaves left but our hike stays right and joins the Bobbitt Hole Trail. Continue cruising hilly, rocky terrain, crossing shallow drainages, shaded by pines and oaks, with a healthy dose of holly and a few cedars.

0.9 Cut back under the power line cut. Descend.

1.1 Come to Piper Creek Campground. A spur trail leads left to tent sites and a restroom. Cross Piper Creek then pass a couple more spur trails leading to campsites. Cruise in bottomland near the Eno.

1.2 Keep straight on the spur leading to the Bobbitt Hole, located just below a rapid.

1.3 Reach the Bobbitt Hole, a bench, and the end of the spur. Backtrack downriver.

1.4 Continue down the Bobbitt Hole Trail, cruising through bottomland in buckeyes galore.

1.5 Bridge lower Piper Creek. Keep along the scenic Eno waters.

1.9 Rejoin the Cole Mill Trail at an intersection. You are very near the power line clearing again. Ahead, squeeze past a hilly section of path mixed with rock outcrops. Be careful to stay on the trail and avoid erosive paths. The trail remains rugged and scenic. Avoid user-created water accesses. Pass a spur trail leading to a picnic area.

2.4 Come to a trail intersection and kiosk. Here a short spur leads left to the lower end of the Cole Mill trailhead. Still other paths head down to the water, including a canoe access combined with user-created trails. Leave the kiosk and join the Pea Creek Trail, continuing down the Eno on a rocky, narrow path. Pass a smaller picnic area. Ahead, across the river, stands the old McCown/Cole Mill site.

2.7 The Pea Creek Trail leads under Cole Mill Road. Steps lead up to the road itself. The path remains rocky.

2.8 The Pea Creek Trail splits. Stay right, along the Eno River. The other way will be your return route.

Cole Mill Loop

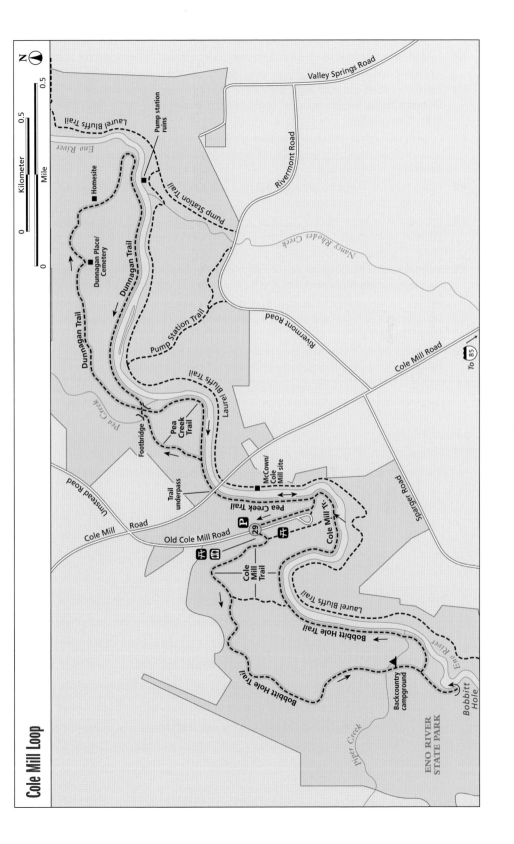

3.0 Pass sheer rock bluffs across the river then curve under a power line clearing. Come along a long pool and flat.

3.2 Turn up Pea Creek and reach a trail intersection. Head right, crossing Pea Creek on a footbridge, joining the Dunnagan Trail. Stay right again, keeping along the Eno River portion of the Dunnagan Trail.

3.9 Come to blasted rock. The stone foundation of the old Durham pump station stands across the river. Ahead, turn away from the river, joining an old roadbed ascending into woods.

4.2 Pass a homesite. A park maintenance road goes right. Stay left with the blazed, now narrower path. Dip to cross a branch.

4.4 Come to the Dunnagan Place. It is marked by a crumbled stone chimney, perennials, and the small graveyard with the marked grave of Catherine Dunnagan. Leave the homesite in pines.

4.9 Reach the end of the Dunnagan Trail. You are back at the footbridge over Pea Creek. Cross the bridge and join the unhiked portion of the Pea Creek Trail, rising on a bluff above Pea Creek.

5.2 Dip back to the Eno River after crossing a power line clearing. Follow the Eno River back toward Cole Mill.

5.6 After taking the short spur to the lower end of the Cole Mill trailhead, complete the hike by taking the road a short distance to the upper Cole Mill trailhead parking.

30 Laurel Bluffs Trail

This is a history-heavy hike, with evidence of the past situated at the beginning and end of the adventure. Start by descending to the Eno River and passing the ruins of an abandoned Durham waterworks operation, then cruise along steep hills and alternately atop bluffs and along the river amid first-rate natural scenery. The undulating terrain leads to the old Guess Mill site, with more ruins to explore. The return trip yields additional human and natural history.

Start: Rivermont Road
Distance: 5.2-mile there-and-back
Hiking time: 2.5–3.5 hours
Difficulty: Moderate
Trail surface: Natural
Best season: Year-round, good summer morning hike
Other trail users: Anglers
Canine compatibility: Leashed dogs allowed
Land status: State park

Fees and permits: No fees or permits required
Schedule: May–Sept: 8:30 a.m.–8:30 p.m.; Mar, Apr, Oct: 8:30 a.m.–7:30 p.m.; Nov: 8:30 a.m.–6:30 p.m.; Dec, Jan, Feb: 8:30 a.m.–5:30 p.m.
Maps: Eno River State Park; USGS Northwest Durham
Trail contacts: Eno River State Park, 6101 Cole Mill Rd., Durham, NC 27705; (919) 383-1686; www.ncparks.gov

Finding the trailhead: From exit 173 on I-85, west of downtown Durham, join Cole Mill Road northbound. Follow it 2.5 miles to turn right on Rivermont Road. Follow Rivermont Road for 0.3 mile. Here Rivermont Road turns to gravel and you will see an alternate trailhead for the Pump Station Trail. Keep going past this shoulder-parking trailhead for 0.2 mile farther to the bridge over Nancy Rhodes Creek and the correct trailhead. Trailhead GPS: N36 3.505', W78 57.938'

The Hike

This hike is an ideal combination of human history and native splendor. There is much evidence of the Piedmont past and a whole lot of Piedmont beauty in this river corridor. The Laurel Bluffs Trail is one of the more rugged paths traveling along the Eno River, with multiple ups and downs, irregular terrain, and narrow shorelines. However, it can be easily done by your average hiker. The varied terrain reveals geologically fascinating bluffs, wildflower-laden flats, small streams sporting modest cascades, and an everywhere-you-look beauty in an ever-changing scene. Much of the history of the Eno River Valley is tied to the mills that were scattered along its banks, and this segment is no different. Upwards of thirty mills were stretched along the Eno from the mid-1700s to the early 1900s.

This particular hike ends at Guess Road, named for the nearby mill constructed by William Guess in 1848. Back in his day there was no bridge over the Eno River near the mill, just a ford. Guess's operation moved along well until the Civil War and he was forced to sell. The mill was located on the south bank of the Eno River and

THE OL' PUMP STATION

When Durham was a young but growing city in the late 1800s, it had a need for a reliable water system. In 1886 a man named A. H. Howland was contracted to build a pump station and dam to provide Durham with water for everyday drinking and living. Down on the Eno River, a dam was built, not to provide a water supply but to provide waterpower to pump water from yet another dam on adjacent Nancy Rhodes Creek, a tributary of the Eno (which you travel by on this hike). The water from Nancy Rhodes Creek would be the drinking water for Durham. The power derived from the Eno River dam would move the water from the Eno up to Durham's high point—Huckleberry Hill—where there was a reservoir. From this elevated reservoir, water would be gravity fed to the city of Durham.

It sounded like a great plan. By April 1888 the water system was operating. However, problems were immediate. A lack of water pressure and inconsistent flow were the primary complaints. Then a series of city fires in 1894 and 1895 underscored the fact that Durham's water system had insufficient pressure for firefighters to combat blazes. And then there was a little problem about the water being muddy and sometimes containing fish. A remedy was sought, and a filtration system was installed, yet inconsistent service continued.

The city of Durham knew when to cut their losses. They moved on to develop other water sources, and though the Eno River/Nancy Rhodes Creek plant continued as a backup, it was ultimately abandoned. Today you can see the ruins of the pump house on the Eno River. The largest ruins are from the large filtration plant near the dam. Curious hikers can take the Pump Station Trail a little ways up the Eno River to find the remains of the dam on Nancy Rhodes Creek, as well as a small circular pond created when the overflow of the dam gouged out the land below. Amateur archaeologists can spend quite a while examining the stone, brick, and metal remains of this early water system. Remember to leave your discoveries at the site, allowing others to enjoy a similar experience.

had two waterwheels, thus doubling its power. A dam extended across the river and curved at an island. A sluice ran along the south bank of the river.

Frederick Geer bought the mill in 1874, and the operation continued in the black. The ford had been replaced by a bridge at this point. Later, Guess Mill changed owners and was finally left to time and the elements in the 1930s, after mills were no longer needed for power. Today the Laurel Bluffs Trail travels by the Guess Mill dam remnants and actually directly through the old millrace. Spot an old millstone

The pump well and "chimbley" on an old hunt cabin ▶

The Laurel Bluffs Trail travels through a tunnel of green.

and other rock construction at the site. Hikers will also walk by an old hunt cabin chimney and foundation, adding more remnants of the past.

This hike is good for summertime, since the Laurel Bluffs Trail faces north and is well shaded in the early morning, plus you can get a little added coolness from being along the Eno River. You first descend along Nancy Rhodes Creek, a good wildflower destination. The next highlight is the pump station, a good place to linger and explore. After that you will be traversing the surprisingly rugged terrain along the Eno River. Natural highlights include flowery rocky bluffs highlighted by Gebel Rock, as well as numerous little streams flowing toward the Eno. One of these streams even has a modest high-flow cascade just above the trail crossing. Finally, come to Guess Mill, soaking in the past there before returning to the trailhead.

Miles and Directions

0.0 From the parking area on the east side of the bridge over Nancy Rhodes Creek, join the singletrack Pump Station Trail downhill. Nancy Rhodes Creek falls away to your left.

0.2 Pass a power line clearing. A user-created trail leaves left to the upper edge of the old dam on Nancy Rhodes Creek. Keep on the official trail and reenter woods. Step over an intermittent branch then veer left as a ranger-only access road comes in on your right.

0.3 Meet the Laurel Bluffs Trail. The pump station ruins are in the immediate area. The Pump Station Trail leads left to the dam on Nancy Rhodes Creek. After exploring, hike easterly in ferny woods downstream along the Eno River, now on the Laurel Bluffs Trail. Watch for user-created trails leading to neighborhoods abutting Eno River State Park.

0.7 Come to a gas pipeline clearing. The trail turns right here and goes along the clearing then bridges an intermittent streambed left. Return to the Eno. From there climb a laurel/beech bluff. The slope is steep.

Laurel Bluffs Trail

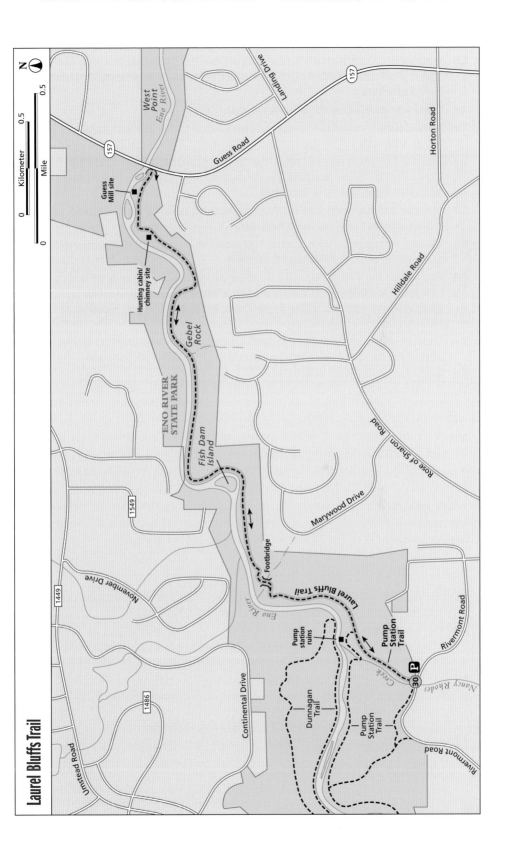

1.0 Cross a spring. Come alongside the Eno and pass near Fish Dam Island. Turn north. Continue to watch for user-created spur trails leading up to nearby neighborhoods. The Laurel Bluffs Trail remains rocky.

1.4 Overlook privately held riverbank across the water.

1.6 A pair of bridges crosses an intermittent stream. Climb over a hill then quickly descend back to water level.

1.8 Step over a very rocky perennial stream that features a cascade at higher water flows. Climb up to Gebel Rock, an outcrop that stands about 30 feet above the river. The riverside terrain flattens out below Gebel Rock.

2.0 Leave the bottomland and make the sharpest ascent yet. Join a bluff clad in Catawba rhododendron and mountain laurel. Keep east.

2.3 Hike directly atop a foundation of an old hunt cabin with the chimney still standing and a pump well exposed. Descend toward the Eno River.

2.4 Return to the Eno River and reach the site of the Guess Mill. Turn down along the tailrace. Look across at standing remains of the old dam as it abuts the head of an island. Continue down the tailrace, looking for other relics and stonework aplenty, as well as a millstone.

2.6 Rise from the river on steps just as you reach Guess Road. The Laurel Bluffs Trail ends at Guess Road. This is also the eastern boundary of Eno River State Park. Backtrack.

5.2 Reach the trailhead, completing the hike.

31 Eagle Trail

This hike starts at Durham's historic West Point on the Eno Park, then heads up the Eno River where you meander along a scenic corridor to Guess Road. From there backtrack a bit and climb into hills, briefly visiting a neighborhood before dropping back to the river, completing a loop. The final part of the hike backtracks to West Point on the Eno, where you can explore the assemblage of historic buildings.

Start: Near West Point Mill at West Point on the Eno Park

Distance: 3.9-mile balloon loop

Hiking time: About 2.0 hours

Difficulty: Moderate

Trail surface: Natural, a little asphalt

Best season: Spring for wildflowers

Other trail users: Joggers

Canine compatibility: Leashed dogs allowed

Land status: Durham city park

Fees and permits: No fees or permits required

Schedule: 8 a.m. to dark

Maps: West Point on the Eno Park

Trail contacts: West Point on the Eno Park, 5101 N. Roxboro Rd., Durham, NC 27704; (919) 471-1623; http://durhamnc.gov

Finding the trailhead: From exit 176 on I-85, north of Durham, take US 501 north for 3.3 miles to West Point on the Eno Park. The left turn into the park is at a traffic light. Drive the one-way park road to circle past the mill and reach the barn-like picnic shelter after 0.3 mile. Official address: 5101 N. Roxboro Road. Trailhead GPS: N36 4.178', W78 54.598'

The Hike

This hike traverses the lesser-visited north side of West Point on the Eno Park along the Eno River. In fact, many people do not even know trails exist on the north bank of the Eno River—except those who live in the neighborhoods nearby, where trails link the neighborhoods to West Point on the Eno Park. This trek utilizes not only the riverside Eagle Trail—named for the Eagle Scouts who constructed it—but also some of these trails linking to the neighborhoods to make a loop hike.

The adventure starts out near the West Point Mill, one of the most historic mills in the greater Triangle area. You may get hung up at the trailhead exploring the preserved old buildings nearby, such as the mill, the blacksmith shop, the Mangum House, and the photography museum. I suggest incorporating time either before or after your hike to visit these park treasures.

Eventually you will be able to break away from the historic part of the park and head north, crossing the Eno River on an iron pedestrian bridge paralleling Roxboro Road. Hikers gain a picturesque view from this span, looking upstream at the Eno and the old West Point Mill Dam. From there the hike heads upstream along the north bank of the Eno, passing the aforementioned milldam. It then crosses Crooked

HISTORY OF WEST POINT ON THE ENO PARK

Before or after your hike, make sure to explore the historic buildings at your embarkation point, West Point on the Eno Park. This 388-acre city of Durham park is situated where old Roxboro Road once crossed the Eno River at Shoemakers Ford. This confluence of river and road made a strategic location to build a mill. Nearby residents flocked here to have their corn and wheat ground.

The first area mill was built in 1752 by Michael Synott. Mr. Synott sold out to the Abercrombie brothers in 1780, but left a corrupted version of his name at the Sennett Hole, where he purportedly drowned trying to retrieve his hidden gold during a flood. The Abercrombies moved the operation to a better site just downstream and built what became known as West Point on the Eno Mill. For 160 years this mill operated, though it changed hands numerous times. One notable owner was a man named Herbert Sims, who was a lawman, county politician, and major landowner during the early to mid-1800s. It was during Mr. Sims's time, 1839 it was, that a post office was set up at the mill site, which had become a regular community with a general store, blacksmith shop, cotton gin, and even a whiskey still. This spot was the last and most westerly stop for the US mail between Roxboro and Durham; thus the community became known as West Point.

In 1888 the mill fell into the hands of Hugh Mangum, known as one of the earliest photographers of Durham. Today a museum of photography stands on park grounds, featuring Mr. Mangum's work. There are also many pictures of the West Point Mill there. He bought the 1840s house that still stands on the grounds. Members of his family lived there until 1968 when the property was abandoned. Later the land was bought by the city of Durham, who reconstructed the West Point Mill, now on the National Register of Historic Places.

Creek and alternately rolls in low hills or along the river. Gain views of bluffs across the river, cloaked in mountain laurel.

The hike continues upriver, passing a chimney from a forgotten dwelling, and makes its way to an access trail leading up to Guess Road and the boundary of Eno River State Park. On your return trip take the loop way back, to pick up a new pathway. A blazed trail curves up from the river then turns east and pops out at Kinlock Drive. Here you follow neighborhood roads for a little less than a half mile before rejoining a woodland footpath returning to the Eno. The whole thing adds up to a fun little hike, and you will have many opportunities for water play and to learn a little history.

An angler as viewed from the iron pedestrian bridge over the Eno ▶

Eagle Trail

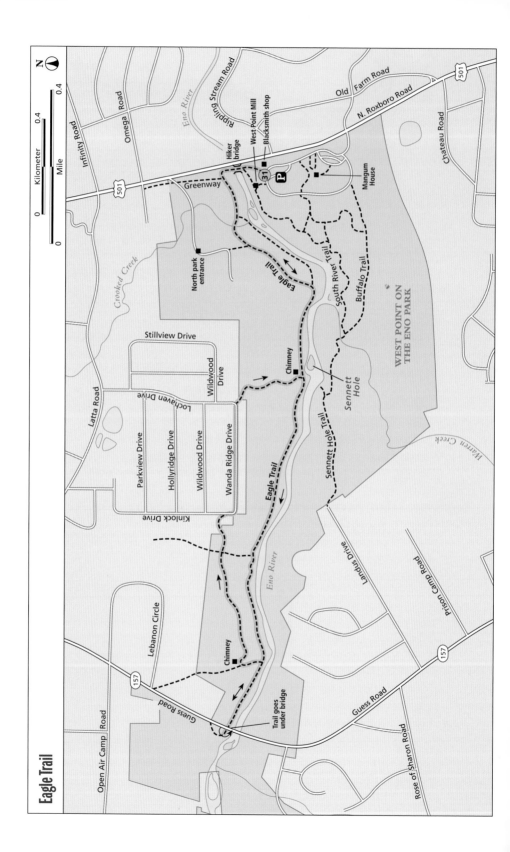

Open Air Camp Road

Latta Road

Infinity Road

Omega Road

501

Crooked Creek

Eno River

Rippling Stream Road

West Point Mill
Blacksmith shop

Hiker
bridge

Greenway

North park
entrance

Stillview Drive

Wildwood
Drive

Lochaven Drive

Parkview Drive

Hollyridge Drive

Wildwood Drive

Wanda Ridge Drive

Kinlock Drive

Lebanon Circle

Eagle Trail

Eno River

Chimney

Chimney

Eagle Trail

157

Guess Road

Trail goes
under bridge

Landys Drive

Sennett Hole Trail

Sennett
Hole

South River Trail

Buffalo Trail

Mangum
House

WEST POINT ON
THE ENO PARK

Warren Creek

Guess Road

Prison Camp Road

Rose of Sharon Road

Chateau Road

N. Roxboro Road

Old   Farm   Road

501

157

N

0   Kilometer   0.4

0   Mile   0.4

Miles and Directions

0.0 From the lower parking area near the West Point Mill, walk toward the mill then take the concrete trail leading north, with the mill on your left and the old blacksmith shop to your right. Soon pass a spur trail along the river then cross the Eno River on an iron pedestrian bridge. Gain a good upstream view of the Eno and the West Point Mill Dam.

0.1 Come to an intersection after dropping from the iron bridge. Here the concrete Eno Greenway leaves right, north, paralleling Roxboro Road. Join the natural surface Eagle Trail going straight.

0.3 Reach an intersection. Here a user-created path goes left to the milldam, while the main trail goes straight to cross Crooked Creek via stepping-stones. Stay with the marked trail, climbing to reach another intersection. A trail goes right to a field accessed via the north entrance to West Point on the Eno Park. Keep left here, continuing up the Eno River Valley. Pass a picnic area and amphitheater on your right, part of the north entrance infrastructure.

0.6 Come near the river as a user-created trail comes in. It has been following a sewer line right-of-way. Keep upriver on the official Eagle Trail, passing bluffs across the river.

0.8 Reach a trail intersection and old brick chimney. Keep straight over rock shoreline, while your return route heads toward Wanda Ridge Drive. Begin a long river walk in woods.

1.2 Bridge an intermittent tributary. Keep hiking among beech, sycamore, and river birch.

1.3 A connector trail leads right, uphill. Stay straight along the Eno.

1.6 Come to another intersection. You will return here later; for now keep straight along the Eno.

1.8 Pass under the Guess Road bridge, reaching the Eno River State Park boundary. A user-created path continues upriver, while an official trail turns right, uphill, via steps and emerges on Guess Road (no parking). From this intersection backtrack toward West Point on the Eno Park.

2.0 Head left, northwest, leaving the Eno on a blue-blazed trail.

2.1 Reach another intersection at an old chimney. One trail keeps straight for Guess Road and the Eno River Association. Turn right here, heading east. Dip across a streambed.

2.4 Keep straight at a four-way intersection.

2.5 Emerge on Kinlock Drive. Join the road, heading right, south, then curve left, east, onto Wanda Ridge Drive. Walk through a neighborhood on the road. City of Durham park property lies to your right.

2.9 Return to woods on foot trail, heading southeast into city of Durham park property, after reaching the end of Wanda Ridge Drive and Lochaven Drive. Descend through pine-oak woods. Note the old bricks embedded into the trailbed to cut down on erosion.

3.1 Return to the Eagle Trail and the Eno River, having completed the loop portion of the hike. Turn left, heading downstream along the Eno, backtracking. You may want to explore the West Point Mill Dam area and the Eno River's confluence with Crooked Creek.

3.9 Reach the trailhead, completing the hike.

32 Little River Regional Park Hike

The hike visits the hills and hollows above the North Fork Little River, using mostly singletrack, natural surface, hiker-only paths traversing pine and oak hills. Parts of the trek visit the North Fork Little River, where you enjoy streamside scenery. Historic sites and interpretive information are interspersed into the trails.

Start: Hiker trailhead off Guess Road
Distance: 4.5-mile double loop
Hiking time: 2.0–3.0 hours
Difficulty: Moderate
Trail surface: Natural, a little asphalt at the beginning
Best season: Spring for wildflowers
Other trail users: None
Canine compatibility: Leashed dogs allowed
Land status: County park
Fees and permits: No fees or permits required

Schedule: Nov–Feb: 8 a.m.–5 p.m.; Mar and Oct: 8 a.m.–6 p.m.; Apr and Sept: 8 a.m.–7 p.m.; May–Aug: 8 a.m.–8 p.m.; closed Thanksgiving Day, Christmas Eve, and Christmas
Maps: Little River Regional Park & Natural Area; USGS Rougemont
Trail contacts: Little River Regional Park & Natural Area, 301 Little River Park Way, Rougemont, NC 27572; (919) 732-5505; www.orangecountync.gov

Finding the trailhead: From exit 175 on I-85, north of Durham, take NC 157/Guess Road north for 10.7 miles then turn right onto Little River Parkway. Follow this two-lane road into Little River Regional Park & Natural Area then dead-end after 0.2 mile. Look for the hiker trail area at the easternmost end of the parking area. Trailhead GPS: N36 9.745', W78 58.231'

The Hike

Seeing how fast the greater Triangle area was developing, Durham County and Orange County teamed up to create and maintain this regional park and natural area along the banks of the North Fork Little River. The boundary between the two counties roughly splits the park in half. It all started when Orange County was looking for a dumpsite. In scouring the area, government leaders realized that open space to create a landfill—or a park—was becoming increasingly limited by ceaseless development of former farmlands and forests. Area residents fought against the landfill, but the valley of the North Fork Little River suddenly became a potential site for parkland. This ecologically significant land abutting the Little River was but 5 miles upstream of Little River Lake, which was part of Durham's water supply.

Feeding Durham's water supply increased the importance of getting land along the Little River. Orange County then partnered with Durham County, and together they worked with the Triangle Land Conservancy and the Eno River Association to make Little River Regional Park & Natural Area come to be. Over time the 391 acres of parkland, once a tobacco farm and pine plantation, was developed as a low-impact park. It now has several miles of hiking trails as well as biking trails and also some historic structures left over from its days as a farm. The property includes over 1 mile of frontage along the North Fork Little River. This waterway is home to four rare freshwater mussels—the yellow lab mussel, Atlantic pink-toe, triangle floater, and the squawfoot mussel. The river frontage and streams that flow into the Little River help keep the waterway healthy and simultaneously protect the drinking water for Durham. The water also provides habitat for fish, beavers, and otters. The land is home to wild turkeys, deer, and songbirds. Over time the park woods are being altered from loblolly pine plantation to natural oak-hickory forest. This will further improve wildlife habitat.

Yet the park has one eye on its past as well. You will use some old farm roads on the hike, and even stop by the preserved Pack

Bluets find their place in the park woods.

House. This building once held tobacco leaves after they had been graded and tied into three-leaf bundles, then piled onto large burlap sheets. The burlap sheets were then tied in a manner allowing a man to move the tobacco leaves without damaging them. These piles of tobacco leaves were packed into this building, giving it the name "pack house." The building was also used to store other farm tools and equipment when not being used as a pack house.

The hike starts on an asphalt path that passes through an old corncrib. Park information is contained in this historic shed-like building. Do not be alarmed if you see lots of mountain bikers at the trailhead. You will be traveling hiker-only trails the entire time. Hikers and mountain bikers each have their own sets of trails, though they do cross a little bit. Enjoy hiking both uplands and along the North Fork Little River, here at this important greenspace for the Triangle.

Miles and Directions

0.0 From the parking area take the hiker-only asphalt trail through a wooden corncrib. Keep straight to come near a bathroom and picnic shelter. Just ahead, paved trails go left, right, and straight (the Bird Trail is the paved path going left; the others are unnamed). Keep straight, entering woods.

0.1 An asphalt trail leaves right, forming a little loop. Keep straight, tracing an old farm road, now leaving the asphalt behind. Pines and oaks shade the trail. Ahead, a gated spur goes left to the park's group camp.

0.3 Come to an intersection and the Pack House. Check out this farm building left over from tobacco-growing days. Just past the Pack House, head left on the Ridge Trail. Your return

DOGWOODS

Hikers will see abundant dogwoods along the Ridge Trail during this hike. Dogwoods are plentiful throughout North Carolina, save for the immediate Atlantic coast and above 4,000 feet in the mountains. The short tree with scaly brown bark and widespread crown is easy to identify, especially with its creamy spring blossoms. Dogwoods are widely regarded as one of the most beautiful trees in the Southeast and are popularly planted in city yards. The tree ranges from eastern Texas north to Michigan, east to Massachusetts, and south to Florida. After greening up during summer, dogwoods produce a shiny red fruit in fall. These small, berry-like fruits are bitter to humans but are an important food for birds. Dogwood is extremely hard and is used to make mallet heads, jeweler's blocks, and spools. It is a very hot-burning fuelwood.

route will bring you back here again. The Ridge Trail quickly becomes singletrack path. Meander in pines and oaks and plentiful dogwoods.

0.4 Bridge an intermittent streambed flowing toward the North Fork Little River.

0.6 Come to a boardwalk and a trail intersection. Here a shortcut trail heads over to the South River Loop. You will be turning here later, but for now keep straight on the Ridge Trail and continue roaming upland woods.

1.1 Come to a trail intersection and kiosk. At this point a trail leads left to a ranger road, but don't take it. Instead, head right and then come to a hiker trail intersection. Keep straight on the Ridge Trail, as the North River Loop comes in on your right.

1.4 The Homestead Trail leaves right. Stay straight with the Ridge Trail, descending for the North Fork Little River. Soon gain glimpses of the river.

1.6 Reach a gate and the park boundary in woods. Split right here, joining the North River Loop. Turn downstream along the North Fork Little River. It stretches about 30 feet across and is clear and quite rocky. Forested bottoms stretch across the river, thanks to a 300-foot conservation easement along the waterway. Travel beside the river for a short distance then climb a bluff.

1.8 Pass a massive tulip tree beside the trail. Also appreciate the copious outcrops along the river.

2.0 Turn away from the North Fork Little River. Ignore park personnel-only roads/trails.

2.1 Meet the other end of the Homestead Trail. Keep straight on the North River Loop. Climb from the bottoms.

2.3 Return to the Ridge Trail. Backtrack south.

2.9 Come to the boardwalk and shortcut to the South River Loop. Head left, taking the shortcut and treading new trail.

3.0 Meet the South River Loop. Head left and begin descending along a branch. This can be a productive wildflower area. A boardwalk takes you over wetter areas.

3.1 Bridge the branch you have been following. Soon sidle alongside the North Fork Little River again, amid rock outcrops and gravel bars.

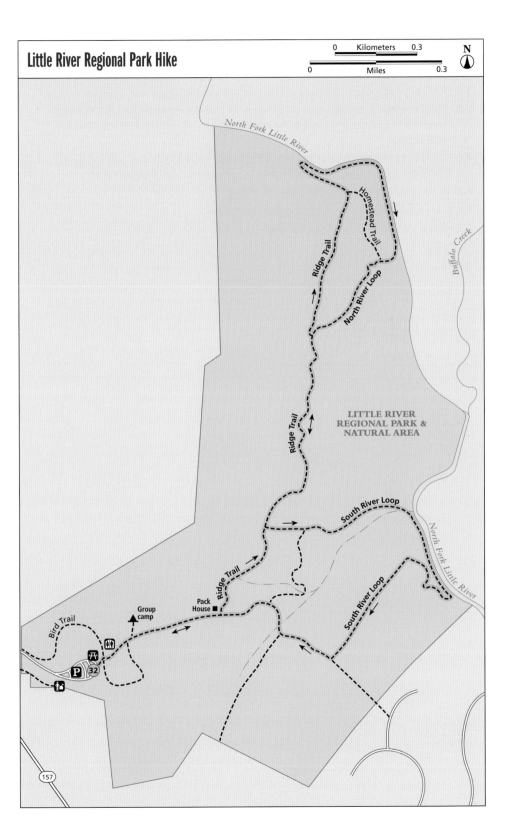

Little River Regional Park Hike

0   Kilometers   0.3

0   Miles   0.3

N

North Fork Little River

Buffalo Creek

Homestead Trail

Ridge Trail

North River Loop

Ridge Trail

LITTLE RIVER
REGIONAL PARK &
NATURAL AREA

South River Loop

North Fork Little River

Ridge Trail

Bird Trail

Group
camp

Pack
House

South River Loop

P   32

157

3.3 Climb sharply up a bluff overlooking the North Fork Little River in some seriously steep terrain.

3.5 Pick up an old roadbed and head directly southwest. The walking is easy.

3.8 Come to a trail intersection. Here a trail leaves left toward a residential area at Mill House Lane. Our hike heads right, meandering over an old, wide farm road turned trail. Make a wide descent.

4.0 Come to another trail intersection. Here a spur heads left to a residential area and Summer Lane. Keep straight and pass over a branch via culvert. Climb from the stream.

4.1 Keep straight as the South River Loop leaves right.

4.2 Return to the Pack House. Keep straight for the trailhead.

4.5 Reach the trailhead, completing the hike.

33 Horton Grove Nature Preserve

Explore a large tract of land featuring varied habitats overlain on one of the largest and most historic plantations in the Piedmont. Your hike first takes you through ecologically significant prairie then curves back along a stream. You then follow this watershed as it cuts a deep hollow before returning up yet another stream. Well-graded and new singletrack paths make hiking here nearly idyllic.

Start: Trailhead off Jock Road
Distance: 4.5-mile loop
Hiking time: 2.0–3.0 hours
Difficulty: Moderate
Trail surface: Natural
Best season: Fall through spring
Other trail users: None
Canine compatibility: Leashed dogs allowed

Land status: Nature preserve
Fees and permits: No fees or permits required
Schedule: Sunrise to sunset
Maps: Horton Grove Trail Map; USGS Lake Michie
Trail contacts: Triangle Land Conservancy, 514 S. Duke St., Durham, NC 27701; (919) 908-8809; www.triangleland.org

Finding the trailhead: From exit 182 on I-85, northeast of Durham and north of Raleigh, take Red Mill Road north for 3.7 miles. Turn right on Teknika Parkway and follow it 0.2 mile then turn left, back on Red Mill Road. Follow it for 0.5 mile then turn right on Old Oxford Road. Stay with Old Oxford Road for 1.7 miles then veer left on Jock Road. Keep straight for a total of 1.3 miles, driving past the first small, shaded trailhead on your left. Keep going to the large, open primary trailhead on the north end of the preserve. Trailhead GPS: N36 8.557', W78 50.609'

The Hike

Horton Grove Nature Preserve comes in at over 700 acres and is linked to Stagville State Historic Site in northern Durham County. These two tracts of land are remnants of what once was a 30,000-acre plantation, one of the largest in the entire pre–Civil War South. Formerly a place for growing crops and worked by 900 slaves, the nature preserve is now a reservation where 5 miles of streams are protected by natural woods and meadows, while the Stagville State Historic Site preserves houses and other buildings and a way of life long past.

Nearly 10 miles of trails wind through Horton Grove Nature Preserve, though you would have to do quite a convoluted hike to walk them all at one time. There are two primary trailheads, with other walking opportunities starting at Stagville State Historic Site. Since these trails were more recently added, they were constructed using smart practices to prevent erosion and not trample biologically important spots while still taking you through a variety of habitats, from great oak forests to piney woods to hardwood bottoms and the aforementioned meadows.

This hiker bridge is set in beautiful beech woods.

Efforts to purchase and preserve Horton Grove began in 2004, and today the trail system is fully developed; however, restoration of natural habitats is a continuing process in this land managed by the Triangle Land Conservancy. Stagville State Historic Site was established in 1976, 200 years after Richard Bennehan bought the initial acreage that would be the heart of what became the massive Stagville tract. After his death in 1825, Mr. Bennehan left his holdings to his son Thomas, who lived at Stagville for his entire life. The family holdings had expanded but grew even more under Thomas Bennehan's nephew Paul Cameron, who inherited the land in 1847. Not only did he enlarge this plantation but he also added other properties in Alabama and Mississippi. By the time the Civil War came, Paul Cameron was purportedly the richest man in North Carolina.

After the War Between the States, the lands at Stagville continued to be worked, though livestock such as cattle, hogs, goats, and horses became a staple rather than just crop raising. Later the estate was slowly broken up, divided among descendants of Paul Cameron until the 1950s, when the properties were sold outside the family. Tobacco was grown on the land after it was bought by Liggett and Myers Tobacco Company.

The historical import of Stagville came to the fore in America's bicentennial celebration. During this year, 1976, Liggett and Myers Tobacco Company donated the land and historic structures of what became Stagville State Historic Site. I highly recommend stopping by and visiting the plantation houses, outbuildings, and preserved slave houses. An additional trail access is located on the north end of the historic site.

This hike starts at the northernmost trailhead on Jock Road. Here you leave north on the Holman Loop (each of the trails at Horton Grove is named for slave

THOSE AROMATIC CEDARS

At the beginning of this hike, you will see scattered cedars rising among the native grasses. The eastern red cedar is the most widely distributed cone-bearing evergreen in the United States, growing in thirty-seven states. Red cedars extend from Maine south to northern Florida and west to Texas, then north all the way to North Dakota. The tough evergreen is resistant to extremes of heat, cold, and drought. The aromatic yet stiff wood is used for cedar chests (which keep the bugs out), fence posts resistant to rot, and cabinets. Early colonists arriving in North Carolina appreciated cedar's hardiness, using it to build fences, cabins, and furniture. The wood also burns hot and exudes sweet-smelling smoke.

Eastern red cedars are perhaps best known for being the wood used in pencils. The cedar, often growing in poor soils, is important for wildlife. The thin, stringy bark of cedar is used by birds for nests. Songbirds eat its berry-like fruit. Deer feed on the green foliage. Obviously there is a lot to enjoy about a cedar tree, whether you are man or beast.

families that once lived on the land). The Holmans were known for their talents as blacksmiths. You travel through a restored prairie featuring native grasses that is favorable for avian life. The Holman Loop then goes to the far northern end of the preserve before curving back south along one of the many streams here at Horton Grove. These streams are tributaries of the Flat River and eventually make their way into Falls Lake. Waterways passing through woodlands such as these are important providers of clean water that eventually gets drunk or otherwise used by Triangle residents.

You then join the Hart Trail. The Hart family was the longest lived at Stagville, with the final slave descendant, Ephraim Hart, residing here until his death in 1998. Hike down the unnamed stream valley then bridge the creek and join the Justice Loop. The Justices were known for being a large family. Continue down the unnamed creek, walking along the rim of a steep hollow. The hike then emerges onto Jock Road and the southern preserve trailhead.

The Walker Trail takes a twisting path as it circles around yet another of the perennial streams of Horton Grove. The Walkers were blacksmiths as well. After going north a ways, the Walker Trail curves around the headwaters of another unnamed stream, then picks up yet a third waterway and travels through a wildflower-rich valley until it reaches the Peaks Loop. The Peaks were a well-represented family who lived all around Horton Grove. The Peaks Loop takes you still farther up the stream then finally curves back to the trailhead. This loop covers a lot of ground, but as you will see, there are still other trails to hike here, and you should return for more trail trekking.

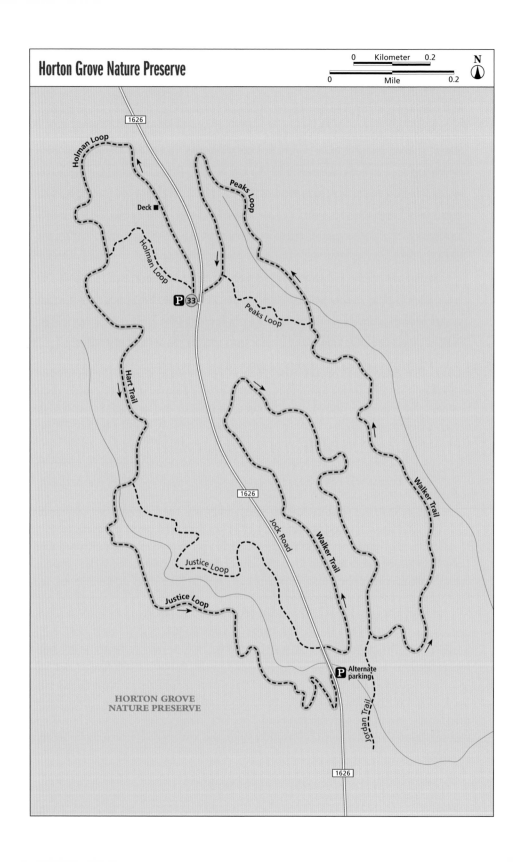

Horton Grove Nature Preserve

0 Kilometer 0.2

0 Mile 0.2

N

1626

Holman Loop

Deck

Holman Loop

Peaks Loop

Peaks Loop

P 33

Hart Trail

1626

Jock Road

Walker Trail

Walker Trail

Justice Loop

Justice Loop

P Alternate parking

Jordan Trail

HORTON GROVE
NATURE PRESERVE

1626

Miles and Directions

0.0 From the parking area take the mown path, hiker-only Holman Loop, north into open prairie. Stay right at the immediate intersection. Wander through open meadows with scattered cedars.

0.2 Pass a bird-watching deck on your left. Shortly enter maples, cedars, and oaks.

0.4 Turn south then come along a snaking stream.

0.5 Bridge a little intermittent streambed. The prairie is to your left. Just ahead, the other end of the Holman Loop leaves left. Stay right, now joining the Hart Trail. Travel hardwoods.

0.7 Bridge an intermittent streambed then bridge another streambed in 0.1 mile.

1.1 Meet the Justice Loop. Head right here, spanning the main stream branch you have been paralleling. Continue south down the west side of the valley in ferny, rocky, tall timber. It is hard to believe this area was ever farmed. The slope steepens radically.

1.7 Briefly turn away from the edge of the creek bluff. Descend in long, loping switchbacks.

1.9 Reach Jock Road and alternate parking. Here the other end of the Justice Loop comes in on your left. Upon reaching Jock Road, turn left and walk north, then pick up the Walker Trail leaving the right side of Jock Road. It is also a singletrack path. Hike north, looking for emergent quartz on the trail.

2.4 Bridge a streambed within sight of Jock Road. Curve back south.

3.1 Come to a trail intersection. Here, the Jordan Trail leaves right, southbound for Stagville State Historic Site. Stay left with the Walker Trail as it eventually turns back north, curving over to yet another unnamed stream, the most easterly in the preserve.

3.9 Come to a trail intersection. Turn right on the Peak Loop. Bridge the stream you have been paralleling in an attractive beech forest. Continue up the stream valley.

4.2 Bridge the stream yet again. Climb into pines.

4.4 Reach the other end of the Peak Loop after turning south. Stay right, heading toward Jock Road.

4.5 Reach Jock Road, completing the hike. The trailhead is a just a little south on Jock Road.

34 Pennys Bend Nature Preserve

Explore an 85-acre parcel circled on three sides by the Eno River. Near the trailhead you pass the remains of Camerons New Mill. From there trace the Eno upstream bordered by riverside flats on one side and a rising rocky hill on the other. Pass a pine savanna and wildflower areas, soaking in river views. Finally, cross the hill creating the river bend, visiting meadows before returning to the trailhead.

Start: Parking area on Snow Hill Road
Distance: 1.8-mile balloon loop
Hiking time: 1.0–1.5 hours
Difficulty: Easy
Trail surface: Natural
Best season: Fall through spring
Other trail users: None
Canine compatibility: Pets on leash only
Land status: US Army Corps of Engineers property

Fees and permits: No fees or permits required
Schedule: Sunrise to sunset
Maps: Pennys Bend Nature Preserve; USGS Northeast Durham
Trail contacts: North Carolina Botanical Garden, 100 Old Mason Farm Rd., Chapel Hill, NC 27517; (919) 962-0522; http://ncbg.unc .edu; also Eno River Association, www.enoriver .org

Finding the trailhead: From exit 177C on I-85, northeast of downtown Durham, follow Roxboro Road north for 1.5 miles to turn right on Old Oxford Road. Follow Old Oxford Road for 3 miles then turn left on Snow Hill Road, just after crossing the Eno River. The parking area is on your left just after turning onto Snow Hill Road, before reaching Wanderlust Lane. Trailhead GPS: N36 4.403', W78 51.802'

The Hike

Owned by the US Army Corps of Engineers and managed by the North Carolina Botanical Garden, 85-acre Pennys Bend Nature Preserve is bordered on almost all sides by the Eno River, forming a near island where soils unusual for the Piedmont give rise to prairie-type wildflowers such as blue wild indigo, hoary puccoon, and smooth purple coneflower. A more common species, the wildflower called Dutchman's breeches, is rare for the Piedmont but grows in large patches here at Pennys Bend. Of course, such things botanical are mostly left for biologists to peruse, but we can appreciate the rare wildflowers and see for ourselves the restoration of a pine savanna as well as a grassy prairie atop the hill around which the Eno River flows. Hikers can also enjoy following the curves of the Eno as it makes an arc, displaying aquatic scenes from rocky rapids to quiet pools where turtles perch on logs in sunny repose. The preserve is popular with anglers who use the trails to access fishing holes.

And what is a preserve like this without a little history thrown in? How the river bend got its name is lost to time, but Camerons New Mill is named for Duncan Cameron, who in 1836 built this grist- and sawmill near the ford of Old Oxford Road, now a bridged crossing. The mill was ideally located, being near the road, which helped business, but architecturally speaking it was in an area without a geologically sound foundation; thus the milldam was repeatedly blown out from floods and the mill buildings continually damaged. Repairs were expensive, and the mill was eventually abandoned. Today you can see the stones scattered at a rapid where the mill once stood. During this time settlers located on Pennys Bend, growing crops and running cattle on the property. Despite extensive agricultural operations over two centuries, the use of prescribed fire has helped restore the native prairie grasses on the bend as well as aid reestablishment of the pine savanna, making the preserve a critical habitat for unusual Piedmont species.

It is the rock that made the Eno River curve in the first place. A volcanic, erosion-resistant stone called diabase made the Eno go around it instead of through it, creating this ultra-sharp bend and resulting peninsula. It is this rock from which the soil of Pennys Bend is formed. Unlike the low pH soils typically found in the Piedmont, the soils here at Pennys Bend are high pH and thus the basis from which the unusual plants grow.

So when you add up the rare plants, the diverse plant communities, the unusual geological foundation, the historic mill, and the aquatic features of the Eno River, it is easy to see that Pennys Bend is not only worth preserving but is worth a visit as well.

The hike starts at the often busy parking area off Snow Hill Road. You may be surprised by the number of cars, but most of their owners will be fishing the Eno

ABOUT DUTCHMAN'S BREECHES

This pretty flower growing at Pennys Bend Nature Preserve is named for its resemblance to upside-down pantaloons worn by eighteenth-century Europeans. It blooms in late March through mid-April. If you think the Dutchman's breeches is an odd flower name, consider its secondary name— Little Blue Staggers. This comes from the poisonous alkaloids found in the plant, which cause cattle to roam about as if they were drunk after ingesting Dutchman's breeches. This wildflower grows throughout the East, though it is much more common in the mountains of North Carolina than the Piedmont. It also can be found in lesser numbers in the Pacific Northwest. Legend has it that aboriginals thought of the wildflower as a love charm. So if your love life is on the rocks, consider taking your other half here to Pennys Bend for a little romance, aided by Dutchman's breeches.

Pennys Bend is known for its displays of Dutchman's breeches.

View of a river bend at Pennys Bend Nature Preserve

River, especially near the Camerons New Mill site. Join the Pyne Trail. You are soon alongside the Eno River on a singletrack path. User-created trails head to the Camerons New Mill site. Check out the remains of this historic structure before resuming your hike. After a short distance the Cash Point Trail leaves and crosses over the backbone of the bend. We stay with the Pyne Trail, still cruising alongside the river. At the most southerly point of the bend, you come to the pine savanna. Note the blackened bases of trunks here. Prescribed fire is used regularly at Pennys Bend.

The trail then turns north, following the Eno River upstream. It is in this area where the Dutchman's breeches are so prevalent. You soon pass the other side of the Cash Point Trail. It may be worth your time to climb to the open meadows featuring native prairie grasses. Otherwise continue along the riverside flats, which become increasingly hemmed in by steep rock outcrops of the resistant diabase. Wildflowers are found among the crevices of these rocks. Just before reaching the preserve boundary, the Natural Heritage Trail returns you to the hilltop of the bend. The Mountains-to-Sea Trail, which has been using the Pyne Trail through the preserve, continues its way along the Eno River, leaving the preserve.

From there you turn left on the Cash Point Trail, passing a road that leads to a pond. This road is closed to the public and is used to maintain and restore the preserve habitats. The Cash Point Trail descends through woods, returning to the Eno River. From there it is but a short backtrack to the trailhead.

Miles and Directions

0.0 With your back to Snow Hill Road and facing the Eno River, look right for the Pyne Trail as it leaves westerly. Walk along the edge of woods with a field to your right. Soon reach a

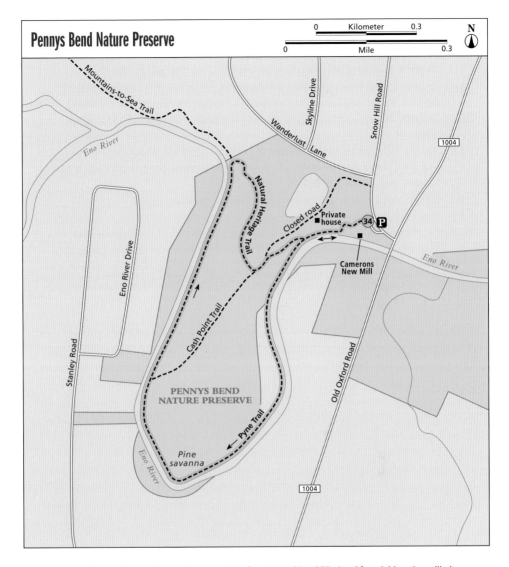

Pennys Bend Nature Preserve

0   Kilometer   0.3

0   Mile   0.3

N

trail kiosk. Spur trails go left toward the Camerons New Mill site. After visiting the mill site, continue on the Pyne Trail, bridging a little intermittent drainage. A hill rises to your right. Look for a house on the hill.

0.1   Reach a trail intersection. Keep straight on the Pyne Trail as the Cash Point Trail leaves right to cross the hilltop bend. The flowing Eno is interspersed with rocks. Ahead, the Pyne Trail passes through a dark cedar grove, yet another habitat on the preserve.

0.5   A rock outcrop and scenic bluff rises across the river, which sings over numerous shoals. Continue on a level track in narrow riverside flats. Look for piled logs and other evidence of sporadic floods.

0.7   Begin to curve northward. Walk within sight of the pine savanna to your right. Note the evidence of prescribed fire in the savanna area.

0.9 Reach a trail intersection. Here the Cash Point Trail climbs to open meadows and a shortcut back to the trailhead. The hike stays straight on the Pyne Trail, passing scads of Dutchman's breeches. Ahead, a rocky hill squeezes the trail close to the Eno River. This section is most attractive. Riverside rocks lure hikers into playing in the Eno.

1.4 Come to another intersection. Here the Mountains-to-Sea Trail goes straight, leaving the preserve and heading up the Eno River Valley, while our hike turns right on the Natural Heritage Trail. Climb a rocky hill. Top out at a stony perch. Head southeast in oaks and pines.

1.6 Reach a trail intersection after opening to a meadow. Head left, joining the Cash Point Trail. Soon pass a closed doubletrack heading to the preserve pond. Reenter woods on a narrower path, dropping toward the Eno.

1.7 Return to the Eno River and the Pyne Trail. Head left, backtracking.

1.8 Reach the trailhead and the end of the hike.

Wake Forest and Falls Lake Area

Pine pollen gathers on the shore of Falls Lake (hike 37).

35 Falls Lake Trail at Rollingview

This hike explores the shoreline of Falls Lake at Rollingview, a unit of Falls Lake State Recreation Area. Leave the main trailhead and roll through woods. Traverse fire-managed pine lands, coming to a cascade then reaching a small beach and extensive shoreline lake view. From there backtrack then make a loop, visiting a pond and coming to an old homesite. Enjoy more lake views before turning around.

Start: Trailhead at Rollingview Recreation Area entrance
Distance: 5.1-mile balloon loop
Hiking time: 2.5–3.5 hours
Difficulty: Moderate
Trail surface: Natural
Best season: Year-round
Other trail users: None
Canine compatibility: Leashed dogs allowed
Land status: State recreation area and North Carolina game lands

Fees and permits: No fees or permits required
Schedule: Nov–Feb: 8 a.m.–6 p.m.; Mar and Apr: 8 a.m.–8 p.m.; May–Aug: 8 a.m.–9 p.m.; Sept and Oct: 8 a.m.–8 p.m.; closed Christmas Day
Maps: Falls Lake State Recreation Area Rollingview, Falls Lake; USGS Creedmoor, Bayleaf
Trail contacts: Falls Lake State Recreation Area, 13304 Creedmoor Rd., Wake Forest, NC 27587; (919) 676-1027; www.ncparks.gov

Finding the trailhead: From exit 9 on I-540, north of Raleigh, take NC 50/Creedmoor Road north for 5.1 miles to NC 98. Take NC 98 west for 4.2 miles to turn right on Southview Road. Follow Southview Road for 1.1 miles to turn right on Baptist Road. Follow Baptist Road for 2.1 miles to reach the entrance to Rollingview Recreation Area. The Falls Lake Trail trailhead is on your left just before passing through the gate of the recreation area. Official address: 4201 Baptist Road, Durham, NC 27703. Trailhead GPS: N36 0.245', W78 43.682'

The Hike

Rollingview is a unit of the greater Falls Lake State Recreation Area, located on big Falls Lake, north of Raleigh and east of Durham. The state recreation area has numerous units stretched along the impoundment, each offering different outdoor opportunities. Rollingview is one of my favorites because it has a little bit of everything, including a fun hike that unrolls from one end of the peninsula that Rollingview occupies to the other. The hike uses the Falls Lake Trail, a path traveling the south shore of Falls Lake for some 60 miles. This is also part of the Mountains-to-Sea Trail, North Carolina's master path running from the Smokies to the Outer Banks. Since the Falls Lake Trail and the Mountains-to-Sea Trail run in conjunction, the names can be confusing to people who don't hike and write about it for a living. Just know that the Mountains-to-Sea Trail in the vicinity of Falls Lake is also named the Falls Lake Trail.

Sunrise over Falls Lake as seen from the trail

Names aside, the trek offers a lot for the local hiker or someone who is staying at Rollingview Campground. The trailhead is accessible without actually entering the recreation area. The hike begins on a connector trail then joins the Falls Lake Trail. Hikers first head west, undulating through hills and hollows, Falls Lake shimmering in the distance.

After a while the Falls Lake Trail enters North Carolina game lands. These lands are not managed as a recreation area, such as Rollingview is managed; rather the area is managed for the enhancement of flora and fauna. You will notice this immediately, since the North Carolina Wildlife Resources Commission uses prescribed fire here in restoring the pine forests as well as improving habitat for deer, which you will almost surely see. The trail comes closer and closer to Falls Lake, until it drops to the water's edge in a little hollow. Here a small beach opens up to the bulk of Falls Lake. This parcel of public land is narrow at this point, and a house stands well above, but the view is worthy nonetheless.

From this spot hikers backtrack to Rollingview, this time using the Falls Lake Trail the entire route. It leads to the main park road then splits off to formerly settled terrain, highlighted by an old farm pond by which grows a massive oak. From there an easy walk leads down to the Lick Creek embayment of Falls Lake. Enjoy more water vistas before stopping at the state park boundary. After backtracking, your return route adds a little more new trail, as you skirt around the pond a final time on a connector trail. Pass a small cemetery just before reaching the trailhead, still more trailside evidence of the past here at Rollingview.

Miles and Directions

0.0 From the parking area take the signed trail northwest. Skirt along the edge of the recreation area boundary in a mix of pines and hardwoods. Shortly come along a small branch. Mostly descend.

0.5 Reach the Falls Lake Trail, which is also labeled Mountains-to-Sea Trail. Again, do not be confused, as they are one and the same path here. Turn left on the Falls Lake Trail, westbound. Pass over a couple of small hollows.

0.8 Cross a wide, wet bottom, hopping a stream without benefit of a footbridge. Climb sharply from this bottom.

1.0 Cross a closed forest road delineating Rollingview Recreation Area from North Carolina game lands. The change in habitat is immediate and apparent as you leave thickly growing, dense forest to open, partly wooded pine savanna with a mix of oaks. Land managers are using prescribed fire to restore the forest to its native state. Descend. Partial views open right of Falls Lake.

1.2 Step over a streambed just above an 8-foot waterfall. This cascade can be especially scenic in winter through early spring or after thunderstorms. At other times it can slow to a trickle or even dry completely. Continue on sloped wooded ground, eventually leaving the fire-managed lands.

1.7 Come to the shoreline of Falls Lake after descending a very narrow little hollow. A small beach is located here, and you have far-reaching north views of the impoundment. The game management land boundaries are very near to the water here; thus there is a house standing sharply uphill above you. Turn around here and begin backtracking eastbound on the Falls Lake Trail.

2.9 Return to the intersection of the Falls Lake Trail and the connector trail. This time keep straight on the Falls Lake Trail, crossing an intermittent streambed then rising.

3.2 Reach the primary road at Rollingview. Head right on the paved road, passing the road leading left to the Rollingview Campground. Keep straight beyond the campground road, passing the recreation area entrance station.

3.3 At the intersection of the main recreation area road and Falls Lake Road (the road to the recreation area marina), pick up the Falls Lake Trail. The singletrack path passes under a small transmission line then continues southeast.

3.6 Come alongside a huge white oak tree and a farm pond. Here the Falls Lake Trail veers left, south, from the pond.

3.7 Pass a connector trail leading right, back to the parking area. You will be returning here, but for now continue straight on the Falls Lake Trail.

4.0 Pass near an old homesite. Look left for a chimney, leftover roofing, parts of a car, and more artifacts.

4.1 Join an old road. Head left then quickly leave right from the old roadbed, then descend.

4.2 Rock-hop a branch. Come along the Lick Creek embayment of Falls Lake. You are close to the water, making it easy to access.

4.3 Reach a sign indicating North Carolina game lands. Turn around here as the Falls Lake Trail continues its quest for Falls Lake Dam.

4.9 Return to the pond and big white oak. This time split left on the connector trail, circling around part of the pond.

Falls Lake Trail at Rollingview

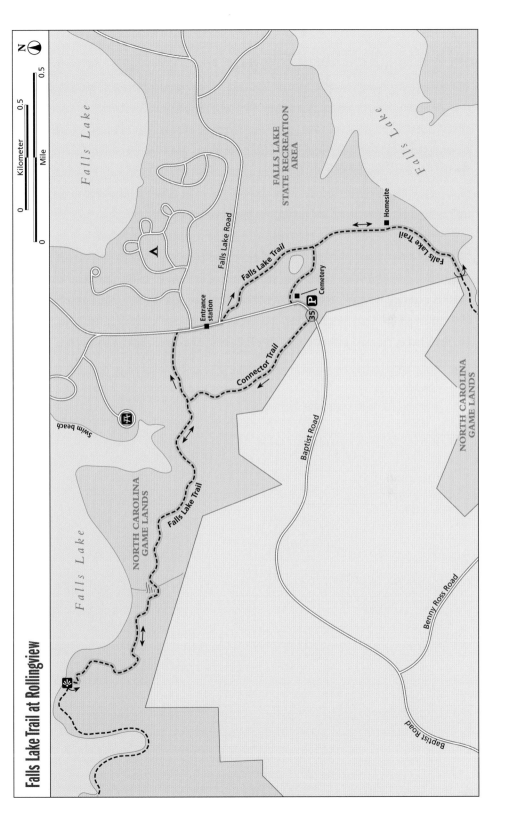

N

Kilometer
0   0.5   0.5

Mile
0   0.5

Falls Lake

Falls Lake

Falls Lake Road

FALLS LAKE
STATE RECREATION
AREA

Falls Lake Trail

Entrance
station

Falls Lake Trail

Cemetery

Homesite

35 P

Connector Trail

Falls Lake

NORTH CAROLINA
GAME LANDS

Falls Lake Trail

Swim beach

Baptist Road

NORTH CAROLINA
GAME LANDS

Benny Ross Road

Baptist Road

THE WAY TO ROLL AT ROLLINGVIEW

Rollingview is my favorite camping area on Falls Lake. I like it because there is so much to do in one area and civilization is not far off if you need supplies and such. For starters the campground is very appealing. It is broken up into three separate wooded loops. The first two loops are equipped with water and electricity, keeping RV owners and electricity lovers together. The third loop has no electricity and is for tent campers. This arrangement keeps like-minded campers together. All three loops have hot showers and water. Hiking trails course through the campground. A playground and fishing pier also serve campers.

Beyond the campground the recreation area, set on a peninsula, has a boat ramp, multiple picnic areas, picnic shelters, and even a community building. A large swim beach is located in a cove and offers sunbathing and swimming opportunities. The recreation area also has a marina. The quiet roads within the recreation area make for fun, casual bicycling. Short pathways link everything together, creating an "all-inclusive" camping resort of sorts. And don't forget the main path—the Falls Lake Trail—adds even more allure to Rollingview.

5.0 Pass a small cemetery just before coming to the main recreation area road. Follow the road left.

5.1 Reach the trailhead, completing the hike.

36 Falls Lake Trail from Boyce Mill

This trek on Falls Lake explores relatively remote terrain. Leave Boyce Mill Road then descend to alluring Laurel Creek. Beyond the waterway rise to find an old homesite with several barns and structures worth exploring. Continue rolling through quiet, contemplative woods, finally dipping to a rocky stream and small cascade, a good place to turn around.

Start: Dead end on Boyce Mill Road
Distance: 5.4-mile there-and-back
Hiking time: 2.5–3.0 hours
Difficulty: Moderate
Trail surface: Natural
Best season: Year-round, winter for viewing old buildings
Other trail users: None
Canine compatibility: Leashed dogs allowed

Land status: North Carolina game lands
Fees and permits: No fees or permits required
Schedule: Sunrise to sunset
Maps: Falls Lake; USGS Creedmoor, Bayleaf
Trail contacts: Falls Lake US Army Corps of Engineers, 11405 Falls of Neuse Rd., Wake Forest, NC 27587; (919) 846-9932; www.saw .usace.army.mil

Finding the trailhead: From exit 9 on I-540, north of Raleigh, take NC 50/Creedmoor Road north for 5.1 miles to NC 98. Take NC 98 west for 2.3 miles to turn right on Boyce Mill Road. Follow Boyce Mill Road for 0.6 mile to a dead end. The proper segment of the Falls Lake Trail leaves right as you reach the dead end. Parking is limited, so be courteous. Trailhead GPS: N35 59.468', W78 43.188'

The Hike

Judging by the size of the parking area here at the dead end of Boyce Mill Road, not many people are hiking this segment of the Falls Lake Trail. And that may be a good thing. This is one of the quieter, more remote stretches of the Falls Lake Trail, as it travels through a relatively wide swath of US Army Corps of Engineers land. Although public lands border the entirety of Falls Lake, much of this shoreline land is but a thin strip. These narrow passages avail public access and a route for the Falls Lake Trail as it makes its way 60 miles along the south shore of the lake from one end to the other, but some thin margins of forested terrain bordering neighborhoods lack a sense of wilderness and a larger natural realm in which to hike.

This segment, however, bucks that trend. In fact, the only residence you will see along this hike is the one next to the trailhead. Along the way you will view evidence of former homesteads, lands sold to the Corps before damming the lake. The owners moved on, and some left their buildings standing, seemingly taking only their clothes on their backs, as you will see on this hike. A little over halfway through the trek, the Falls Lake Trail leads to such a former farm set atop the hill. Here hikers will find

Relics like this can be found at farm sites along the trail.

several structures, including a tobacco barn, formerly found at farms throughout the Piedmont. There is also a generic barn and yet another wooden outbuilding. Interestingly, a half-constructed concrete block structure stands mute in the forest as well. Its purpose is known only to the former owner, who apparently gave up constructing his final building, perhaps upon learning he would have to sell his land because it was in the condemnation zone for establishing Falls Lake. This condemnation zone—the entire shoreline—is nothing but woods now, mostly managed by the North Carolina Wildlife Resources Commission as game lands, though some locales are state, county, or municipal parks.

It's good for us to simply strike out into nature. This hike is nothing more than a linear trail coursing through forestland. Former habitations are revealed in clues like a line of barbwire, a rusty washtub, a faint old farm road, or a crumbled wooden outbuilding. And nature has reclaimed the former fields in a striking manner. Regal forests of oak and pine rise to sway in the wind and tower where tobacco, corn, and cotton once grew in straight rows. Sun-burnished streams are now shaded again and are thriving with minnows, crawdads, and salamanders.

After leaving the end of Boyce Mill Road, the Falls Lake Trail dips off a ridge to reach Laurel Creek, a significant and scenic stream following gravity's orders to feed Falls Lake. Other small and clear tributaries also find their way off the hills above Falls Lake, and you cross them usually on footbridges.

One of the literal and figurative high points of this trip is the former farm site with the intact tobacco barn. Be careful exploring the area, as the previous owner didn't leave his beloved farm with an eye toward future hikers/explorers traipsing among the brush, trees, and vines that have slowly overtaken the clearing where the structures stand. Beyond the homesite you continue winding in rising hills then dip to a rocky stream, with natural stone seats lying beside the waterway. Here an angled cascade drops about 6 feet. This makes for a good turnaround point, though this segment of the Falls Lake Trail does continue 3 more miles to busy NC 50. On your return trip look for other evidence of the past.

Miles and Directions

0.0 From the parking area take the signed singletrack Falls Lake Trail northeasterly toward NC 50 (the incorrect segment of the Falls Lake Trail leaves the parking area north around a gate and follows the roadbed of Boyce Mill Road, now closed at this point since it heads directly into Falls Lake). Skirt the edge of the last residence on Boyce Mill Road in tightly growing young forest reclaiming former pastureland. Begin to drop off a ridgeline. Come near an old homesite, the most prominent remains of which is a collapsed shed.

0.5 Pass another ramshackle shed alongside the trail.

0.6 Come to Laurel Creek just as it is making a little bend. There is no bridge here, and you have to cross the creek the best way possible. Most of the time it is a simple rock hop, though changing flows alter the gravel rocks and water. Consider taking your shoes off and walking through the water if it is too high to get across dry footed. This is the only potential ford on the hike—other smaller creek crossings are bridged.

0.8 Bridge a tributary of Laurel Creek. Watch for big cedar trees in this area. A large, forested flat stretches off to your right.

1.0 Bridge a pretty, clear but small tributary of Laurel Creek. Join an old roadbed now growing up in sycamores and head directly for Falls Lake.

1.2 Come to the shore of Falls Lake. A view opens into the Laurel Creek embayment of Falls Lake. Walk along the shoreline. Note that this embayment is actually part of the greater Lick Creek arm of Falls Lake. When looking at a map of the lake, the impoundment actually comprises multiple narrow arms and embayments and thus never looks huge, not revealing its 38,000 acres of land and water spread amid Durham and Granville Counties.

1.3 Bridge yet another tributary of Laurel Creek. Prescribed fire has been used in the adjacent pine-oak woods, testimony of this being a larger tract along the lake. (They don't use prescribed fire in narrow, smaller parcels of lakeshore due to proximity to private homes, etc.) Climb away.

1.5 Reach the old tobacco barn and other structures at this "newer" historic site. Note the large shade trees that once helped keep those pre-airconditioning Piedmont summers at bay. Be careful of nails and such while exploring the site. Leave any artifacts for others to discover and enjoy for themselves. Bisect an obvious former road after leaving the farm site. Descend.

1.7 Cross a small branch. Ignore any user-created mountain bike trails, as the Falls Lake Trail is clearly marked with circular white blazes. Look for quartz in the trailbed as you stay atop uplands.

2.4 Make a sharp turn to the right, heading southbound, still in uplands.

2.7 Come to an unnamed stream with a very stony bed. Here a rocky cascade flows just alongside the trail. This is a good place to turn around. You can see a power line clearing in the distance. From this point the Falls Lake Trail continues downstream along this creek

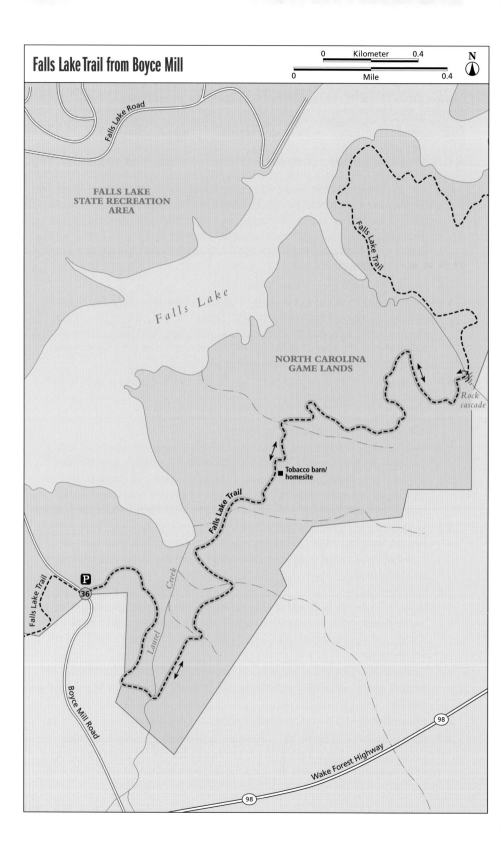

0   Kilometer   0.4

0   Mile   0.4

N

FALLS LAKE
STATE RECREATION
AREA

Falls Lake Road

Falls Lake

Falls Lake Trail

NORTH CAROLINA
GAME LANDS

Rock
cascade

Tobacco barn/
homesite

Falls Lake Trail

P

36

Falls Lake Trail

Laurel Creek

Boyce Mill Road

Wake Forest Highway

98

98

An old barn is painted in streaks of sunlight.

a short distance then crosses it, continuing on to NC 50. There is natural stone seating around the rocky cascade. Take a break here and absorb nature before backtracking.

5.4 Reach the trailhead, completing the hike.

37 Blue Jay Point County Park

Set on the shores of scenic Falls Lake, this trail-laden park offers a fun loop hike using the long-distance Falls Lake Trail combined with other shorter nature trails. Your circuit hike leaves the inviting environmental education center, passes a wildflower garden, then works down to Falls Lake, where it skirts the shore and heads out to sandy points. More views await at other overlooks as you walk the edge of the lake. Climb hills back to the trailhead.

Start: Blue Jay Center for Environmental Education
Distance: 2.9-mile loop with spurs
Hiking time: 1.5–2.0 hours
Difficulty: Easy
Trail surface: Natural
Best season: Year-round
Other trail users: None
Canine compatibility: Pets on 6-foot leash only

Land status: Wake County park
Fees and permits: No fees or permits required
Schedule: 8 a.m. to sunset
Maps: Blue Jay Point County Park; USGS Bayleaf
Trail contacts: Blue Jay Point County Park, 3200 Pleasant Union Church Rd., Raleigh, NC 27614; (919) 870-4330; www.wakegov.com/parks/bluejay

Finding the trailhead: From exit 11 on I-540, north of downtown Raleigh, take Six Forks Road north for 2.4 miles then turn left at a four-way intersection, still on Six Forks Road, as Possum Track Road goes straight. Stay with Six Forks Road for 1.4 more miles then turn right on Pleasant Union Church Road. Keep straight on Pleasant Union Church Road and follow the signs to the park and the Blue Jay Center for Environmental Education. Trailhead GPS: N35 58.150', W78 38.584'

The Hike

Blue Jay Point County Park was formed after Falls Lake came to be. Falls Lake was established after the US Army Corps of Engineers condemned the land currently under Falls Lake and the surrounding shoreline of what was then the free-flowing Neuse River. The Neuse River is formed at the confluence of the Eno River and the Flat River. This confluence occurs at what is now Falls Lake. The condemned land around the lake was completely under the umbrella of the US Army Corps of Engineers, who then parceled out parts of the shoreline to North Carolina state parks as well as Blue Jay Point County Park.

The whole idea for Falls Lake came to be when communities downstream on the Neuse were damaged during floods in the early 1900s. The river then came under review for being dammed. In 1945 the Homestead Hurricane flooded the Neuse

A small beach on the peninsula of Blue Jay Point ▶

River again. This high water event gave engineers an idea of how big a reservoir was needed to slow down hurricane level floodwaters.

The Homestead Hurricane dumped 8 inches of water over the Triangle area on that fateful September 17. And this was on top of heavy rains earlier in the month; thus the soils and streams could absorb no more and just pushed the floodwaters into the Neuse, Cape Fear, Lumber, and Pee Dee river basins. To give an example of this extreme storm, the Cape Fear River crested at 68.9 feet at Fayetteville with flood stage being at 35 feet. That is over 33 feet above flood stage! It was this type of flooding that ultimately led to Falls Lake being constructed, which ultimately led to the creation of Blue Jay Point County Park.

The building of the Falls Lake Dam was authorized by the US Congress in 1965, but it was another thirteen years before construction began on the dam. The dam was finally finished on February 26, 1981, and the Neuse River began to back up at Falls Lake. It took nearly three years for the lake to reach full pool, and ever since then Falls Lake has been a significant outdoor resource for Triangle residents. Of course, the primary purpose of the dam project was not recreation first but increasing the drinking water supply, reducing flood damage, enhancing water quality, enhancing fish and wildlife, and lastly recreation.

Blue Jay Point County Park is a good example of recreation on Falls Lake. Set on a peninsula jutting into the Neuse, bordered by the Upper Barton Creek embayment and the Lower Barton Creek embayment, Blue Jay Point County Park has miles of shoreline and miles of hiking trails. It also features a quality environmental education center where programs are held for the public. There is a variety of playgrounds and open play areas, and multiple picnic areas too. Anglers can walk to shoreline access points to fish, but there is no boat ramp here. Though swimming is not allowed in the park, it does have a very popular zip line traveling through the trees.

The Falls Lake Trail is the primary park path and runs along the entirety of the shoreline of 236-acre Blue Jay Point County Park and beyond for 60 or so miles along Falls Lake. Of course, the Falls Lake Trail is part of the greater Mountains-to-Sea Trail, North Carolina's master path, which when complete will travel from the Tennessee state line in the Great Smoky Mountains all the way to Cape Hatteras on the Atlantic Ocean.

The hike at Blue Jay Point County Park travels well-marked and maintained trails, all with color-coded blazes. The trek first leaves the environmental education center and passes through a garden with native plants and wildflowers. Take the time to learn about the labeled plants here. From there the walking adventure joins the Azalea Loop Trail before connecting to the Beaver Point Trail, where you gain your first glimpse of Falls Lake. The hike then picks up the Falls Lake Trail and meanders along the shoreline, sometimes curving inland as it works around drainages topped with footbridges. The walk out to Blue Jay Point is a highlight. Here you tightrope a slender swath of land bordered with beaches on both sides, ending at a rocky, partly

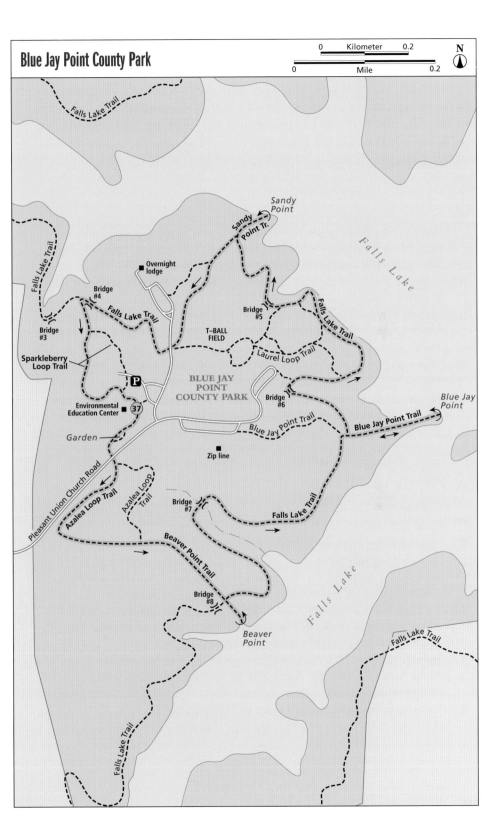

Blue Jay Point County Park

Falls Lake Trail

Falls Lake Trail

Sandy Point

Sandy Point Tr.

Falls Lake

Overnight lodge

Bridge #4

Falls Lake Trail

Bridge #5

Bridge #3

Falls Lake Trail

Sparkleberry Loop Trail

T–BALL FIELD

Laurel Loop Trail

Falls Lake Trail

P

BLUE JAY POINT COUNTY PARK

Bridge #6

Blue Jay Point

Environmental Education Center

37

Blue Jay Point Trail

Blue Jay Point Trail

Garden

Pleasant Union Church Road

Zip line

Azalea Loop Trail

Azalea Loop Trail

Bridge #7

Falls Lake Trail

Beaver Point Trail

Bridge #8

Falls Lake Trail

Beaver Point

Falls Lake

Falls Lake Trail

0   Kilometer   0.2

0   Mile   0.2

N

wooded knoll. Enjoy hanging out beside the water, watching motor boaters whizz by or birds in season.

Next, curve around a steep drainage and return to the lake, soaking in more views, and then make a side trip out to Sandy Point, a truly sandy part of the shore. From there the Falls Lake Trail takes you through hills away from the water before heading even farther inland to join the Sparkleberry Loop Trail, which returns to the environmental education center.

Miles and Directions

0.0 As you face the education center building, head left on the asphalt path toward the wildflower and native plant garden. After walking through the garden, leave it via a gate then cross Pleasant Union Church Road and join the Azalea Loop Trail. Head right on the Azalea Loop Trail, running roughly parallel to the road, then turn east toward Falls Lake.

0.3 Reach the other end of the Azalea Loop Trail. Continue toward Falls Lake, now on the wider Beaver Point Trail.

0.5 Meet the Falls Lake Trail but keep straight for the moment and head down to Falls Lake, grabbing a view of the impoundment. Backtrack then head right, joining the Falls Lake Trail, northbound.

0.8 Cross Footbridge #7 after turning into a hollow. The park zip line is nearby, uphill, and you may see/hear zip-line enthusiasts zipping through the tree canopy.

1.2 Turn right on the Blue Jay Point Trail, heading east to a narrowing peninsula that becomes a sandy beach with a small wooded knoll at the end. Enjoy stellar lake views then backtrack and rejoin the Falls Lake Trail.

1.6 Cross Footbridge #6 after turning into a hollow then continue just a short distance and pass a red-blazed trail leading left to a parking area. Descend the hollow back toward Falls Lake.

1.7 Pass another red-blazed spur trail leading left to the Laurel Loop Trail. Stay with the Falls Lake Trail. Curve near the lake to an overlook and continue past a second junction with the Laurel Loop Trail.

1.9 Cross Footbridge #5. Wander hills above the lake.

2.1 Meet the Sandy Point Trail. Turn right here and head downhill on a narrowing spit that becomes very sandy. Enjoy the views to the north of the Upper Barton Creek arm of Falls Lake and to the south of a small cove. Backtrack, rejoining the Falls Lake Trail.

2.3 The Sandy Point Trail splits right toward a parking area. Stay with the Falls Lake Trail to emerge at a parking area for the T-ball field. Cross the park road, staying with the Falls Lake Trail. This segment of trail traverses a steep-sided slope.

2.7 Leave the Falls Lake Trail left, just after Footbridge #4. Join a red-blazed connector, reaching the Sparkleberry Loop Trail. Head right on the Sparkleberry Loop Trail, turning into a steep hollow.

2.9 Reach the environmental education center, completing the hike.

38 Falls Lake Trail at Falls Lake Dam

This hike starts at the recreation hub that is the Falls Lake Dam tailrace area. Here adventurers can fish the tailrace, paddle the Neuse River, bicycle the Neuse River Trail greenway, and, of course, hike. This walk takes the Falls Lake Trail from the tailrace area up to the dam visitor center, then travels along the shore of Falls Lake. The return route leads past other trail connections via the Blue Dot Trail and back to the trailhead where you can tack on other adventures.

Start: Tailrace fishing area
Distance: 1.7-mile balloon loop
Hiking time: About 1.0 hour
Difficulty: Easy
Trail surface: Almost all natural
Best season: Year-round
Other trail users: None
Canine compatibility: Leashed dogs allowed
Land status: US Army Corps of Engineers property

Fees and permits: No fees or permits required
Schedule: Sunrise to sunset
Maps: Falls Lake Dam Trails Map; USGS Wake Forest
Trail contacts: Falls Lake Dam Visitor Assistance Center, 11405 Falls of Neuse Rd., Wake Forest, NC 27587; (919) 846-9332; www.saw .usace.army.mil

Finding the trailhead: From exit 14 on I-540, northeast of downtown Raleigh, take Falls of Neuse Road north for 3.2 miles to turn left on Old Falls of Neuse Road. (The right turn at this intersection is Wide River Road.) Follow Old Falls of Neuse Road for 0.3 mile to the tailrace fishing area. This final left turn is just before Old Falls of Neuse Road bridges the Neuse River. Trailhead GPS: N35 56.391', W78 34.855'

The Hike

I still remember being stunned when pulling up to the Falls Lake tailrace fishing area to make this hike for the first time. I expected to perhaps see anglers milling around the parking area and a stray hiker or two, but I did not expect to see so many bicycles and cars with bicycle racks. It was confusing! Then I recalled that the Neuse River Trail, a popular bicycling greenway and part of the greater Capital Area Greenway network, starts here and heads almost 28 miles along the Neuse River to the Johnson County line, making connections to other greenways along the way. I even saw someone unloading a kayak, fixing to embark on a paddling trip down the Neuse from the canoe/kayak launch here.

Despite being a fishing, paddling, and bicycling trailhead, it is also an important hiker trailhead. This is the eastern terminus of the 60-mile Falls Lake Trail, which stretches along the south shore of Falls Lake all the way to Pennys Bend Nature Preserve, also detailed in this guide. Just so you know, the Falls Lake Trail and the Mountains-to-Sea Trail run conjunctively, so you may see signage and references to

PRIDE OF THE RALEIGH TRAIL SYSTEM

Starting at this very same trailhead is the capital area's premier greenway, the Neuse River Trail. Leaving from the tailrace below Falls Lake Dam, this almost 28-mile greenway is the pride of the Raleigh trail system. The paved path crosses wetlands on boardwalk bridges, passes historical sites, and goes along agricultural fields as well as along the river, through forested floodplains, and over tributaries. The greenway also crosses the Neuse River twice on pedestrian bridges. Finished in 2014, the Neuse River Trail was over forty years in the making. The Capital Area Greenway System was adopted as an idea by the Raleigh City Council in 1976. It was another twenty years before they finished a master plan for what they called the Neuse River Corridor, a sort of linear regional park. Their goal was to preserve the full width of the floodplain along the Neuse River while putting in an asphalt trail extending the entire length of the Neuse River from Falls Lake Dam to the Johnson County line. And along this linear regional park, the city council wanted to have larger, more traditional parks at a spacing of every 2 to 3 miles. This would not only deliver additional activities for visitors to the Neuse River corridor but also provide access points for users of the greenway. The plan was adopted, and the city of Raleigh purchased over 2,000 acres of land along the Neuse River floodplain. Other greenways connect to the Neuse River Trail, including the Abbotts Creek Trail, the Crabtree Creek Trail, the Walnut Creek Trail, and others. Adjacent Johnson County has gotten in on the act and extended the trail 5 miles from the Wake County line to the town of Clayton, making the route 33 miles. The trail also has the honor of being the longest greenway in North Carolina. Plans call for an extension to Clemmons State Forest.

For those coming to enjoy the Falls Lake Trail near Falls Lake Dam, a bicycle trip on the Neuse River Trail is a welcome addition to activities from this trailhead. Savvy paddlers embark from this very same location, float down the Neuse River in canoes or kayaks, then use the greenway to walk or pedal back to the tailrace area. Come to think of it, outdoor adventurers could come here and engage in a triathlon of sorts, hiking the Falls Lake Trail, paddling the Neuse River, and bicycling the Neuse River Trail greenway—all from the same trailhead!

the Falls Lake Trail also being the Mountains-to-Sea Trail. It is also at this trailhead where the Mountains-to-Sea Trail begins tracing the Neuse River Trail greenway. No need to worry about names, though, because the hike is well marked and well maintained. However, do consider incorporating other immediate activities into your adventure, since the hike is relatively short.

Falls Lake Dam

Also, make sure and stop at the Falls Lake Dam Visitor Assistance Center either during your hike or beforehand. They have interpretive displays, maps, and other worthwhile information to help you better appreciate and enjoy the area, which includes not only the tailrace but also all the activities on the lake itself, such as motorboating, sailing, swimming, fishing, and waterskiing.

The hike joins the Falls Lake Trail from near the restrooms, following a gated track south, away from the tailrace, greenway, and parking area. It soon splits to singletrack trail and climbs toward the visitor center, passing through a meadow and beside a massive tulip tree. After nearing the visitor center, the loop comes along a rocky slope overlooking Falls Lake. Good still water views can be appreciated here. It is not long before you are heading back toward the tailrace area via the Blue Dot Trail, which slips down a hollow on its return trip. With a hiking time of plus or minus an hour, you will have an opportunity to engage in other outdoor pursuits from the recreation hub that is Falls Lake Dam.

Miles and Directions

0.0   From the parking area leave south from the tailrace area restrooms. Pass around a pole gate, joining a gravel roadbed on the Falls Lake Trail. Travel just a short distance on the gravel road then split left as the path becomes singletrack. Climb a bit then look right for a huge rock outcrop standing on the hill to your right.

0.2   Come to a trail intersection. Here the Falls Lake Trail leaves right, and your return route, the Blue Dot Trail, comes in on your left. Stay right with the Falls Lake Trail. Climb in a mixed forest of hardwoods and evergreens.

0.3   Reach and cross Falls Dam Road. Veer right after crossing the road. Wander through a small meadow, cultivated with wildflowers in season. Reenter woods. Hop over a little rocky

Falls Lake Trail at Falls Lake Dam

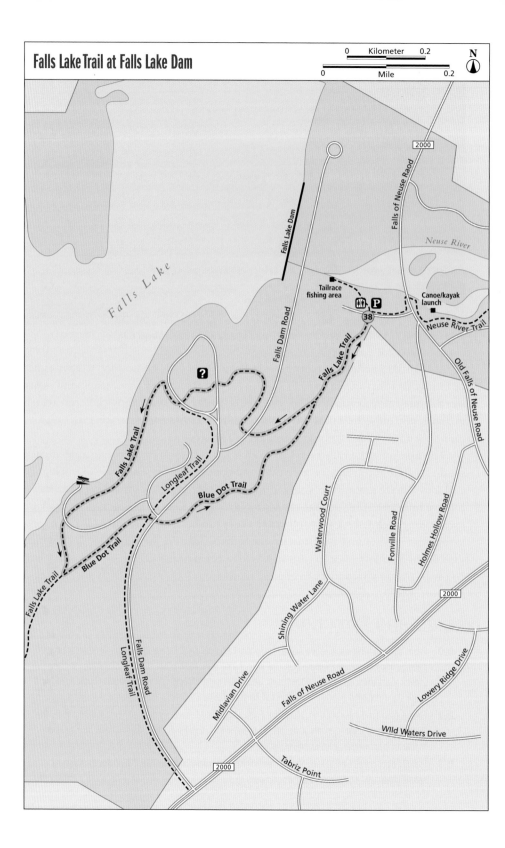

0   Kilometer   0.2

0   Mile   0.2

N

Falls Lake Dam

Falls of Neuse Raod

2000

Neuse River

Falls Lake

Tailrace
fishing area

P

38

Canoe/kayak
launch

Neuse River Trail

Falls Dam Road

Falls Lake Trail

?

Old Falls of Neuse Road

Falls Lake Trail

Longleaf Trail

Blue Dot Trail

Waterwood Court

Fonville Road

Holmes Hollow Road

Falls Lake Trail

Blue Dot Trail

Longleaf Trail

Falls Dam Road

2000

Shining Water Lane

Midlavian Drive

Falls of Neuse Road

Tabriz Point

2000

Lowery Ridge Drive

WIld Waters Drive

branch and find a huge trailside tulip tree. It may have not been cut since the trunk is split down low, making it less valuable, and therefore was left behind when this locale was logged.

0.5 Reach the visitor center access road. There is alternate parking on the right. Consider going in the visitor center and absorbing the interpretive information. Restrooms and drinking water are also available. Climb into pines.

0.6 Cross the other end of the visitor center access road. Here the asphalt Longleaf Trail leads left 0.8 mile to Falls of Neuse Road. Turn right here on an asphalt path then reach an elevated boardwalk. Split left on the boardwalk, descending toward the steep hillside. A user-created trail drops steeply toward Falls Lake. The Falls Lake Trail, however, turns south, paralleling the lakeshore. The slope beside the trail is rocky to the extreme for the Piedmont. Holly trees are nearly as prevalent as the rocks.

0.9 Cross a boat ramp access road.

1.0 The Falls Lake Trail meets the Blue Dot Trail, your return route. If you wish to continue on the Falls Lake Trail, it is 2.7 miles farther to Raven Ridge Road. For this loop turn left and join the Blue Dot Trail as it turns back northeast.

1.2 The natural surface Blue Dot Trail meets the asphalt Longleaf Trail. Keep straight, crossing the visitor center access road a final time. Resume singletrack natural surface path. Descend in deep woods. Come alongside a perennial branch.

1.5 Meet the Falls Lake Trail, completing the loop portion of the hike. From here backtrack toward the tailrace fishing area.

1.7 Reach the trailhead, completing the hike.

39 Wilkerson Nature Park

This newer nature park on the north side of Raleigh presents an interconnected set of paths exploring woods and fields of a former farm. The park, big on ecological learning, makes for a fun little day hike and a great place to take younger nature enthusiasts.

Start: Wilkerson Nature Park office
Distance: 1.7-mile loop
Hiking time: About 1.5 hours
Difficulty: Easy
Trail surface: Natural
Best season: Year-round
Other trail users: None
Canine compatibility: Leashed dogs allowed
Land status: Nature preserve

Fees and permits: No fees or permits required
Schedule: 8 a.m. to 5:30 p.m.
Maps: Annie Louise Wilkerson Nature Preserve Park
Trail contacts: Annie Louise Wilkerson, MD Nature Preserve Park, 5229 Awls Haven Rd., Raleigh, NC 27614; (919) 996-6764; www .raleighnc.gov/parks/

Finding the trailhead: From exit 14 on I-540, north of downtown Raleigh, take Falls of Neuse Road north for 1.5 miles to turn left on Raven Ridge Road. Follow Raven Ridge Road for 0.3 mile then turn right onto Awls Haven Road and enter the park. Follow Awls Haven Road to the park office. Trailhead GPS: N35 55.403', W78 35.966'

The Hike

Annie Wilkerson started her medical career in 1940, back when women were rare in the medicine field. She practiced for fifty-three years. The practice she established thrives to this day. But Annie Wilkerson had another side. She loved nature and loved her farm on the north side of town. During her career Raleigh kept creeping toward her farm. She knew her parcel of green just south of Falls Lake would be better appreciated by the public than would another subdivision, so she willed the land to the city for a nature park. Annie stipulated in her will that the park be set aside as a "nature preserve park," with its primary purpose being nature and wildlife education. No new buildings were to be built. The city honored her wishes, renovated her home and another residence on the 157-acre property into the park office and classroom, and established Raleigh's first nature park. Interestingly, until Wilkerson made her donation, Raleigh had no classification for a nature preserve park, but has since added new nature preserve parks and reclassified others. So this donation to Raleigh had a ripple effect.

Now Raleigh has a nature park with its primary purpose to "help groups and individuals foster a connection with the natural world through public, group and self-guided programs." You can create your own self-guided tour of the park utilizing informative pamphlets and displays to learn more about the flora, fauna, and geology

WHY VISIT WILKERSON NATURE PARK

So why do it? Why visit a place like Wilkerson Nature Park? After hiking here I know it is good for your body. Hiking, biking, camping, hunting, fishing, and paddling are opportunities to get exercise, to reach our physical potential. In today's world we are always encouraged to reach our mental potential, but what happened to reaching our physical potential? To be in great shape is not only a healthy choice, but it also helps carry us through our daily lives in pursuit of our mental potential.

Exploring the outdoors positively stimulates your senses. Smell the autumn leaves on a crisp afternoon. See deer bound through a meadow. Hear birdsong echo in the woods. What a contrast to smelling auto exhaust, seeing trash on the street, or being pounded by endless noises from your smartphone!

The great outdoors puts our hurried lives into perspective. Nature moves at its own pace, with no regard to hourly schedules and appointments, only following the changing seasons, guided by the sun. A respite at Wilkerson Nature Park revitalizes your spirit and frees you of time constraints. It is a chance to get away from work stress, bills, and the everyday hassles that sometimes bind us.

Exploring the outdoors is great for your mind, too. Once out there you can unleash your brain: let it roam where it wants to go—no screen time, no commercials—allowing you to think in continuums without interruption. When was the last time you did that?

We Americans are restless by nature; we settled this continent from the Atlantic to the Pacific. Getting outside feeds our restlessness, our desire to explore. We see what is around the bend, climb the mountain to get the view, float the river to see where it leads. Starting here and ending up there puts together the pieces of the geographic puzzle that make up the Triangle.

Exploring the outdoors leads to preserving our natural wonders, of which North Carolina is rich. It is one thing to generically say, "Let's preserve the environment," and entirely another to want to safeguard what you have seen with your own eyes. Getting into nature provides "tangibility" to natural preservation.

Finally, the outdoors is a great venue to make memories. Most of us don't remember what we did last week—it probably involved a lot of time on your television, computer, or phone screen. Watching television together is a passive shared activity. However, hiking to the pond at Wilkerson Nature Park, finding a wildflower in the woods, or seeing the rock outcrops here is an active shared experience that creates bonds between you and your fellow outdoor enthusiasts. And those last a lifetime.

The hike passes by an old farm pond.

contained within Annie Wilkerson's former farm. Exhibits are designed for adults and kids.

This hike links up the three primary park trails. After stopping at the office and getting a park map and additional interpretive information, take the Epps Forest Loop south and quickly meet a connector leaving to overflow parking. The Epps Forest Loop rolls through hardwoods, coming near Bartons Creek. It then meets a link to North Carolina's master path—the Mountains-to-Sea Trail (MST). The path, when completed, will run all the way from Clingmans Dome at the Tennessee state line in the Great Smoky Mountains National Park east to Cape Hatteras and the Atlantic Ocean. If the Wilkerson Nature Park hike is too short, you can stretch your legs on the MST as it wanders some 60 miles along the shoreline of Falls Lake, more than even the most ambitious day hiker can tackle.

Should you decide to stick with Wilkerson Nature Park, the Epps Forest Loop passes a massive white oak tree then opens to meadows. Trace a mown path back toward the park office before turning toward the park pond. The hike loops around the pond, coming close to Annie's home-turned-classroom. It then joins the Hidden Rocks Loop, reentering forest. Here you cross a city of Raleigh water pipeline delivering 48 million gallons of drinking water per day from Falls Lake to a water treatment plant and then to homes throughout the area.

Next, come to an exposed rock garden as well as rock piles from long-ago agricultural days. The park has specific information about these boulders for junior geologists. Interestingly, much of the exposed rock is magnetite, the most magnetic naturally occurring mineral in the world. Stick your compass next to the mineral and the compass arrow will move. You leave the rock to cross the waterline again. A final

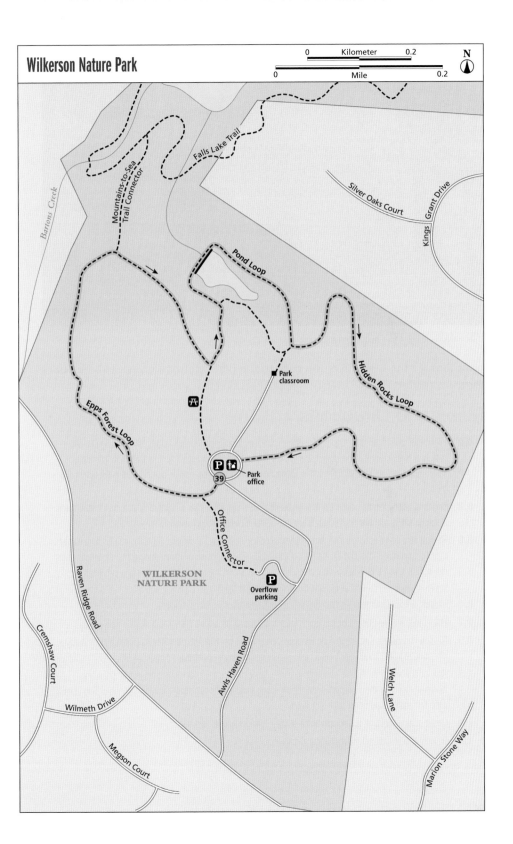

Wilkerson Nature Park

N

0   Kilometer   0.2

0   Mile   0.2

Barrons Creek

Mountains-to-Sea Trail Connector

Falls Lake Trail

Silver Oaks Court

Kings Grant Drive

Pond Loop

Hidden Rocks Loop

Park classroom

Epps Forest Loop

Park office

39

Office Connector

WILKERSON NATURE PARK

Raven Ridge Road

Cremshaw Court

Wilmeth Drive

Megson Court

Awls Haven Road

Overflow parking

Welch Lane

Marion Stone Way

The author sizes up a mighty white oak tree.

jaunt through the forest takes you back to the office, perhaps loaded with questions for the naturalists who are there to help. After all, this is a nature park.

Miles and Directions

0.0 From the south side of the park office, pick up the Epps Forest Loop. Hike 115 feet then reach a trail intersection. Here the Office Connector leaves left to the overflow parking area. You turn right and follow the Epps Forest Loop. Hike under beech, red oak, and tulip trees.

0.3 Cross a plank bridge over an intermittent drainage after the singletrack dirt path descends. Ascend from the plank bridge. Bartons Creek flows through woods to your left.

0.5 Reach the connector to the Mountains-to-Sea Trail. This is where you can really add mileage to this hike. It is but 0.2 mile to the MST, and it goes for miles along the shore of Falls Lake. However, the Wilkerson Nature Park hike stays right here, ascending a bit. Ahead, pass a huge white oak just before opening onto field.

0.6 Reach a T intersection in the field. Turn left toward the Pond Loop.

0.7 Head left at the Pond Loop. Cut through woods then cross the pond dam.

0.9 Reach the other end of the Pond Loop. Head left on the Hidden Rocks Loop. Enter woods of pine, maple, sourwood, and oak. Cross another streambed.

1.3 Bisect a waterline. Curve through a rock garden. This outcrop is much larger than you normally see in the Raleigh area. Look for quartz veins running through the boulders. Look also for rock piles from farming days.

1.4 Cross the waterline a second time. Angle left back into woods.

1.7 Reach the trailhead, completing the hike.

40 Durant Nature Preserve

This former scout camp turned nature park is laced with trails centered on a pair of lakes. This loop hike explores the 237-acre park from head to toe. From the park office you head to Lower Lake, making a near circle around the tarn. Pick up the aptly named Border Trail and circle around the park, passing Upper Lake along the way. The last part of the hike traces Simms Branch, a rocky and scenic stream, back to the trailhead.

Start: Park office
Distance: 3.1-mile loop
Hiking time: About 2.0 hours
Difficulty: Easy
Trail surface: Natural
Best season: Year-round
Other trail users: None
Canine compatibility: Leashed dogs allowed

Land status: Nature preserve
Fees and permits: No fees or permits required
Schedule: 8 a.m. to 5:30 p.m.
Maps: Durant Nature Preserve
Trail contacts: Durant Nature Preserve, 8305 Camp Durant Rd., Raleigh, NC 27614; (919) 870-2871; www.raleighnc.gov/parks/

Finding the trailhead: From exit 14 on I-540, north of downtown Raleigh, take Falls of Neuse Road north for 0.8 mile to Durant Road. Turn right on Durant Road and follow it 1.5 miles to turn right on Camp Durant Road, then follow Camp Durant Road 0.4 mile to enter the park. From the parking area walk to the park office, then join Charlies Service Road southeast. Trailhead GPS: N35 53.672', W78 34.701'

The Hike

The town of Raleigh has been rapidly growing from its downtown core for decades. With the addition of I-440 and I-540, the growth sped up. What once was a rural getaway for the Boy Scouts at Camp Durant, a place where they could grow and interact with nature in the back of beyond, was becoming crowded by roads, warehouses, and subdivisions. Therefore, in 1979 the Boy Scouts sold their 237-acre wooded tract, with two lakes and a camp infrastructure, to the city of Raleigh.

Since then it has been a place for area residents to hike, paddle, fish, and get back to nature. In 2010 the park officially became a nature preserve. With the new designation the emphasis has been changing to not only recreational pastimes but also environmental education experiences, which it presents for school kids and adults alike. Upcoming park programs are listed on their website.

The trail system here is a series of interconnected pathways—so many trails that your first outing may be a little confusing. Definitely bring the preserve trail map with you. They are available online and at the park office. That being said, trail maps are also posted at many intersections, keeping you apprised of your position, so you

SASSAFRAS AND SIR WALTER RALEIGH

On this hike you will run into some trailside sassafras trees. These smallish understory trees are easy to identify. Their leaves have three basic shapes: oval, three-lobed, and mitten-shaped. Mature sassafras trees have a reddish-brown, deeply furrowed bark. Sassafras trees are known for their aromatic scent. Scratch the bark away from a twig and the sweet smell is unmistakable. American natives used sassafras for medicinal purposes. Pioneers, and even people today, make tea from boiling sassafras roots. Sassafras roots were one of colonial America's first exports. Sir Walter Raleigh himself, the man for whom the city of Raleigh is named, touted sassafras tea to be a cure-all and shipped roots to England. Sassafras oil was once a popular perfuming agent for soaps and the primary flavoring in early root beers.

Sassafras trees can be found throughout North Carolina in moist and sometimes sandy soils of uplands, in addition to being on the Border Trail at Durant Nature Preserve. Sassafras is a rather short-lived, usually understory tree here in the Piedmont, though it regularly becomes full sized in western Carolina. The North Carolina record tree stands at Maggie Valley, in mountainous Haywood County. It has a circumference of 16.5 feet! However, that pales in comparison to the world record sassafras near Owensboro, Kentucky, with its 21-foot circumference!

Sassafras trees range from central Florida all the way to southwest Maine, then west to central Michigan and south to Texas. Deer eat sassafras leaves and twigs, while the fruit of sassafras is eaten by birds from woodpeckers to mockingbirds. The wood of sassafras shrinks when dried and is used for fence posts and hand tools, and in boat building. However, since sassafras trees are relatively small, it is hard to get large sized and large enough amounts of sassafras to undertake major projects, unless you want to send their roots to England, as Sir Walter Raleigh did.

won't be lost for long. This hike takes you to the three main water features at Durant Nature Park—Lower Lake, Upper Lake, and Simms Branch—as well as the wetlands around them. Along the way you will enjoy traipsing through the woods as well as alongside the stream and lakes. Just make sure and learn something as you go, keeping with the mission of this nature park.

Miles and Directions

0.0 From the park office join paved Charlies Service Road southeast. It quickly becomes gravel. Just ahead, Pine Ridge Connector leaves left. Stay straight.

Park visitors relish the warm fall day at Durant Nature Preserve.

0.1 Reach another intersection and Lower Lake. Turn right, joining the North Lakeside Trail. Head west along the north shore of Lower Lake. Immediately pass a dock. Intersect the Lake Access Road but keep straight, passing the park boathouse. Parallel the shore.

0.3 Walk through the park group camp, with multiple shelters, just after intersecting the Campsite Access Trail. Beyond the group camp the Nature Trail leaves right. Stay alongside the wooded shores of Lower Lake.

0.6 Intersect White House Road (closed to private vehicles). Turn left here, crossing the dam for Upper Lake. Look west on Upper Lake.

0.7 Turn left, joining the South Lakeside Trail. Meander through wetlands below the dam spillway then keep east along the south shore of Lower Lake. Soak in good views of the lake.

0.8 An unnamed spur trail leaves right. Stay straight along Lower Lake.

0.9 The trail splits. Stay left, now on the Fishing Trail.

1.0 Leave left from the Fishing Trail then split right and head uphill to come very near the Spottswood Street trail access, information kiosk, and trailside parking. Meet the Border Trail and head right, southwesterly, away from the Spottswood Street trail access. Pass through hardwoods scattered with sassafras trees.

1.3 Come to a four-way intersection. A short spur leads left to Spottswood Street, while another trail leads right toward Lower Lake. Keep straight with the Border Trail.

1.4 Pass a second spur leading left to Spottswood Street. Cross a tributary by bridge then ramble through upland woods.

1.5 Reach Upper Lake again, and a four-way trail intersection. White House Road heads right across the Upper Lake Dam, while the Border Trail goes left. Stay straight, now joining the Beaver Pond Trail. Meander parallel to the shore of Upper Lake on an elevated path.

1.6 Bridge an intermittent tributary entering Upper Lake. Come alongside wetlands above the impoundment. Pass a short spur to an overlook of a willow marsh.

Durant Nature Park

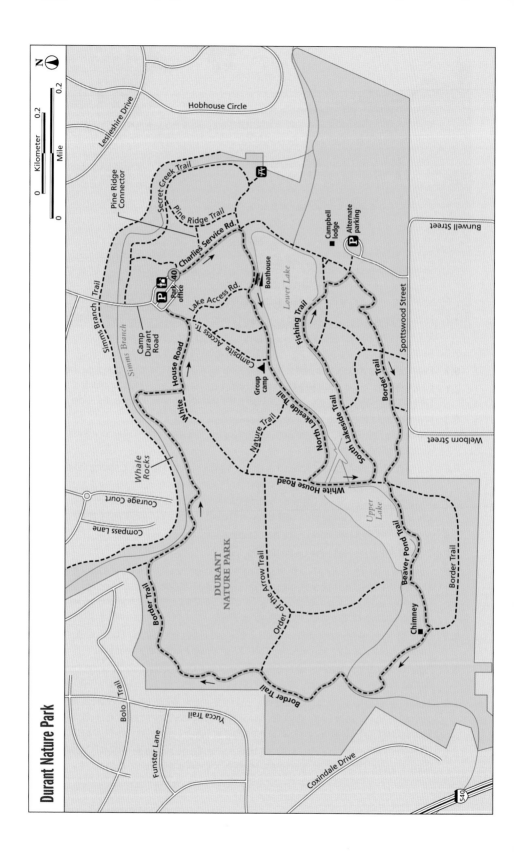

1.8 Reunite with the Border Trail at an old cabin site. Note the chimney stones of the forgotten Ponderosa Farm. Walk northwest on the Border Trail.

1.9 Make a rock hop of the unnamed stream feeding the lake of Camp Durant. Boulders have been strategically placed to help you cross the stream, but at high water the route will be impassable in this floodplain. Turn downstream and follow the creek. A sewer maintenance road leaves left. Do not take it; instead follow the trail sign left, beyond the sewer maintenance road. Turn away from the stream and lake.

2.2 Meet the Order of the Arrow Trail near the park boundary. Stay left with the now narrower Border Trail. Hike north. Houses are visible through the trees.

2.3 Cross an intermittent streambed twice in succession. Turn easterly.

2.5 A spur foot trail leaves left to Clivedon Drive. Turn right here and begin walking downstream along Simms Branch. Walk through tall bottomland of sycamore and tulip trees. Notice the Simms Branch Trail across the creek, part of the Capital Area Greenway System. The 1.7-mile path connects to the Abbotts Creek Trail, another greenway, near Durant Road. Walk alongside Simms Branch, with its extensive boulders and sandbars. This is a good area for wildflowers. The flat shortly closes, and a hill rises on trail right.

2.7 Pass the Whale Rocks to the left of the trail. One of the boulders resembles the upper half of a whale emerging from the sea.

2.9 Fully turn away from Simms Branch. Climb a hill, heading south.

3.0 Meet the White House Road. Take it left, easterly.

3.1 Meet the Campsite Access Trail just before emerging on the west side of the parking lot, finishing the hike.

Hike Index

About the Author

Johnny Molloy is a writer and adventurer based in Johnson City, Tennessee. His outdoor passion started on a backpacking trip in Great Smoky Mountains National Park while attending the University of Tennessee. That first foray unleashed a love of the outdoors that has led Molloy to spend most of his time hiking, backpacking, canoe camping, and tent camping for the past three decades. Friends enjoyed his outdoor adventure stories; one even suggested he write a book. He pursued his friend's idea and soon parlayed his love of the outdoors into an occupation. The results of his efforts are more than sixty books, which include hiking guidebooks, camping guidebooks, paddling guidebooks, comprehensive guidebooks about a specific area, and true outdoor adventure books throughout the eastern United States, including hiking guides to North Carolina's national forests, Great Smoky Mountains National Park, and the Triad.

Molloy writes for various magazines and websites, and is a columnist/feature writer for his local paper, the *Johnson City Press*. He continues to write and travel extensively throughout the United States, participating in a variety of outdoor pursuits. His non-outdoor interests include American history and University of Tennessee sports. For the latest on Johnny, please visit www.johnnymolloy.com.

THE TEN ESSENTIALS OF HIKING

American Hiking Society

American Hiking Society recommends you pack the "Ten Essentials" every time you head out for a hike. Whether you plan to be gone for a couple of hours or several months, make sure to pack these items. Become familiar with these items and know how to use them.

1. Appropriate Footwear
Happy feet make for pleasant hiking. Think about traction, support, and protection when selecting well-fitting shoes or boots.

2. Navigation
While phones and GPS units are handy, they aren't always reliable in the backcountry; consider carrying a paper map and compass as a backup and know how to use them.

3. Water (and a way to purify it)
As a guideline, plan for half a liter of water per hour in moderate temperatures/terrain. Carry enough water for your trip and know where and how to treat water while you're out on the trail.

4. Food
Pack calorie-dense foods to help fuel your hike, and carry an extra portion in case you are out longer than expected.

5. Rain Gear & Dry-Fast Layers
The weatherman is not always right. Dress in layers to adjust to changing weather and activity levels. Wear moisture-wicking cloths and carry a warm hat.

6. Safety Items (light, fire, and a whistle)
Have means to start an emergency fire, signal for help, and see the trail and your map in the dark.

7. First Aid Kit
Supplies to treat illness or injury are only as helpful as your knowledge of how to use them. Take a class to gain the skills needed to administer first aid and CPR.

8. Knife or Multi-Tool
With countless uses, a multi-tool can help with gear repair and first aid.

9. Sun Protection
Sunscreen, sunglasses, and sun-protective clothing should be used in every season regardless of temperature or cloud cover.

10. Shelter
Protection from the elements in the event you are injured or stranded is necessary. A lightweight, inexpensive space blanket is a great option.

Find other helpful resources at AmericanHiking.org/hiking-resources